"Not enough people plan for the future. Joe uses irreverence and hilarious analogies to help fellow Millennials learn how to improve financially. Joe's unique voice works to drive his points home."

Mike Frerichs
Illinois State Treasurer

"Lucid, funny, and serious at the same time. This is a rare combination for a personal finance book, but that's exactly what this is."

David Aronson
CEO, Peanut Butter

"Joe's book is the perfect guide to finding a practical approach toward financial well-being. It is a critical time for young professionals to start making incremental and positive change toward their futures. This book will lead a conversation about millennials fueling a new economy thanks to his understanding of money and finances."

Aerial Ellis
Author, *The Original Millennial*

"I expect Rogue Finances to shake things up and trust that many of Joe's ideas and prescriptions will improve your financial confidence and beliefs as you build your financial dreams."

David Marzahl
President & CEO, Center for Economic Progress

ROGUE FINANCES

THE "UN-SYSTEM" DESIGNED TO HELP YOU BECOME FINANCIALLY HEALTHY, SUCCESSFUL, AND AWESOME

JOE HOLBERG

Published by Blog Into Book
1871: Holberg Financial
222 W Merchandise Mart Plaza
Chicago, IL 60654

ISBN: 9781619846043
eISBN: 9781619846050

Printed in the United States of America

To my Mom and Dad

FOREWORD

What we know at the Center for Economic Progress (CEP) is that it is never too early to start planning one's financial future. Younger Americans, whether recent college graduates, or early in their careers, are uniquely positioned to make smart, high-impact financial choices that can pay off over a lifetime. From basic budgeting—what we call a spending plan, to understanding credit and debt, to savings and investing, these are the building blocks of financial success and the ability to achieve one's dreams. Or, alternatively, if ignored or done wrong, they can be precursors to financial ruin and a lifetime of falling behind. That's why I find Rogue Finances so exciting; it promises to address all of these issues head-on, with humor and verve and in a way that you will inspire you to take action.

Much of what we see in the media or read in social media about finances are either wrong or based on mistaken assumptions. Behavioral finance further teaches us that decisions of the moment or guided by emotion are often objectively wrong and can lead to selecting the wrong financial product or service. Human emotion, and the tendency towards procrastination, present another set of risks for many of us. This furthers the need to act now and seek out trusted sources of information while time is still on your side.

Joe Holberg, a long-time volunteer with the Center for Economic Progress, brings a new, different and exciting perspective to financial advice and planning. When I survey the landscape of financial advice, it's apparent that too much is geared towards older and wealthier consumers and misses the younger generation. From my experience leading CEP and providing trusted financial advice to thousands of consumers each year, the inflection and decision points for Millennials present an opportunity to make choices that could reap benefits for a lifetime. We need to acknowledge the financial challenges facing Millennials, from having $1.3 trillion in student debt to feeling that homeownership isn't a realistic option. At the same time all of us need to take action and own up to the reality that we own our financial future. I expect Rogue Finances to shake things up and trust that many of Joe Holberg's ideas and prescriptions will improve your financial confidence and beliefs as you build your financial dreams.

David Marzahl
President & CEO
Center for Economic Progress

Acknowledgements

To begin to thank everyone who has contributed to this undertaking is a fool's errand in that I surely cannot extend my gratitude far or wide enough to encompass each integral thought, word of encouragement, and prescient suggestion that ultimately coalesced into the pages constituting Rogue Finances. Alas, but a few of the many who have guided this work in one form or another include my insightful editor and publisher, Blog Into Book, whose staff and leadership wrought from my rough edges a smooth and palatable piece that is of much higher quality than I could have hoped. To my admirable friend, Marisa Rademacher, for without her relentless accountability and 6:00 AM texts to drag me from slumber into a writing posture, this book would not exist. And finally to the guiding lights of both my history and my present: my parents, the DeBows, Grandma Grinnell, Rose Tropp, my Advisory Board, and too many friends and family whose footprints are cherished impresses on my heart. This, to acknowledge each of you who never once waivered in your steadfastness nor belief in me and my crazy dreams.

Most Humbly,
Joe Holberg

Table of Contents

Part 1
Ready, Set, Go!

1. MENTALITY MATTERS MOST

You're Behind and We Both Know It

You're behind the proverbial 8-ball financially and we both know it. Part of it is your fault and part of it isn't. That's quite an off-putting way to start a book isn't it? I mean, seriously, why would you want to read any more? It's certainly a little disheartening to be told right away that you're financially lagging behind where you should be at this point in your life. Sure, I could have opened this book with some fluffy story about how magically your life is going to change if you believe in yourself and read each page attentively to the end. Sorry to disappoint. This isn't that book. So if you're looking for a book that is going to leave you warm and happy inside, put this down and go search for *Chicken Soup for the Teenage Soul*[*] or go find yourself one of the over 39,000 books[†] about finances that give you dry textbook definitions of boring financial terms and prescriptive formulas like, "Do A, B, C and achieve 1, 2, 3." Poof, magic, and... you're going to be a millionaire!

This book is not that. Instead, it is a dissection of why it is so hard to get ahead financially, *and* it provides useful, concrete steps (as well as warnings on missteps) that you can use to become better off. This is a high-density, information-packed, astute diagnosis of where we're at and how to move forward most effectively. No

---

[*] Admittedly, I used to read those books all the time and yes, they made me feel warm and happy inside.

[†] This number was found by searching for personal finance books on amazon.com on 9/13/2016.

more being stuck in a rut financially where, from month to month, your aspirations are there, but your finances seem to lag perpetually behind. This book will show you how to break all the financial rules you thought you knew so you can play the game successfully and come out on top – no matter who you are, how bad you think your situation is, or how big your dreams may be.

So embrace the fact that you're currently behind and that it is up to you – exclusively you – to do something about it.

Why does this even matter? It matters because once you realize that *you yourself* need to take direct action to get ahead, you must own the fact that the person who cares most about your financial progress and success is in fact *you*. I don't mean that Mom and Pop don't care about you having a job so you can finally pay your own cell phone bill. They do care about that. And I don't mean that people aren't genuinely invested in your success as a person – they are. But at the end of the day, you need to make sure that *you* are equipped individually – all by yourself – with knowledge, skills, and confidence to manage your own situation now and going forward.

The litmus test of being financially savvy, knowledgeable, and independent is simple. Ask yourself, "If all of a sudden the people that care about me disappeared," how would I do financially? Would I know everything I need to know to be truly independent and successful? If you answered yes, you might be right and you might be fine, but then again, you're reading this book presumably because you aren't a financial genius who knows every single concept out there (arguably no one knows them all, myself included). If you answered no, pat yourself on the back for being honest. You win this round, and if you keep the mindset that there is something to learn, you'll do well.

---

* Think about the enrapturing *Left Behind* series or the distortedly hilarious *This Is the End* movie with Seth Rogen & Co.

By the end of this book my goal is to get you into a position where you can more confidently answer the litmus test question in the affirmative rather than in the negative so that you are in fact empowered financially.

Further, if we look beyond ourselves and those most proximal to us and look at society and the economy at large,* we have to realize that we aren't doing so hot as individuals. As a group, Millennials and young professionals are *way behind*. We have massive amounts of student loan debt, credit card and personal debt, very little savings (along with almost no emergency savings), we're behind on making retirement progress, and it's becoming even more difficult to garble together a healthy down payment for a home which we are buying later and later in life. These are but a few of the bleak components that add up to a perfect storm, leaving people pinched each month and struggling to get ahead even if they have a decent job earning a healthy amount.

The tough part in thinking about this is that we are teetering on the sharp blade of a double-edged sword. On one side we have the most successful and prosperous economy in human history and on the other side, individuals are for the most part only *surviving* but not *thriving* financially. This leaves people financially exposed and brittle.

I'm the last person you will find diatribing against the merits of capitalism and the free market – they have literally built the vast majority of the world's wealth since my main man, Adam Smith, wrote about them in *The Wealth of Nations*. However, the caveat that we'll run with as a theme in this book is to make sure you are cognizant and attentive to the implications of this system on your day-to-day life. You must safeguard yourself against the modern design of a system that encourages, thrives on, and ultimately relies upon you spending your hard-earned money and remaining generally complacent for years on end.

---

* I could feel you shudder ever-so-slightly at this notion of macroeconomics. Eww... don't talk about economics, please – anything but that class-that-must-not-be-named. #Voldemortonomics.

It's not like I'm going to sit here and wag my finger at spending and people's lifestyles. But I will help to dissect the pros and cons of *not being mentally aware of the long term implications of such actions.* We'll get into specifics later, but for now, realize that I'm your new BFF (best financial friend,* FYI) and you need to keep reading this book so you don't get tricked into a life of financial mediocrity and repetitiveness like the metaphorical rat on the wheel who is destined to always be on the move, but who never makes any substantial progress. It's time to get out from behind the 8-ball, catch up, and get ahead...

I'm Your New BFF

I live in Chicago and I love it here. It's the Second City, but to me, it feels like the center of the universe.† Millennium Park in the summer evenings listening to (free) live music is epic and throw in a blanket and a cheap bottle of wine on the Great Lawn, and you'll feel like you are hanging out in a more divine moment in time than Woodstock in the summer of '69. The streets are alive, craft beer and local coffee roasters provide a palatable array of beverages to top off and compliment an already renowned food scene with hot dogs on the street (no ketchup in this city unless you're willing to commit a heinous faux pas). On top (literally) of all this is the SkyDeck at the Willis (I still call it the Sears) Tower. It looms large and was the tallest building in the world from the time of its creation in 1974 until 1998 when the Petronas towers went up in Malaysia. It has been a beacon and an inspiration in the city and it dwarfs almost every other building in the city. Every once in a while,‡ I'll go up to take in the view. It's stunning. Whether you go up for fireworks on

---

* It's worth pointing out that I am as corny and filled with roll-your-eye puns in real life as in this book. Ultimately, if I make myself laugh, I'm good to go and if you laugh along the way, enjoy the ride.

† While Galileo is certainly turning in his grave at this notion, even his less informed predecessors, Copernicus and Ptolemy, would give me a nice slap for this idea. Although, Socrates and Plato might be inclined to agree with me on a philosophical level. #EpicRapBattle idea? YouTube it...

‡ I've literally only been 3 times in my life, so once every 9.3 years would be more accurate. For you math whizzes out there, you now know my age.

the Fourth of July or for a sunset show by Apollo himself drawing the sun below the horizon in his horse drawn chariot, it'll take your breath away. The height itself gives you an unprecedented view of the city and the large glass windows allow for unobstructed visual glory.

Each time I've been there, I've been struck by the *inability* to actually take it all in at the same time. Just changing a couple of degrees to the left or right can wildly change what you're seeing. Looking straight down grounds you in the heart of the city and yet looking blocks away, you can see the formation of distinct geographical features that govern many industrial areas, neighborhoods, residential areas, and of course, a giant lake to the East.* Depending on your perspective, everything can change when you're 1,353 feet up in the air.[1]

Likewise, a slight alteration in the perspective of this book can change quite a bit for you as the reader. I am writing this book for my friends and the people I know. I'm writing this because after years of helping my friends with their finances, I realized that we all have the same questions and because of everything that has led up to this point in my life, I seem to have a lot of the answers. This is the same reason why I started my company, Holberg Financial. We exist to help millions of people, primarily in their 20's and 30's, increase their financial health and ultimately achieve their financial and life goals. It was surprising to me to learn that my friends had so many questions about money, about finances, about spending, saving, travel, and retirement. After wondering how we were all out there in charge of our own income, expenses, and financial life (to varying degrees, which is fine), I realized that none of us actually got any formal or extensive education related to money or finances.

Yeah, yeah, you might have done some type of fun, light program in middle school or high school (and I'm not knocking them, I did one and it was great) that taught you how to save in a piggy bank. And

---

* Lake Michigan, which to date, still doesn't have Asian Carp. Yet another crazy thing to look up on YouTube.

yes, you might have taken an econ class in high school or college that alluded to investing or had some stock simulation game where you got fake money to invest. But really, none of us, virtually no one in the U.S., received what could rightfully be considered an actual and effective *personal* financial education class. If we note the italicized "personal" in the preceding sentence, it will become even more painfully obvious that we missed out on what could be considered a core life skill. To accentuate this point, think of all the people (myself included) who got an economics, accounting, or business degrees and can help consult and manage the financial books of multi-billion dollar corporations, but still don't really know the ins and outs of their credit score or how much to save each month for a down-payment on a house or for retirement. And if they struggle (which is no fault of their own – we simply don't know what we don't know), just imagine the struggle for the "non-financial" among us: biology majors, doctors, psychology majors, technical or community school grads, etc. What are we doing? Why do we (as a country) allow this?

Unfortunately, you would be hard pressed to go to any university and find a personal finance class or course. If you were lucky enough to stumble upon one, you'd quickly realize that it's *optional* and that a very small – arguably tiny – fraction of students actually take it. Maybe a couple hundred per year. Proportionally, if we look at society at large, that implies that that same tiny fraction of the U.S. population actually knows what the hell is going on with their personal finances. This just can't remain true.

Now, I do not think universities should bear this responsibility alone. Even if 100% of college students took personal finance, that would still leave roughly 30% of the population[2] without the skills and knowledge since many people don't go to college in the first place. Then, the question becomes, is it the public education system's responsibility? I think we can safely say that it is, most likely, something that middle schools and high schools should teach so that at least when you graduate with your high school diploma, you can name the inner workings and components of a cell in your body, but you also understand interest rates, basic retirement investing, what and how much to save, the true cost of credit, etc. Oh, and maybe throw in a lesson or two about paying taxes – that seems pretty practical…

Ok, so we've squarely placed the burden on the school system. Fair enough. But the real question now is whether or not "they" will rise to the occasion and provide a high-quality, useful personal financial education for our nation. To that, our answer is two-fold. First, by virtue of the fact that this book is primarily for people that are already in their 20's, 30's, and beyond, we have missed our opportunity at a formal personal financial education. Therefore, it's a moot point. From an individual perspective, we missed out on a good personal finance class that would teach us enough to make really well-informed choices, and we are where we are now and we can (and should) deal with it accordingly. That just means it's up to you to do it individually. Secondly, and while we ourselves may not really care or control whether or not this happens, perhaps some magical switch will flip where we start teaching people about personal finances in high school. But at this point, we have enough historical data to assume that this isn't going to happen any time soon so we personally have to find better information and answers as do those that follow in our footsteps. In the long run, yes, we'll have to invest a lot of time and resources to solve this massive problem, but for now, we can only take one small step.

As our educational sidewinding analysis comes back to our original place in this train of thought, I return to the statement that, "I'm writing this book for my friends." Now, you and I may never meet, but that doesn't mean I'm not your BFF. "How do you figure?" you may ask. Well it goes like this: When I was living in Charleston, South Carolina, I rented my place out via Airbnb.* A couple who was renting my place showed up and knocked on my door. I welcomed them in and the first thing they saw was a picture

---

* I made almost $10,000 in less than a year. I love it. I'm a die-hard Airbnber and totally think you should give it a go if you haven't already. Try staying with a host next time you travel, and if you like it, consider hosting yourself (which has the upside of earning you some extra moola).

frame with a photo of me teaching.* They said they were teachers in Oklahoma and I asked if they knew a teacher named Johnnie Appleseed.† Coincidentally, they knew good ole Johnnie and what do you know, all of the sudden we're all chummy with each other. This all took less than 30 seconds.

I didn't even know these people, and yet, we had a mutual friend. Like the random couple who knew Johnnie Appleseed, you and I could play the same game and most likely find some mutual friend or a friend-of-a-friend³ that we have in common. It might be a little challenge to do manually, but we could hop on LinkedIn or Facebook and connect the dots. In essence, I think one of the pitfalls of a lot of other personal financial books is that the authors write about topics only. While this is great if you want a reference tool or a quasi-textbook, it misses the mark on what I know to be true: you (and everyone else) wants to know that the book they are reading is relevant and meaningful to them. You aren't looking for an academic text book loaded with jargon that comes down from on high or from the Ivory Tower of academia. You also aren't looking for another cheap trick or a gimmick-ridden book that says you can have it all just by following some format or strategy that may or may not work for you. Those books have been written for years, and no doubt, people will continue to write them en masse. Go get one if you want. They're probably $15 at Barnes and Noble,‡ maybe $14 on Amazon. Who knows?

---

* For what it's worth, I taught math for a couple of years in Chicago and as an overlap between this and that, I had an artificial economy for my students: they had class jobs, made "money," rented their desks, etc. so they could learn *and* practice personal finance. So if you hear the teacher in me coming out as I write the book, you're not imagining things.

† Johnnie Appleseed is a fictitious name for my friend's actual name.

‡ A quick R.I.P. to Borders Bookstore. They went bankrupt and closed all their stores around 2013. While I was a student at the University of Michigan I worked at Store #1, where all the magic began. Ironically, I got in trouble a lot for reading on the job and may or may not have hidden from my manager in the children's section of the bookstore to read in peace (I assumed that would be the last place he would look for me).

As such, you're stuck with me, your new BFF (best financial friend). And let's get one thing clear. I'm the financial friend you love to hate because you know I'm right and I'll always tell it like it is, even if you'd rather have soothing words to comfort you. Go find someone else for that. If you're looking for someone to paint you a pretty picture with roses and rainbows, go pick up a different book that promises something like "6 things you need to do to get rich" or "the simple way to be a millionaire."

Our Brash Approach

Let's get one thing out in the open: this book is not the sugar-coated bull crap that you'll find in other books on personal finances. I could weave a web of hope and prosperity about how if you just do a couple of things differently, you'll reach your goals and dreams. But I'm not into being a lollipop of irrational optimism. It might taste sweet and be delicious, but after a couple of licks, you're left with nothing but useless sticks.

I will remain honest and brash with you and this leads to an effective blended cocktail of the above hope, mixed with a salty dose of fear.* Why is this concoction important? We could sit here and look to lessons in psychology, motivation, societal constructs, and evolution all day (or for many years or a lifetime), but I have distilled it down to one comment on why we need each of the main ingredients of hope and fear.

First, fear. We need a little fear woven into this book because from an evolutionary standpoint, we are not that great at planning for the future. We are pretty good at procrastinating, delaying action, being lazy, and living in the moment. There hasn't been a single person, probably in the course of human history, who ever completely avoided procrastinating or being lazy at some point. I mean, Olympians, celebrities, presidents, athletes – they've definitely had that thought in their head at least a couple of times, "F*** it, I don't want to do it," or "It would be easier just to watch a little TV." Everyone wants to be lazy sometimes.

---

* For some reason this description, with its adjectives, made me think of margaritas.

This isn't always a bad thing. We just have to own up to the fact that we all procrastinate and struggle with delayed gratification and thinking about the future. We're preprogrammed to be lazy because, in our nomadic hunter-gatherer years, it paid off to conserve calories. You never knew when you would need those energy reserves to run and hunt down prey, move your whole tribe because of a flash flood or fire, or go days without food or water (i.e., being lazy allowed us to survive, ironic as that may seem today in the hyper-connected, text-24-7 lifestyle where being lazy is demonized).

Since much of our future financial success depends on strong planning and mitigating some portion of our predisposition to not give two craps about the long run, I will be blatantly brutal with the facts and implications of ignoring that metaphorical light at the end of the tunnel. Sadly, for many millions of Americans, they will never reach the light. If you think you're exempt from this and you will always come out on top, I'd caution you to think again and start considering what you need to do now in order to better prepare for the future.* On the flip side, if you already have a healthy amount of fear in you (*Am I doing it right? Am I saving enough? How do I retire early like a boss?*) then this book will be great because you'll find a lot of information that is designed to help you answer those pesky questions that run wild in your head.†

Secondly, hope. We can't just live a life of fear. It's not sustainable and it's not fulfilling. We need fear in healthy doses to spur action and give us perspective. But a solid amount of optimism and hope is a key ingredient in our journey both in this book and in life. Hope's purpose is to give us something to strive for, to move towards, and to seek when all else is fraught with the trivialities of day-to-day life, the weight of responsibility, or forces that are seemingly aligned to thwart our progress. Hope allows us to realize that saving $5 a month matters, even if it seems like you'll never have your credit

---

*   Technically, that might be our first dose of fear in the book. How'd it make you feel? Did you embrace it, reject it, or feel something else? Try to self-diagnose how you reacted to this (and future) doses of fear.

†   One survey finds that at least 83% of Americans worry about their finances. Let's see if we can lower that number, shall we?

card or student loan debt paid off. Hope gives us the ability to push on towards retirement even if we have $0 and a job we hate. It's an essential ingredient that allows us to overcome challenges and achieve things that we've only dreamed of accomplishing.

If we wrap these two up nicely throughout the book, a very approachable, empowering, and useful theme emerges: we will be able to look at things from a practical standpoint. This viewpoint is based on educating ourselves on where we are as individuals and as a society, and then leads us to develop an understanding of what we have to do about it. I like this approach because it strips away all the bogus ways to write a book. This approach literally adopts a scientific and methodical approach to getting you to where you want (and need) to go financially. It says, "Okay here we are today, why? Where do we want to be 'tomorrow?' Here's how we do it." Sometimes the most elegant solutions are the simplest ones and I'll try my best to act as a reductionist to simplify ideas so they are easy to understand and equally easy to implement, while ensuring that the ideas and concepts are fully fleshed out.

Finally, unlike most other personal finance books, we will move far beyond the *personal* component and look from a bird's eye view at what is going on in society and the economy at large. This is super important because we are all individuals in society and by definition, we cannot remove ourselves from said society. This has massive implications on our lives in that we are greatly influenced – whether we think so or not – by all things around us. This goes way beyond finances. While some areas will be more important to venture into (such as talking about our obsessive compulsion to compare ourselves to others and how that plays out financially), there will be some that we touch on lightly to make a point and provide perspective. It's a fool's errand to approach personal finances without societal commentary, and yet most do so. Most write in a style that treats the individual like a fish in a fishbowl. They comment on how the fish itself can change within the context of the fishbowl, but they never bother to look at what is going on outside the fishbowl and how that influences what is going on inside. There might be a 3-year-old child with a small net outside who thinks today is the day that the toilet will allow you a better swimming experience. Or maybe there's a 50-year-old collector of rare fish who monitors and cares for every aspect of the fishbowl. In either circumstance, using only your newly acquired fish eyes to look through your bowl, you have to realize that we all have a distorted and incomplete view of the outside world and that by knowing more about this outside context (i.e., society and the economy) can greatly aid how we respond to and act within our immediate fishbowl surroundings.

In the name of belaboring this analogy, I would challenge you to do one thing to learn about the "world outside your fishbowl." Go find someone over the age of 35, the older the better.* Ask them just one simple question: "Do you think it's important to start taking your financial situation seriously right now, or should I wait until I am 10 years older to do so?" I can almost guarantee you that none of them will say, "Hey, you know what, you should totally wait to start learning about your finances."

The point of asking such an obvious question is to give ourselves a little slap in the face, a little jolt about reality and to gain from the wisdom of those who have been there and done that and would probably go back and do things just a little bit differently.† I ask older people this all the time and I have literally *never* heard someone say that they are glad they procrastinated. I don't imagine I ever will.‡ In fact, many will go even further to expound upon the importance of "starting early." Not only is this great advice from a general life perspective, it is also the one that mathematically makes life a hell of a lot easier for you and me.

---

* In general, the elderly have so much wisdom and insight and as young people, myself included, we stand to gain immensely by enquiring about said wisdom and listening to sage, time-wrought knowledge. Sadly enough, we seek their counsel far too infrequently.

† Even though it's so hip and cool to proclaim from the rooftops #noregrets, it should be modified to #almostnoregrets.

‡ Perhaps now I've exposed myself to someone acting in spite to disprove me.

In closing, embrace this brash approach. I'm not doing it to be contrarian or self-indulgent. I'm doing it because I know that as your new BFF, you will grunt snorts of disdain throughout the book, but after you're done resisting change, you'll go out and act in your own best interest and you'll start to make some serious progress towards your goals. And that result is why I'm writing this for you in the first place.

Becoming Rogue

I've been up and down, inside and on the outs, with and without, and pretty much everywhere else in between. I've wondered how I was going to find money for my next meal. I've racked up credit card debt paying for college textbooks* with no end in sight, and I've struggled to pay for rent. I lived in a tent and have slept in my car (surprisingly comfortable, I might add). My family qualified for free and reduced lunches at school and I got on food stamps for a year. When I was a senior in high school, I almost missed out on going to college because we couldn't afford the $40 application fee.† Once there, I had to call to drop out of school after my sophomore year because I had exhausted all of my financial ability to pay for my education. Even while working multiple jobs on campus and getting financial aid, it was too much. Fortunately, Fate intervened in the form of the Vice President of the Financial Aid Office Life, who in 30 minutes – with the flick of a wrist – altered my financial aid package and my life to make sure I could stay in school.‡ Life, at times has shit on me. No literally, life shit on me in the form of a seagull. Landed right on my shoulder. (This was one of the easier things to deal with, as gross as it was).

But the glass has constantly remained half full. I found that next meal, I got that degree, and have worked at some of the best

---

* The average college student graduates with $3,000 in credit card debt. Insane.

† Fortunately, my grandmotherly-like neighbor, who I'll never be able to thank enough for an unending and wide array of support, gave me $40 to apply to school.

‡ I don't know how she did this, but whoever she is, I'll forever be indebted to her while simultaneously being much less indebted in regards to my student loans.

companies in the world, including Google – which is as awesome a place to work as it's made out to be – and there's been no sequel to my seagull incident. All the while, I have searched incessantly for ways to improve personally and financially so that I wasn't exposed to uncertainty and financial insecurity. These struggles helped me learn along the way and have put me in a position to give back to others since they helped me to continually ask myself "How could I, in my limited capacity and in my small corner of the universe make a difference?" I was thinking about ways to do this as I was finishing college – ready to receive my cherished Economics degree – when President Obama gave an inspiring and motivational commencement address on the merits of national and international service 50 years after JFK inspired students to form the Peace Corps at 2 AM on the fabled steps of the Michigan Union. I knew that I too would pursue service in some capacity. It was the beginning of the last several years of work that led me to the place where I am now, writing to you about personal finances.

In short, the last several years and the years before that, have taught me how to become rogue financially. They've taught me to break rules, ignore advice, shun the status quo, and they have forced me to see the underlying system as not only the source of our greatest opportunity, but our greatest threat.

I've learned that if we don't learn more about finances, then we are going to end up with too much debt, not enough assets, and we are going to severely compromise our financial future like the 95% of Baby Boomers who don't have enough for retirement.[4] I've also learned, that as alluded to earlier, there is no structured, formal way to actually learn what you need to know about personal finances and how to effectively build a stable and successful financial life – you have to go out and proactively learn independently or informally (from parents, mentors, the Internet, etc.). At each step of the way, I've found that saying screw you to the way we're taught to live financially has been tremendously beneficial and has allowed me to amass the knowledge and skill set to teach you to do the same.

This real education about personal finances started a couple of weeks after I had dried the tears of joy from my face that welled up upon graduating from the University of Michigan. I threw all of my possessions in a U-Haul and drove 800 miles east to Providence, Rhode Island to start my AmeriCorps position at a small non-profit that was engaged in microfinance. The organization was called the Capital Good Fund. It was a quite a young non-profit and that's putting it kindly. Turns out that I was the first full time staff hired besides the founder and I took a whopping $11,000/year salary since I had accepted an AmeriCorps position at the non-profit.* We were constantly getting kicked out of Brown University classrooms and lecture halls that we would sneak into so we could have a place to work and get free Wi-Fi (and air conditioning). We had lots of questions and not a lot of answers and yet, we had a vision, a purpose, and a mission to end poverty and change people's lives. I was totally on board.

I still remember the first business class that I taught to a group of low-income entrepreneurs. Here I was, an overconfident, under-experienced, 22-year-old teaching 35 – 65-year-olds about budgeting, savings, business plans, debt, and so on. I thought there was no way they were 1) going to believe me, and 2) going to learn anything from me because there was no way they didn't already know the concepts and ideas that I was teaching them. Yet, they hung on every word. "Tell us more about how credit scores are calculated;" "How do I set up a savings and checking account?" and "I didn't realize that debt was so expensive to have." These were but a few of the comments and questions that popped up then and throughout the next year as I worked to teach as many people as possible about business and finances. It blew my mind at the time, and it is still wild to me now how valuable these classes were. However, now I have no delusions about how hard it is to learn about money and how much harder it can be to actually do the right things to make sure you are getting ahead regardless of your socioeconomic status or your educational level.

---

* Per the Americorps philosophy and policy, you only get paid a small stipend during your time of service. While difficult, it is truly a wonderful program and I will always highly recommend it to anyone even if the pay is pretty low.

Fast forward through the years. I taught inner city kids about personal finances as a middle school math teacher, served on the Associate Board of the Center for Economic Progress, an organization that provides amazing, free financial coaching and tax preparation to hard working families, and I had a fellowship at Google to bring computer science to nearly a million students around the globe. No matter where I went across the U.S. *everyone had questions:* people with high paying jobs and low paying jobs, people with lots of education and people with not as much, black people, white people, brown people, and purple people. Everyone was looking for answers and time and again they asked me. I had become the resident expert on personal finances. As the questions came in, I just kept answering them. I'm no longer shocked when people who got a 4.0 in Biomedical Engineering or Neuroscience want to know what percent of their income they should save. It doesn't surprise me when computer scientists at Silicon Valley companies who build sweet apps, websites, and Internet tools, want to know how to build a financial roadmap designed to help them become financially healthy so they can retire at some point in the future. I'm no longer dumbfounded when accountants at top tier accounting and finance firms whose job it is to manage the financial books of billion dollar companies want to know how to budget. And I'm certainly not surprised when people want to know how to pay off debt, student loans, and car loans so that they can work towards purchasing a house, travel more to see the world, and not work until it's time to consign themselves to the mansions of rest.*

What I've realized (and what I hope to impress upon you via this book) is that you have to start rethinking what you know, you have to start breaking some rules,† and you've got to go rogue in a system that says just keep running on that metaphorical rat wheel until the end of time. Again, there isn't a silver bullet that is going to magically change your life and make you rich, but if you start

---

* The "mansions of rest" being an elegantly beautiful phrase for death. from George Washington's Farewell Address.

† While I'll encourage you to break a shit ton of societal rules and norms (i.e. social constructs), I will not encourage you to step outside of the letter of the law.

tweaking a couple of things here and there and you keep an open mind, one that allows you to self-diagnose and continually learn, then there is a solid path forward. There is a path and a course that will allow you to buck the system so that you can get to where you want to go. But first, you have to break society's rules and become un-average.

Becoming Un-Average

What does it mean to become un-average? And what are these "rules" that I now have to break? Is this guy as weird as he sounds?*

Let's start with becoming un-average. Right now, you are average. You make an average amount of money, you spend an average amount, you have an average amount of credit card debt, and you have an average amount of student loans. You also have an average diet and average exercise regimen. You do not defy the laws of being average – none of us do. That is literally the idea behind the concept of averageness. Now, I know that as Americans, we're coddled in childhood and in school and everyone gets a first place ribbon for something, but overall, most people are, well, mostly average.

Think about it. I'm not trying to diminish anyone by saying this, I'm just trying to bring up the point that while you might be an Olympic swimmer, you might be average at soccer. You might be taller or shorter than the average, but most of us are within a few inches either way of the general idea of being average. You might be awesome at public speaking, but still be a nice balance between introvert and extrovert. If you work a regular 9 to 5 job and like it enough not to quit, you still might go home and prepare the finest world class cuisine for you and your friends.

---

* While we'll endeavor to answer the first two in the succeeding chapters of this here book, the third one we can almost unequivocally answer yes to. I have one specific friend who, for years, said to me many times, "You're the weirdest person I know." To that, I have always responded. "Thank you."

29

The idea here is that given the several thousand variables and dimensions that we could look at, you will certainly excel at and be awesome at a couple or maybe several, but for the other 95% of the items in the list we'll simply fall somewhere reasonably close to average. This is fine and in fact, it's simply average.

It is tempting to reject this idea and cry out, "I'm special! I'm not average!" Just take a breather and realize that yes, you are special and yes, in some areas, you are not average. Then realize that since everyone is special and in some ways they are not average, this is precisely what makes being special average. If you're sitting there thinking this is a dressed up way of saying that people are unique individuals with various idiosyncrasies, you are correct.

But here's why becoming un-average financially is super important: if you remain average, ignore your finances for even a couple of years, or think that you don't have time, money, nor energy to deal with and be proactive about your financial life, then you'll end up financially average years down the road. Essentially, there are a handful of things that we'll work on uncovering throughout this book that can make positive progress, start to make inroads towards goals, and avoid the disastrous pitfalls of being financially average.

So what does being financially average look like? Let's just look at a couple of key stats. First, the average income is about $43,160 per year.[5] Of these earnings, somehow, only 50% of Americans have managed to save one months' worth of income (a paltry amount compared to what is financially healthy – more on that in a bit). On average, we each have $8,392 worth of credit card debt, the average amount of student loan debt is right around $23,000, and our average credit score is 692 (which isn't all that great).[6] You personally might make more or less than this, you might have more or less savings, or more or less credit card debt. We're not trying to dissect this and say that you are only financially average if your stats line up directly with the ones above. But realistically, we're all going to be at or near the average of many of the categories we could map out in terms of key financial areas (such as the various chapters of the book). The main point here is to get everyone comfortable with the idea that no matter how awesome your finances are, we want you to become even more awesome and move significantly away from financially average.

Similarly, if you're average, we'll move you away from this mediocre position. For those of you thinking that you're already un-average, but not in a good way (mounds of debt, low credit, lower income, etc.), we've got our work cut out for us, but don't worry: *this is a process* and we're in it for the long haul if you are. First step for you – become average, then become un-average in a positive sense.* Regardless of starting position, you aren't a model cut from the finest Roman sculptor's hands. Virtually none of us have chiseled financial features and a smooth perfect finish for the masses to admire. We're more like the raw marble material halfway finished by an apprentice. We're rough around the edges, we've got a ways to go until we're museum ready, but we've got that latent potential ready to be carved and crafted into something truly un-average.

Further, the scariest thing about being financially average is not the stats above (those can all be addressed and worked on), but it is the *mentality and complacency* that we're taught to have when it comes to improving our finances. This can be highlighted by looking at some phrases you've probably heard before, and perhaps have even said or thought yourself. Be honest – I know I've thought almost all of these at one time or another:

- I'm not good at finances.
- I don't have time to deal with my finances.
- I'll do it tomorrow.
- I don't have enough money to think about my finances.
- My parents take care of my finances (or taxes) for me.
- I can think about it later.
- I'm not good at math.
- My significant other/spouse/partner does it for me.

---

* It's my birthday, I can cry if I want to. Equivalently, it's my book, I can make up words if I want to. #Bushisms

- I'll figure it out later; I have time.
- I don't have any debt, so I'm doing well...enough.
- I save some, so I must be doing ok.
- I'm not old enough to need to deal with this yet.
- I have so little saved, it doesn't even matter.
- I have so much debt that I can't think about saving.

The laundry list goes on and on. And yet, truly the first step to becoming un-average is realizing that for the sake of yourself, it is mandatory to refute whatever reasons are holding you back and causing you to delay action.

Ask yourself, "Do I believe that I can improve financially now and in the future, slowly but surely?" If you are honest with yourself and answer "No," then put this book down and go out and buy *Mindset* by Carol Dweck. Seriously, it's ok if you answer no. But there is no point in trying to improve your finances (or anything else for that matter) unless you actually believe you can do so. The book, *Mindset: The New Psychology of Success* (2007), explains how to change your mind and work towards your goals. *Mindset* blew my mind when I read it and has forced me to think about and identify whether or not I have a *growth mindset* or a *fixed mindset*. A growth mindset is simply one that you hold when you believe that you can learn, practice, and improve over time in any given task, activity, area, etc. I have a growth mindset when it comes to learning, exercise, writing, diet, and relationships. I think and believe that I can get better at each of these things. The fixed mindset, on the other hand, says that you are currently as good or as bad at something because of static factors. You are as smart as you are now because of some innate amount of "intelligence." Or you were "born to run" so you became the star athlete. The fixed mindset is one in which you already are who you are and the world around you influences most of what happens in your life rather than being someone who can go out and change things yourself. I personally struggle with and have a fixed mindset around art and music. I literally draw stick figures and that's about the best I can do. Sure, I want to believe that I could get much better at art and learn to play an instrument, but I struggle to identify as someone who can do so.

Finally, on Dweck's idea of mindset, it's important to note that everyone holds both growth and fixed mindsets in different areas (such as my growth mindset in finances and fixed mindset in art) *and* that this will change over time as mine did with computer science and programming. Initially, when I started working at Google, I couldn't code to save my life. I was asked in my interview what 4 lines of code meant. It looked like a dang Martian language and I sputtered for a few minutes before my gracious interviewer pulled the paper away and said, "It's ok. The code just counted the numbers from 1 to 5." Clearly, I barely knew what programming was. I thought that it was some special skill that these elite programmers knew and had some secret handshake between them to help keep the coding secrets in their group, hidden from the rest of the world. How wrong I was. Before work, I'd go in and watch YouTube videos of Stanford's CS106a course led by the brilliant and articulate Mehran Sahami* and I'd code. I'd get pissed off, I'd fail, and I'd want to quit. But each day I was there, for months, teaching myself this strange new language, Java, with several cups of java to keep me focused. Soon enough, I had programs bending to my newfound will. I went from not even knowing what application to use for programming to learning Java, (some C++), Python, SQL, cloud computing, and analytics. In his opening lecture, Professor Sahami says, "Sometimes you have to unlearn what you've learned," and I couldn't agree with him more. I'm sure Carol Dweck would concur.

You too will want to bash your head against the wall, when you're improving your finances, like I did when I got error messages galore in my programs. You'll set a savings goal and you'll miss it. You'll pay off a credit card and 6 months later, have some more credit card debt. You'll want to buy a house in 2 years and it will take 3 or more. It will be messy, imperfect, and a long, winding course will be charted as you steer towards your vision and goals. But if you really embrace a growth mindset and are willing to work towards becoming un-average, then you have already won half the battle.

---

* All of the CS106a course materials are online and public so you can not only watch all of his incredible lectures, but you can actually do the coursework. The first lecture is here: https://www.youtube.com/watch?v=KkMDCCdjyW8

Now that you are sufficiently versed in becoming un-average, let's look at how to win the other half of the battle: breaking society's rules. It will suffice to do a quick mental exercise. Let's ask ourselves the simple question: What are some financial rules that society puts on us? Another way of asking this same question is, what are some financial things that most people, including myself, are doing or not doing? Once we have generated a decent-sized list, we'll just group them into two categories: 1) maintain rule (i.e., it's a good rule) or 2) break rule (i.e., it's a bad rule). Ready?

Take 60 seconds to think about major financial things that you do or don't do and things in society that are promoted or not promoted (like "you should open a bank account" or "travel today while you're young, but worry about retirement later").

Here is a list of some rules that I see in society as they relate to finances:

- Get a checking account.
- Get a savings account.
- Save a little each month.
- Get experiences in your 20's and 30's, then start to focus on retirement after.
- Travel while you're young; you won't be able to once you're married, have kids, etc.
- Maybe know your credit score, but don't explore enough to know what it really means.
- If you have debt, try to pay it off, someway, somehow. P.S. All debt is bad.
- If you've got a retirement plan at work, use it.
- Track your monthly spending somehow.
- It's probably a better deal to get a new car anyways...
- Buy the biggest house you can afford.*
- It's not socially appropriate to ask someone how much they make.

---

* I'm sure you don't think that you follow this rule! Right? But remember that little financial crisis back in 2008? Yeah...that was (mostly) because people bought houses they couldn't actually afford. And yes, there is a large fraction of blame to place on financial institutions and government for allowing this to happen in the first place.

- Don't talk about how much you have (or don't have), how you are investing, or about where you're struggling financially (i.e., keep your finances secret).
- If you save money, that means you can't spend it.
- If you are financially responsible, that means you can't have fun.
- Oh...and spend less than you make.
- And always, always, always, make sure you are keeping up with the Joneses next door! You wouldn't want people thinking you don't have as much as them right?

As you went down the list, which ones did you nod your head affirmatively to? Which do you follow? Which do you break already? This list is surely incomplete, but the overwhelming take-away is that there is a fuzzy list out there that we all subscribe to by default. These rules themselves may seem good or bad, right or wrong, but each one of them are topical. But they only tell a portion of the story. Take the top three on the list. They are fairly easy rules to follow and while they are certainly good things to do, they just scratch the surface of the underlying reason why they are important. For example, if you have a savings account, you get an automatic B grade for opening it. Most* of us have a savings account already, but are we using it properly and are we saving a healthy amount?†

We could go line by line in our lists of what society says are rules that we should follow and quickly we would find out that most of the rules that we're actually following are superficially incomplete (such as, just get a savings account and you're good to go) or downright pernicious (such as buying into the belief that it's socially inappropriate to talk about wages, finances, and money with your family, friends, and colleagues). What we have to realize is that we have to break away from just taking all these rules in and using them as default settings and as "givens" that we don't delve into

---

* 21% of people don't have a savings account – and by other measures, this is a really low estimate. Just think of all the people that have them, but rarely use them or just have low balances.

† The answer to this is unfortunately, no, we're not. According to a survey, 62% of people don't have more than $1,000 in savings - leaving us "living right on the edge," vulnerable to unexpected emergencies (which almost all of us will face sooner or later).

deeper. If we don't move beyond accepting these default settings, we are doing ourselves a disservice by remaining in the dark* financially and we simply let things happen to us in a passive way. Instead, we should be proactively going out to learn new things and to truly understand how to create a more secure and fruitful financial life.

Take the very popular societal rule and paradigm, "all debt is bad." We view debt in such a way as to vilify it, scorn it, and avoid it like the Black Plague. And yet, where would millions of us be without student loan debt? Less educated? Fewer universities? Surely, this type of debt isn't all bad. What about a mortgage? We have a crap ton of mortgage debt and it's our single largest debt holding in the U.S.,† but should we be trying to avoid it? Not necessarily; this debt has been a major part of the backbone of the American Dream for the past 2 centuries. The nuances for each of the examples above become apparent when we think a little deeper about them. This additional amount of thinking is what will drive us to realize that we have to start breaking said rules and crafting a more complete picture and understanding for ourselves. This will allow us to avoid the traps, the pitfalls (and the financial predators and sharks out there), and the sheer mediocrity that comes with ignoring our personal financial reality.

With each of these rules comes a standard way of operating and a belief system about how to think and act financially. At this point, we just have to ask, "Is it working?" The clear answer is no, it's not working. Things that worked 40 years ago for our parents aren't necessarily going to hold true for us (think about the almost complete extinction of pensions, for example) and like previous systems of evolution, you can either "adapt or die"

---

* The allusion to the cave in Plato's Republic here seems quite appropriate in that most of us are living in an unformed and ambiguous financial world where we haven't been exposed to the real implications of our actions.

† Collectively we have over $8 Trillion in mortgage debt, which is over 68% of all of personal household debt owed, according to one of my favorite entities, the Federal Reserve Bank of New York.

financially. This book is designed to help each of us adapt to the changing world around us rather than sit idly by as the world passes us by.*

In essence, our challenge is to start questioning what is going on individually and around us. You and I have to deal with our finances. There is no way around it. We stand to gain by being proactive, rather than dealing with it later. Once we desire to do something, we might as well approach it with the attitude that we can change it and get better (i.e. deploy a growth mindset). And as we look to better our situation and create more financial success in our lives, we need to go rogue, become un-average, and break some rules and societal paradigms that aren't really helping us as much as we think they are.

If you're on board, you should expect to improve. It'll take time and it's not going to be all roses and fairy tales. But once you start learning and crushing some small goals, you are going to notice a big switch: you're going to switch from being like Sisyphus† to feeling like someone whose financial rolling stone gathers no moss. Personally, I don't have the answer to why you want to improve your finances – only you can answer that. While we are all playing the Game of Life,‡ the end goal and vision you craft for yourself (and those that are playing the game with you) is going to serve as the motivation and the driving force that keeps you going when times get tough.

For me, while I'll give you my two cents' worth on how to improve, I couldn't give two craps about having money, believe it or not. I don't want to teach you how to amass hordes of cash so you can log into your bank account each day and simply look at some number on a

---

* "As the world passes us by" is quite an intriguing idiom if you really think about it. In order for the world to literally pass me by, I'd have to be hanging out in space (hopefully in a NASA space suit) long enough to watch the world go by in its elliptical orbit. Alternatively, I could imagine myself as Saturn since it has a longer orbit around the sun than the Earth.

† In Greek Mythology, Sisyphus was punished by being forced to roll a giant stone up a mountain only to watch it roll back down, repeating this for all of eternity

‡ If only it were as simple as the game of *Life*, we'd all be able to retire to Millionaire Mansions. Oddly enough, as a kid, I usually opted for Countryside Acres so that I could have way more cash on hand – I think I'll try to do the same in real life.

screen. I want to give you the knowledge and skills to put you in a position to *choose* what you want to do with your life and with your financial wealth. If you gain this choice and freedom, things start to open up – all kinds of things. Things that used to be dreams and wishes start to become feasible and attainable. I don't want to impose an end destination on you. You get to envision and seek that yourself. But I do want to impose information on you so that you can figure out how to get to wherever you want to go. I have a pretty high degree of confidence that you are on board with this and if you stick with me, I'll do my best to get you all the information you need so you ultimately have more choice and freedom.

What This Book Is Not

One thing that needs to be made abundantly clear is that this book is *not* advice. This book is primarily information and education. While the lines between these two may seem initially blurry or inconsequential, I find it stark and important enough to address. The reason for this is I want to avoid having you fall into the very real, time tested trap of a very normal and blasé situation: person reads book, likes it, gets excited to implement tactics, does so for a while, falls off, and is back to square one. This is what happens when you think that a book is both simultaneously advice and information/education.

Marathon running is the same. If you dare to undertake the challenge and physically demanding requirements, you can't just successfully prepare by yourself by running and reading online blogs. I've had friends train for marathons and yes, they first sought out information, but then they took the necessary many other steps to make sure they were successful. You need to know how to pace yourself so many get a watch. If you're going to pound the pavement with your feet for 26.2 miles, you better have the right shoes so you get a shoe that works (and most likely consult someone who specializes in running shoes). You also need to figure out a training regimen to build stamina, create reliable habits and actions, and ultimately to build up, slowly over time, the total distance you can run in one session. The type of clothes you select becomes important, as does the frequency and amount of water you consume (and even the method of consumption). Many training for a marathon create systems of accountability to further enhance the likelihood of success. They form running groups, they give themselves special rewards if they meet goals (perhaps a chocolate bar after certain goals are met), they build in rest days, etc., etc., etc.

What separates these marathoners from those who desire to complete the trial, but ultimately fall short, is that they make sure that they embark upon *both* the informational acquisition and research portion of the endeavor (i.e., reading this book), as well as seeking professional advice and guidance to develop a training *system* to increase the probability of success (i.e., using financial technology tools, setting up reward/punishment incentives, using a company such as Holberg Financial,* etc.).

Now if we take a step back, think of all the activities and pursuits out there in the world besides running a crazy long distance. There's Crossfit, Tough Mudder, cycling races, and tons of things that aren't as physically related like performing at work, starting a company, getting a promotion, raising kids, being active and committed volunteers and board members at non-profits, local community organizations, or religious institutions. Just think of all the time and energy you spend trying to be active and successful in life. It's hectic, hopefully fun, and a lot of times things come up that either facilitate or detract from what we're trying to accomplish. Regardless of what you're involved in or what your current situation is, I have a hunch that you'd prefer to be *more* effective/successful than *less* effective/successful. Knowing this, we can't simply read a book and think our financial life is going to become better. We have to be willing to embody all of the above to become rogue, become un-average, and be willing to defy society's rules that shackle us to perpetually running on the metaphorical rat wheel. Strong systems and support are necessary

---

* While I'm very well aware of the self-serving nature of referencing my own company here, it is merited both because 1) we help our users achieve goals they otherwise aren't meeting, and 2) consistently throughout the book I'm going to qualify that we aren't the only route to becoming financially successful. As a broader caveat, it should be noted that in fact you absolutely do need more things to becoming financially successful than just our book, services, support, etc. We are only part of the solution.

around the financial information you are about to learn so you can significantly increase the probability and likelihood that you make real progress towards your financial goals and dreams.

There are many routes to actually achieving this, and just like marathon running, everyone is going to have to craft a system that works for them individually – there is no cookie cutter answer that exists. Over time, you'll find things that don't work for you (discard and move on) and those that do (keep and enhance). Further, this is not an end all be all, nor is it the only good source of information, nor is it the "only system." You will need to constantly refine your knowledge and behaviors to stay on top of your finances (in small doses, so don't freak out) over the course of your lifetime. You might be a Mint.com + Holberg Financial type of person or a Dave Ramsey Apostle + manual bill paying or maybe you use Wealthfront for your sophisticated investing needs, but keep your savings under your mattress (the latter is a terrible idea, btw). As mentioned before *this is a process*. And it is one that is not one-and-done nor static, it is active, alive, and it resembles a science experiment more than a picturesque two-story house with a white picket fence and 1.8 children and a puppy lolling happily in the blissful sun. It will be messy and hard, but it will be worth it.

With that, welcome to your new rogue financial life and our "un-system." The following chapters are going to equip and empower you with rock solid information that almost every company and system in America is banking* on you not realizing until it's far too late. While not as exciting as getting an invitation to Willie Wonka's Chocolate Factory, you just found your very own Golden Ticket.

---

* Gahh - I love financial puns!

2. LIFE'S FORMULA

I speak a lot. For better or for worse. When it's for better, I'm generally giving presentations about financial health and teaching people how to get a better handle on their finances so they can work towards their dreams more confidently. I've been fortunate to have spoken at some of the best universities in the world to hungry and eager students, to individuals who dreamed of a better future, and to employees at companies that bring in hundreds of millions of dollars in revenue each year. No matter where I go and no matter who I talk to, I always share with them a secret that I am honored to share with you now: Life's Formula.

Don't freak out – for those of you who have slight to severe arithmophobia,* it doesn't even have any numbers in it. It does however, govern almost 100% of all of us in the U.S. (and in fact, the world). There is a very, very slim percentage of the population that can claim not to be encapsulated by this formula. Not even 0.001% could realistically claim to be outside of its influence. It is simple, comprehensible, and at the broadest level, it is quite comprehensive and complete. When I discovered it, I realized I was a genius; then quickly discarded this notion in favor of thinking that I just put words to something that is almost painfully obvious.

With all of this build up, you're probably ready to be shocked and awed by a revelation, that once known, will make you question how

---

*   As a former math teacher, perhaps my next book will be about destroying the pernicious effect of how we teach girls to fear math at a much higher rate than boys in the US. This is a nonsensical societal narrative that we've honed for centuries that cramps an individual's potential as well as our nation's GDP.

you ever made it so far in life without it.* Without further delay, I present to you, Life's Formula:

$$\text{Learn} \rightarrow \text{Career} \rightarrow \text{Earn} \rightarrow \text{Spend}$$

It's fantastic isn't it?! If we take a step back for a second to dissect the formula a little more intensely, you will find that there are two parts in particular we care about in this book – and they happen to be the last two in the formula. Starting at the beginning, you are either currently learning or have learned. Learning is a lifelong pursuit, no doubt, but in this formula, we are going to assume that it is weighing more towards the formal side of the learning spectrum (i.e., being in high school, technical school, college, etc.). In fact, everyone in the United States is legally mandated to be in formal education up to some point,† which turns out to be a pretty solid idea.

This book is not about the first part of Life's Formula. There are tons of other books and resources that cover this and it is an increasingly important and fascinating part of the formula. It is also riddled with controversy such as how much learning should cost (think student loans and private schools), how much of it we should each have (what is the value of a high school diploma, a college degree, a Ph.D., etc.), and to whom and by whom it should be received and given (traditional classrooms, teaching methodologies, or massive online open courses, a.k.a. MOOCs, etc.). While this raging debate will continue to escalate in the nation's discourse, we are going to move past it to look at the next part of the formula.

Career. It really is a sucky word when you think about it. What does it even mean? Millions of us in the "Millennial Generation" (people between the ages of 18 – 35ish) have almost completely rejected this notion of a "traditional career." When I think of a career, I think of Don Draper‡ in Mad Men, or Homer shuttling to and from his factory

---

* This happened to me when I ate my first avocado at the age of 22.
† You have to go to school until you are 16, in most states, but it varies state by state.
‡ I've been told (only a handful of times) that I resemble Jon Hamm, the actor who portrays Don Draper. In all reality, I probably more resemble Homer Simpson than Draper, who seems to have been cut from the bust of a classical Greek statue.

job in the Simpsons. Then there is this increasingly antiquated notion of popping out of high school or college and starting at a company in your younger years knowing that the only way to achieve the American Dream is to stay at that same company for 30 plus years until the ripe old age of retirement when you are finally released from Labor's burden. Even though we are a rebellious group of rogue anti-careerists, we are all really still pursuing some notion of a career. No matter how hip it is to shun the traditional notion of a career, we ultimately end up working somewhere* and whether or not our career is satisfying, ideal, or perfect, we work each day. Sure, you might be doing some volunteer work, working at some job you hate, or only temporarily working at the job you love knowing that you'll leave it to pursue another path at some point in the future – but almost everyone is doing something that, in exchange for your time, mental/physical energy, skills and knowledge, you are paid. We could poke holes in this portion of the formula all day (and believe me, I do). The point is easy enough to understand in that we all have some type of career path that we are on, whether or not we can see the light at the end of the tunnel, or feel trapped in some digression of what we really want to be working on.

Unless you are one of the random, isolated people that choose to eschew the predominant societal, economic, and political order by cutting off all ties to everything, then you fit into the formula. There are square pegs in this round hole system, but you're not one of them. Even Henry David Thoreau, who cast himself as a romantic recluse in *Walden*, at one with nature, was still walking into town, checking his mail, and bartering. He took a temporary hiatus from work, but ultimately was still governed by Life's Formula.† Finally, even people who don't fit the traditional notion of "employee" still are on some career/work journey. The list of economic creators and deviants is long: entrepreneur, business owner, solopreneur,‡ or independent consultant, designer,

---

* Forgive me for glossing over unemployment and underemployment here. A warranted discussion. However, I am trying to focus more on what happens at the end of said formula than its other components that are equally important in a much larger context.

† I apologize to all the ardent romantics out there whose lofty idealized notions of a simple and pure life I just crushed.

‡ Or any other hideous and gross abuse of the word entrepreneur.

developer, etc. You may be your own boss and call your own shots, but you are still participating in the economy, trading in whatever you have of value for money. My intent here is not to demean these worthy pursuits, whatever they may be, but to make sure we're all on the same page in understanding this simple formula that governs us all.

Now that we have squared away the first two components, namely we learn stuff and then we go get paid, we can look into the last portions of the formula.

Once we go to work, we expect to be compensated. It would be a pretty raw deal if we showed up, created value and worked hard only to find out that we weren't going to get paid. Personally, I'd be pretty pissed and eventually each of us would run out of that precious patience reserve even if it was a cherished virtue. Alas, in fair exchange, we are paid. Now I'll assume you hate getting a physical check as much as I do, so we'll talk as if that money you just toiled for is going to get direct deposited into your checking account[6] (as a quick side step, there are over 30 million American households comprising 90 million adults who are either unbanked or underbanked[7] – which means they don't have or aren't effectively using banking services such as a checking or savings account[*]).

We'll certainly talk more about adjusting the amount that actually comes into your checking account each pay period later, but for now, we'll just treat it as "some amount." You might already have health care, retirement, and insurance costs coming out before your direct deposit or maybe you do that after, but "some amount" comes in more or less regularly. Finally, once that money comes in and your balance increases for the better (even if temporarily!), we are flooded with choices. Some of them we have on autopilot (such as transferring an amount to savings, auto bill pay, etc.) and

---

[*] As an aside to the aside, this is a particular area of interest to me. I spend a lot of time and energy trying to address this, mainly via a fantastic non-profit organization called the Center For Economic Progress (www.economicprogress.org) that I'd highly encourage all of you to check out. If you are compelled to do so, you can donate and help vulnerable families in Chicago and Illinois get access to much needed financial and legal services. It's my book, I can cry (or solicit donations) if I want to.

some of them we consciously have to enact (such as going out to eat, paying credit cards, buying gas for the car, etc.). Whether or not it's automatic, we are looking at the final part of life's formula and this is where the end of the rope is in terms of our process. These last two sections, especially the final one – spending – is where we will hone in and focus our discussion for the majority of the book.

To be clear, a lot of people begrudgingly assume that managing your personal finances is all about "spending less" and that is the only way they are going to improve. That's bogus, and honestly, quite ill-informed and naive. So if you are sitting there thinking that the only way to achieve your goals and dreams is to spend less, you need to take a serious step back and realize that for once in life, you can "have your cake and eat it too." This may come as a shock, and disbelief might be rampaging through your mind, but it's true. This is where the ubiquitous maxim comes to the forefront: everything in moderation. To summarize the "earn → spend" portion of the formula more accurately, you could employ a quote from Ben Franklin: "By failing to prepare, you are preparing to fail." This harks back to and emphasizes the previous point about becoming un-average.

Millions upon millions of Americans are blindly allowing Life's Formula to passively happen. I'm guilty of it too at times – we wake up, go to work, get paid, go out to eat, buy something at Target, save a little (or none?), then we conveniently press the repeat button and do it all over again next week. Just like Adam Sandler in *Click*, we can get so caught up in the ever-accelerating pace of life that we might find ourselves waking up one day and realize an entire year (or lifetime) has gone by without a more intentional view of what we're trying to achieve. Sandler lies down on a mattress in (if my memory serves me well) Bed Bath and Beyond where he proceeds to slowly fade off into a dream. In said dream, he's able to hit fast-forward through some of the more humdrum (mowing the lawn) and stressful situations (babies crying). And before we know it, he's spiraling out of control towards the end of his now squandered life. Some people fall into this pattern financially and delay taking life by the reins. They wind up 5, 10, 20 years later like a financial Rip Van Winkle waking up to rub their hazy eyes and long grey beard and wonder where the time went. While many people will find some fire burning their rear end that helps them to act and be more intentional, there are still those out there who really do just press fast-forward and let life happen to them. It's my hope that by more fully understanding what is happening at each of the last two components of Life's Formula, we're able to edge away from average and more fully take control of what happens to us financially.

Now that we have a solid understanding of our position and focus, we can start to make incremental and positive change financially by going through each of the following chapters to better learn not only about actions that can lead to more financial success and security, but also about what the common mistakes and pitfalls are and how to avoid them. We'll cover many topics that fit into three major sections so that the material is structured to convey the relative chronology *and* weight when approaching and building a strong financial life.

The first section, *Financial Foundations*, is really the intro crash course to personal finances. This section can be viewed as the mandatory stop-gap measures that *must* be put in place to in address a hemorrhaging wound. This section is equivalent to cleaning up the scraped and bleeding knee that occurred after your first bike crash or slip and fall on a cement sidewalk. There is no point to really talking about how you're going to run in a race next week until you've cleaned up and bandaged your wound. This section of the book is the most vital to establishing your initial financial security and a base upon which you can build a more robust and successful financial future. These are the concepts such as savings, paying off debt, and setting up a basic plan for retirement, that you have already heard *ad nauseum* since you were a kid. It will be inviting and tempting to breeze through this section with a nod of assent, as in, "Yes, I know this already, what's next?" However, as a self-examination to see how you are doing, all you have to retort to yourself is, "Am I actually *doing* each of these things?" As we'll see more fully, these are also areas in which we are financially exposed, vulnerable, and anemic – even if we think our knee isn't bleeding that badly. As you peruse* the chapters in this section, recognize that many of these things will take time, lots of time in some instances. While you will be able to act immediately on many topics (i.e., setting up an emergency savings account), others will help you set up correctly for the long run (i.e., paying more than the minimum on a credit card each month). This financial foundation, as you attend to it, will become stronger over many months and years and can significantly prepare you for life's unknowns. Finally, as you understand and complete many of the aspects of this section, you'll be ready to tackle the remaining two sections which can significantly enhance your overall financial situation and wealth over the course of your lifetime.

The second section, *Financial Fitness*, is what it sounds like. It's about becoming fit financially. Our crashed bike rider, whose tears are now dried, is ready to hop back in the saddle and crank their way forward to new speeds and heights.† Financially, this means that we've addressed any initial items that were essential to getting us in a position to look further forward. We have taken care of and are continuing to work on the immediate and important basics. Now we are thinking about what we can do to move away from being a passive reactor to life to one who is actively choosing what to do financially. In this section we are going to start to create a more robust financial life that incorporates many items to enhance our ability to move away from being average. In this section, you'll start to learn how to control what is going on in life and it's a sweet stage to be at because it feels like you just hit that coveted speed boost in Mario Kart that will allow you to start making headway towards first place.

---

* While the colloquial and familiar use of peruse is "to skim over something lightly," I am using it in its original sense of "to studiously and judiciously examine in detail."

† As a child, my brothers and I used to build bike ramps in our driveway out of discarded plywood and bricks. 9 times out of 10, our delicately constructed ramps did allow us to soar to what felt like infinite, new heights. But let me tell you, that 1 time out of 10 that it collapsed was inevitable and quite painful. In retrospect, I think it was worth it to push the boundaries even amidst the risks that resulted in more scraped knees and hands than my mom and dad probably cared to deal with.

In the third section, *Advanced Financial Fitness*, we will work on going from stable and secure to a place where our focus is about maximizing and optimizing your financial life. All too often we want to jump right to this section and talk about things like investing in real estate (other than a house that you plan on living in), putting lots of money into the stock market to test your trading game, or maybe throwing some money at your long lost cousin's new exciting business venture. You. Will. Get. There. Trust me. It might feel like ages before you have enough money to even think about investing in stocks and bonds, but you'll get here. Further, it might seem like, as a young financial grasshopper, the concepts such as Efficient Market Hypothesis, are beyond your intellectual ability, but they aren't. You. Will. Get. There. Again, while you can read through the book quickly enough, it might take years – and in the digital age of instant gratification and Instagram (a.k.a. "instagramification") this feels nearly impossible – to actually get to the place where you are engaged in and actively working on some of the concepts in this section. But, like a fine wine, as you age, you'll get better and eventually, you'll be the master sommelier of your own finances.

In closing, as you progress through the book and actually put the ideas and information into practice, you will be following a much less traveled pathway that is both actionable and attainable. Don't doubt for a second just how challenging and difficult it can be to take the seemingly "self-evident" text and put it into practice in real life. Many have read books, year after year, about self-help, self-improvement, etc. and have remained static at the point where they initially embarked upon. While inertia will condone being average, I'll prod and implore you, via my brash verbal abrasions and cajoling, to strike out into rogue un-averageness and into a life that you more fully control and develop. My hope is that you embrace this "un-system" and really wake up to the fact that many forces in society rely on you not knowing the information contained here. Throughout this book, you need to embrace becoming a rogue rule-breaker and one who is willing to shun the prevailing ideas that are ultimately detrimental to your own financial health. It's time to become un-average. Let's Go.

Part 2-Financial Foundations

3. FINANCIAL FOUNDATIONS 101

The Essentials

Imagine if the architects of the Tower of Babel* decided that, in pursuing the heavens, it would be wise to skimp on the foundations of their edifice in favor of building a leaner structure. "We'll save time!" one shouts. "Yes, and we'll save material!" another joins in the chorus advocating for using less resources. "We'll need less people too, and we'll be able to build taller!" says a third. You can almost see it now as they decide to forgo a wide base in favor of further heights. Out comes an unstable needle that wavers and quakes in the slightest breeze. It is doomed to topple during the first minor storm. "Crash, ye weak men of folly!" the revered Babylonian philosophers cry out as they look down from a hillside upon the builders who were so brash and naive to think that a solid foundation wasn't necessary...

In terms of physical buildings, a solid foundation is something no architect or engineer would dream of skipping – it just doesn't make sense. The Egyptians understood this when they built the Great Pyramids of Giza almost 5,000 years ago. The Great Ziggurat of Babylon wouldn't have stretched to an impressive height of 300 feet without its trusty foundation (massive at the time). Now we don't build skyscrapers – such as the Space Needle in Seattle or the 2,722 foot Burj Khalifa in Dubai – without first driving massively tall support

---

* The construction of the Tower of Babel was an attempt of old to create a tower tall enough to reach the heavens. In the book of Genesis, God confounds these builders by making them speak different languages.

structures deep into the ground so that buildings can tower over the earth with structural integrity, fearing not the breeze nor the elements.

Even non-physical structures need foundations. Our government, which was built upon a core foundation enshrined in documents such as the Declaration of Independence and the Constitution, is a good example.* The notion of a free and just society seeking to guarantee life, liberty, and the pursuit of happiness are foundational structures upon which our country relies. Where would we be without these documents, tenets, and beliefs that underlie our modern pursuits as a country? We'd probably be begging Britain to take us back and make us colonies again. Or maybe, we'd be in some perpetual disarray resembling anarchy instead. We'll never know because some people back in the day decided to build a strong foundation upon which to build a modern country (however ineffective and utterly incompetent today's political system may seem). Harking back to an earlier example, without a foundational training plan, would our elite marathon runner break world records? No. Would Facebook be anything without its foundational idea of a social network, one in which you can message and post on your friend's' wall? Heck no – without their respective foundations, each of these would suck.

So why would we, as individuals, skimp on building ourselves a strong, sturdy, and resilient financial foundation upon which we can construct a future and, even more immediately, deal with the myriad of situations *right now* that require our cornerstone to be secure? The fact that we know that, *at a minimum*, 83% of Americans worry about finances[8] should leave us nonplussed, confused, and driven to act in our own self-interest to mitigate weaknesses and to improve our current state of affairs.

As we dive into this first section of the book, it will help to outline the three components that comprise your financial foundation so that we can work on becoming less worried about money and become

---

* Lest we not forget what Thomas Paine aptly pointed out in his revolutionary pamphlet *Common Sense* – and we'd be remiss to forget – "society in every state is a blessing, but Government, even in its best state, is but a necessary evil."

more financially healthy. Each of these three areas, if addressed, can significantly lead to better outcomes in both your short term and long term horizons. This will be a quasi-painful process for many to actually get moving on these processes, but those who do will find their security and success in life improving.

The first component that we'll look at together is savings. While savings can certainly be interpreted in a broad sense that encompasses many different reasons for and areas of savings, I want to create a much narrower and more defined meaning of savings. You and I both know that savings is a good thing, but we struggle to figure out how much to save, where to save it, and what we're saving it for. As such, we will be looking explicitly, in this first section, at two main areas of savings: *general* savings and *emergency* savings. Without going into much more detail now, it will suffice to say that these two areas, if attended to diligently, can revolutionize the way you approach life and your finances. We'll go further momentarily, but creating a habit of savings is the anatomical equivalent of having a heartbeat – without it, we're dead.

After we get going with an inspection of savings, we'll look at debt. Scary, I know. But instead of covering it up, selectively ignoring it, and attempting to relegate it to the infantile "I'll deal with it later" mindset, we'll face it head on so that we can see it more clearly and get ahold of it. The ancient frescos of the Minoan civilizations found on Crete depict heroic people running straight at a bull. In a celebrated ritual, they would leap up straight over the horns of this fierce animal in order to springboard off the bull's back in an acrobatic display of agility and power. Just imagine how fearful they were in the moments before – staring down a feverish and gigantic bull, trying to conceive of leaping over its massive frame. The task ahead of them loomed large and I can hardly leap over a short, stationary fence, let alone a raging, charging bull. I give them due credit.

So too it can be with debt. It can feel overwhelming and depressing, a seemingly unconquerable task like a bull charging at us full speed, but by working on ways to handle it, you will lessen that weighty feeling of doom. Instead of being confined to perpetual servitude to your bull of debt, you'll start to figure out ways to tackle a formerly formidable task. Admittedly, dealing with debt isn't fun. It's so much easier to delay action here – to run the other way. But getting ahead of your debt can be a massive opportunity in life. So we'll face the huffing nostrils and horns of our bull of debt together. Debt takes all types of forms and comes in varying amounts.* It might be student loan debt, credit card debt, a mortgage, or any number of things that we have to pay for, but regardless of what it is and how much you owe, you can develop strategies to become an agile, acrobatic bull-hurdler of your own debt.

Finally, while savings helps give you a necessary cushion for life and paying down debt makes life easier, the third component of your financial foundation centers on retirement and long term wealth building. These are not terms reserved for the rich. They are concepts for all of us. The best part about being younger is that you have *time* on your side. But don't be fooled just because you have time. It does not allow for the justification of delaying action from a financial standpoint. Rather, time is our biggest opportunity and asset to be capitalized on. As we dissect retirement further, it will become excitingly obvious that this is no Herculean task and that even us mere mortals can accomplish big things in our own lives. Sure, when dealing with retirement, the many-headed Hydra† flails around waiting to attack from various angles to thwart our success, but once you learn a couple of key things about retirement accounts, investing, and how to harness the power of time and compound interest, the battle for long term wealth accumulation becomes

---

* Importantly, for those that are in the minority and have no debt, this section is still important so that you can arm yourself with information. There is a high probability that at some point in the future you will have some type of debt such as a mortgage or something else so bone up now.

† The mythological Hydra was the guard the entrance to the Underworld at Lerna. It had poisonous breath and even the scent of it could kill unassuming victims. If you were able enough to cut off one of its many heads, it would simply regenerate. Thankfully, Hercules slayed it during his Twelve Labors. This makes LeBron James' conquest of the NBA look relatively easy if you ask me.

much more manageable. Our loathsome retirement Hydra will reduce from a many pronged, regenerating, and infinite problem, to a manageable pack of puppies, which to me, seems like much less of a nuisance and way more adorable and valuable.

In closing out the framing of Part 2, I'd like for us to think about these three key areas of our financial foundation, savings, debt, and retirement, as a three-pronged stool. The key to the success of having a sturdy stool here is that each of the legs provides the necessary strength *and balance* so that it is a functional piece of furniture. Like this three-legged stool, our financial foundation is comprised of three equally important aspects. In understanding the balance of both the stool and our financial foundation, it is painfully obvious what happens if we remove any one of the given legs: we fall down and wind up hurt and bruised. Right now, many of our financial stools are unstable or already broken and in need of repair. On top of having to work to rebuild and fix our stool, we have to simultaneously guard ourselves against those companies who are explicitly waiting to capitalize on and take advantage of those whose stool is broken. As if life weren't challenging enough, right? As we think about becoming rogue financially and playing by our own new rules, it is absolutely essential to make sure that your financial foundation is strong and able like a well-made stool, a trained marathon runner, a nimble surgeon – do whatever you have to do to convince yourself that this is important and that you're going to pursue it. It's now time to start building your own financial skyscraper.

Joe Holberg

4. SERIOUSLY, SAVE

The Savings Tub

Remember when you were a kid and there was the little yellow rubber ducky floating in the tub next to you? Bubbles everywhere, not a care in the world.* You could fill it up super high and create a mini-ocean of sorts where your most creative imagination could run wild (or swim) for hours: submarines and oceanic battles of pirates and the Spanish Armada, diving competitions for GI Joes, and Barbie in search of Olympic swimming glory. Or, you could fill it up just enough to get in and out as quickly as possible, perhaps in time for your favorite TV show or nightly board game. Whatever it was, the tub was a versatile mix of functional cleaning arena and play station and while most of us opt for the quicker shower these days, we'll talk about your savings – a core pillar of your financial life – in terms of a bathtub. Odd as it may seem, this will help us understand how we're interacting with and developing our savings accounts.

Right off the bat – in the name of being jarring and slightly combative – I want to tell you something: you're not good at saving. No offense, it's just true. Cry out in resistance to this notion if you will, but consider this simple thought experiment and ask yourself, "How much do I make in one month?" Figure out your annual salary and divide by 12. For the sake of using some real numbers, let's assume that good ole Deborah makes $60,000 a year. That comes neatly to $5,000 a month (before the hideous and horrendous notion of taxes

---

* That is unless you hated baths, of course.

– which we will completely ignore here). Now, the vast majority of financial planners, advisors, experts, or whatever else you want to call the people who "know about money" will say that you should have 6 months' worth of this income saved up in a savings account. Mind blowing, right?! Think about Deborah. This means that she should have 6 times her monthly income of $5,000 in savings which is an immense $30,000 (and note, this is just in savings; this doesn't include her checking, retirement, and other investments).

Now let's imagine various levels of savings Deborah could have. She might have one month's worth of her annual income saved ($5,000), maybe she has done a solid job saving and has 3 months packed away ($15,000) or maybe she is set with a really healthy amount and has already socked away the full six months' worth of income in her savings account ($30,000). She could be any number of places, including not having any savings at all. So where might she be? If Deborah is like 62% of Americans, she we will have *at or below $1,000.*[9]

This amount is actually scarier than it might seem at first blush. This means that if Deborah's car breaks down, she might not be able to afford the fixes. She might have a medical emergency and not be able to pay the bill. And because, like half of Americans, she doesn't have much saved, she is going to struggle to cover other "emergencies" and unknown expenses that crop up here and there like little financial wildfires that need to be doused out before they rage and become giant conflagrations. This is precisely the reason why we're starting our financial foundation discussion around savings. It is quite critical for a variety of reasons. Not least among them is being able to quickly and adequately deal with emergency situations. The thing is, bad stuff happens and if you're prepared for it with savings, you can better deal with it. If you're not, then things can spiral out of control pretty quickly.

You have probably heard lots of buzz words about savings, such as an "emergency fund," a "rainy day fund," or more recently, the "F*ck Off Fund" by Paulette Perhach.[10] But what do they actually mean and why do financial people, myself included, preach about the necessity of saving? It is because you are going to need it. Maybe not right this second, tomorrow, or next month, but you are going to need it at some point. The problem is, if you don't have a small savings cushion, then life gets a lot harder, more uncertain, and ends up costing you more in the long run. Until I was about 25, I thought I was invincible and that I didn't really need savings (even though I had it) because emergencies just didn't happen to young people like me. But there are studies out there that show that you can have two or more significant spikes or dips in your expenses or income in a given year.[11]

A spike in expenses might leave you short on cash one month as might a dip in income (especially if you aren't a salaried employee). These natural oscillations – that the research shows happens in almost everyone's life – are hard to see coming in terms of their magnitude (i.e., how much it costs) and frequency (i.e., how often it happens). And yet, however unpredictable the actual event is, we can be almost certain that *something* is going to happen. Knowing that something will happen, even if you don't know exactly who, what, when, why, or how, leaves us in a great position because we're able to proactively plan for it, rather than passively waiting to react to it. This natural vulnerability and likelihood of having some uncertainty and unknown events happen on a *regular* basis shows just how naive I was in the past to think that I didn't need savings (and that I was invincible). I don't know about you, but given life's uncertainty, I'd rather be more prepared to handle these types of situations than less prepared – it just makes sense.

So, what is the monthly income number that you calculated (a quick way to do it is just multiple your biweekly paycheck by 2)? Then, ask yourself the final follow up question: how does this compare to my current level of savings? Do you have at least one month's worth of income saved? Maybe 4 or 2.5? Maybe 0? Be honest with yourself here. Just log on to your bank account and look at the number in your savings account. If Deborah has $2,500 saved up, then she has half a month's worth of income saved and she's already eclipsed the

62% of Americans who have less than $1,000. It's a good start, but she probably needs to save more over time. In time though, she can build her savings up, just like you can.

Regardless of where you are currently with your savings, we can do stuff now to make sure that you can handle bad stuff later. There is an interesting paradox, I believe, when it comes to savings. The concept of savings is probably one of the *easiest* of all financial topics to understand. We need savings to help plan for and fund a whole host of things in life. And yet, as our national inability to save shows, it is one of the *hardest* of all financial goals to actually achieve, even if we do understand it on a conceptual level.

So what's going on?

Let's return to the bathtub analogy to see more clearly why saving is so hard. The water level in your bathtub is the current amount of savings. If you have no savings, there's no water in your tub. If your goal is to have $30,000, like Deborah, and you have $15,000 currently, then your tub is 50% full. So on and so forth. Use the numbers that you have from the earlier questions to think about your own tub. If we walked away and never did anything again, our tub would just stay the same.* Next, note that there is a drain in our tub and when we take money out of our savings account, we are effectively opening the drain and letting our savings dwindle out. Don't view this entirely in a negative light. Sometimes this has to happen and it is actually much preferable to use funds in our savings tub than it is to say, swipe our credit card and have to pay interest for using it. After all, if we've planned and saved well, our savings will be serving its intended use after all. Alas, our drain is a tricky feature and sometimes it isn't as tightly closed as we thought it was and it could be the case that while

* Technically, and as a fun real life extension of the tub here, the water will actually slowly evaporate over time until it's all gone (it might take a while), but the financial parallel here is that due to the slow, but sure rise of inflation that has been a consistent Federal Reserve and national target for decades, your funds would slowly, but surely lose purchasing power over time until your savings dwindled to virtually nothing as well. Assuming that your savings account interest rate is below the inflation rate, which has been the case for almost a decade post-Great Recession.

you think you have good savings habits, your tub might slowly be draining with or without your knowledge. You might put in $200 a month and pat yourself on the back. But then, a couple of days later, you grab $100 out of the ATM on the fly during the weekend to take your lovely significant other out to dinner and the movies without really paying that much attention. Or maybe your savings account is hooked up to Netflix, or was it Spotify, or...well, it's only $10/month anyways so it's fine. Or is it? Your goal should be to *plug this drain in your savings account and try to have it come out of your checking account instead.*

With two features discussed now (our tub water level and the drain), let's turn to the faucet. This is where the fun begins. The faucet itself is either on or off. Pretty obvious right? So ask yourself, "is my savings faucet on or off?" If you currently transfer money from your checking to your savings account, then your faucet is on. If you haven't transferred money from your checking account to your savings account recently (like 2 – 4 weeks or so), then your savings faucet is turned off. We have to dive in a little deeper here to really get at what is a weakness in millions of people's savings habits: lying to ourselves about our savings habits (I do it too; we all do). Most people will self-select into the first savings style of saying that their faucet is turned on. However, like an irascible and impatient child filling up the tub, we might be going at savings in a really ineffective way. Essentially, if you constantly have your hand on the faucet twisting, tweaking, and modifying how much spills out, then you are setting yourself up for failure because you can just as easily turn your faucet off at any time, just as you can turn it on. Further, it takes way too much energy and thought to continually play with the faucet and how much money you are saving each month.

To be crystal clear, if you manually choose how much to save each month, your bathtub is not going to fill up the way you want it to. And year after year you'll be looking at that water level wondering why it's virtually unchanged. If you have to actively save each month – and that means logging into your account and physically clicking buttons to transfer money from your checking to your savings – then you are most likely doomed to stay in the category of the 62% of Americans who don't have enough saved (arguably this may even be a higher percentage than 62%). Just think about how many people are prone to this: America has 245.3 million adults[12] which means that about 152 million people haven't figured out how to save well.

What is the solution to this?

The solution lies in *automating* your faucet rate and the contribution that you make to your savings account. This is mandatory, crucial, beyond important. I have watched people for years try to save – ineffectively – and one of the fastest ways to get them on a path to actually filling their savings tub is to get the faucet turned on to a methodical, healthy flow rate from their checking account to their savings account.

There are a couple of subtle key tricks to fine-tuning the filling of your savings tub so make sure you duly consider each one and see whether or not you are currently doing them. If you're not, just fix it so that you are (you'll be that much more un-average if you can master these simple steps). The first trick to automating is syncing up your transfer from your checking account to your savings account with your paycheck deposits. The vast majority of people get paid twice a month on Fridays. Maybe you get paid once a month or weekly, but you just have to account for the slight difference. Going back to Deborah, if she gets paid every other week on Friday, her first step is to go set up an automatic transfer for every other week on the same day that she gets paid. Now, a lot of people will get paid on Friday and their funds won't technically settle until Monday, so if you're worried about this, then set up your auto transfer from your checking to your savings for every other Monday. One of the main reasons this step is so important is that you will be timing your savings with the corresponding income *increase*. It helps to smooth out the pain of savings. For Deborah, if she gets $2,500 deposited and immediately and automatically saves $250, her checking account will look like it went up $2,250.

Psychologically, it is much easier to see your bank account increase (albeit by a slightly smaller amount) than it is to see your checking account balance decrease (which would be the case if she saved in off weeks, for example). It's a subtle distinction, but this timing helps to make saving easier when it is paired with your income increase.

Before moving on, it is worth noting that not everyone has a steady paycheck like this, so for those who don't, you'll have to be a little more adaptable. At the same time, it's feasible, even if it is a smaller weekly amount to set up automatic and recurring transfers from checking to savings.

Going forward, as we look into extending our savings discussion, we will break down our savings accounts into two distinct and equally important types. The first type we'll discuss is the well-known "emergency savings account" that has already been alluded to and a second savings account blandly named the "general savings account." Two accounts? You might be thinking, "I barely have any in just my one savings account – give me a break!" Yes, two accounts. It is entirely possible to have all your savings in just one account, and millions of people do this, but I will encourage you to make sure that you have two savings accounts and not just one. The reason for this, as will become apparent, is that each of these two accounts serve very *different* purposes and if we keep them in one account we run the risk of falling victim to psychologically commingling the funds and this detracts from our overall financial health and ability to systematically save more effectively. Let's tackle them in turn; first the emergency savings account and then the general savings account.

Emergency Savings Account

The emergency savings account (a.k.a. rainy day fund, F*uck it fund, etc.) serves the purpose of creating savings that are used for *unexpected* expenses. The key here is the italicized word. We need to be ready for that unknown future and all the crazy crap that life throws at us. Last minute travel to see a sick loved one, job loss, car breakdowns, emergency health costs (as opposed to routine expenses like medications, annual checkups, etc.), needing to quickly move across country for that dream job (or at least a better one), or needing to escape a toxic work or personal relationship. Whatever it is, it's the use of funds towards *unplanned* things that crop up like a vampire in a horror movie – you knew it was coming, but you didn't know when, where, or how nasty it was actually going to be. Fortunately, you've got your garlic savings to ward off the perils that lurk around the corner ready to strike.

This account, most likely a) doesn't exist yet for you or b) is underfunded. If you already have one current savings account, then you don't have an emergency savings account. What you have is a general savings account that we will cover next. I don't care if you already have $20,000 or some large number in a savings account, until you have two savings accounts, you don't have an emergency savings account in my book. The simple solution is to open a second savings account that will serve as your emergency savings account. A lot of people ask me, should this emergency savings account be at the same bank that I have my other savings or checking account at? To this, I'll simply say, do what works for you. Almost all savings accounts are super basic and they should be free. If you are paying for one, it might be time to look elsewhere. On top of that, savings rates are really low right now, we're talking like almost 0% interest* so don't go out there trying to find something that is going to earn you tons of money. The point of setting up this emergency savings account isn't to earn money (although we will try to earn as much as possible). It is to have funds set aside for emergencies and when we keep funds in savings accounts, it is highly accessible (aka *liquid*),

---

* As of June 2016, this is primarily due to the Federal Reserve keeping the interest rates low, which banks respond to by lowering savings and deposit account interest rates (bad for us, the consumer, better for banks). Since they are still able to increase rates on their products such as credit cards, mortgages, etc. this generates a higher profit margin. Don't get me wrong, I love banking – it has helped build the modern financial world and I wouldn't put my cash under my mattress for any reason. But wow, are they making killer profits in the post-Recession world: http://www.forbes. com/sites/billconerly/2015/09/08/bank-profit-outlook-2016-earnings-could-rise-50-percent/#6dde5e934bdc

but not very return-oriented (aka earning interest).

If you have accounts at a versatile bank, setting up two separate savings accounts should be relatively easy and (almost) pain-free. You probably don't even have to go to the branch or make a phone call, you can log on to the site, click click click, and boom, 5 – 10 minutes later you have a second savings account. While I very rarely suggest specific companies or products, I will here. One of the highest interest earning savings accounts out there is Ally Bank (www.ally.com) whose current interest rate is at ~1.0% (compared to many others that are offering a dismal 0.1 – 0.5%). The account is free as well – bonus land. If that doesn't seem appealing, check out Goldman Sachs (GS) Bank (www.gsbank.com)

Once you have this second savings account set up, the questions become a) how much should I have? and b) how much should I be saving each month? The first question is answerable here, but the second question and answer is more individualized to each person. In terms of how much you should have, we can answer it just like a marathoner would read about the training schedule on an online blog. A couple of articles later and basic facts are known which covers the first question. But the second question gets into the area of needing real people to form a support group, some friends to run with, and maybe even a coach. Everyone's answer to the second question is highly contingent on individual circumstances and it would be a fool's errand to attempt to answer it within the confines of this book.

As mentioned before, almost all financial professionals will recommend having between three and six months' worth of your income saved in an emergency savings account. This range is going to fluctuate based on your own needs and situation, but it's a solid target to shoot for. It also might change over time as you either add funds or actually use some in the unfortunate case of an actual emergency. Going back to Deborah, this meant having between $15,000 to $30,000 in her emergency savings account. This number should look large and your own number, whatever it is, will look large as well. That's the point. It is a large, emergency reserve that can help you handle life's wacky ways. Once we figure out this number (as a reminder, take your monthly pay and multiple by 3 to find the minimum and 6 to find the maximum for this account), we can start working towards it.

One of the most important things here is to realize that you aren't going to magically have this amount anytime soon (and if you do, congrats). Again, it is more about getting the faucet system set up so that you are *slowly building your emergency fund over time.* Just like climbing Mount Everest, savings is about putting one foot ahead of the other repeatedly. No one in their right mind is going to expect you to climb it all in one day (in fact, you would most likely die due to the change in atmospheric pressure*) nor do I expect you to save all of your emergency funds immediately. It. Takes. Time. Read those last three words again.

How much time it takes to get there will be determined not only by how much your faucet puts in each month (or biweekly), but on how many times the drain is forced open. For simplicity's sake, let's try to answer the first part related to how much to put in regularly while assuming that we don't experience any draining of our funds. This obviously doesn't accurately reflect reality, but it is close enough to be useful. Harking back to Deborah, let's assume that she just opened that Ally savings account and is in the process of setting up her automatic, repeating transfer from her checking to savings. As a reminder, she brings home $2,500 every two weeks ($5,000/month) and she wants to save 10% of her earnings. But this just feels a little too ambitious (there's no harm in starting small and working your way up gradually. In fact, it's more prudent to do this than to over-save and have to backtrack later). Instead she is going to save 5% of her monthly take home pay which amounts to a bi-weekly transfer amount of $125 (or $250/ month. Mathematically, 10% would have been $250 bi-weekly or $500/ month).

Deborah sets up the timing to coincide with her paycheck deposit

---

* If you're looking for an amazing (and devastating) book on Mount Everest, read *Into Thin Air* by Jon Krakauer.

and boom, she's on autopilot. Now that she doesn't have to manually remember to do this every two weeks or each month, it'll start to build more quickly and regularly (which is what we're hoping for after all). Since her emergency savings account is growing at a rate of $250 each month, we can quickly see that every 4 months she will have saved $1,000. That's pretty cool. She logs in months later and sees that and already feels better about her ability to cope with rainy day events. This rate of savings will build her to $3,000 after one year. Sure, it has taken her a year to build up her funds, but she's further along now than she was before. If we look at her original target goal of getting to $15,000 (which is three months' worth of her income and the recommended minimum for emergency savings), it will take her 5 years to accomplish this. Granted, this may seem like an incredibly long time, but there are three extremely compelling reasons why this is worth pursuing:

1. She is continually increasing her capacity to deal with emergency situations. This gives her more resources, choices, and power over her own situation. Not every emergency will decimate her fund, so even if she experiences some along the way, she is continually replenishing and growing her fund.

2. As she gets to this goal, other goals will be met faster. By being able to deal with emergencies efficiently, she is able to stay on track with her other financial goals and need not slow down or deviate when things get tough.

3. Once she has a solid emergency fund built, she only has to do it once. If you're 25 and spend 5 years until you're 30 building your account up, you've got about 3 other decades of working life where you won't be frantically putting out metaphorical fires. That tub is full and ready to douse a nasty blaze.

For a moment, let's imagine Deborah decided to transfer 10% of her paycheck to her emergency account. She would have had twice as much as her 5% rate so instead of $3,000 saved after a year, she would have $6,000 saved. A pretty big difference for just a year. In terms of meeting her long term goals, it would take half as long. So, in 2.5 years (instead of 5), she would have saved $15,000 and in 5 years (instead of 10), she would have saved a full six months' worth of income ($30,000). This is quite a big difference which increases your financial health that much quicker. So as you look to figure out how much you can realistically save each paycheck, be reasonable with yourself, but also try to push yourself a little. You don't have to break your back and never do anything fun, but trimming the fat is a reasonable approach. Just think about it in a slightly different way: if you go out to eat twice a week, that's 8 times a month and if you spend $25 each time (a drink or two plus an entree) you're spending $200 a month just to eat out. Now, if you went out 6 times a month instead, you just found a way to increase your savings by $50 a month on top of whatever else you were already able to carve out towards your establishment and building of your emergency fund. And that's just the tip of the iceberg in terms of creatively increasing savings.

In closing out the discussion of your emergency fund, I cannot overstate the importance here. Yes, it may seem daunting now, but small actions will lead to long term big results. You don't have to move heaven and earth to save every last penny, but you do need to turn on your faucet and make sure that it is automatically and regularly helping you in the background so that you don't have to think about it and it just starts to happen. In terms of making you feel less stressed about your financial situation, this is it. This is the area that can help you move away from being financially average like at least 62% of Americans who are living on the brink financially. On top of that, you can work to avoid being one of the 83% of Americans that admit to worrying about a lack of savings.

At the end of the day, just ask yourself which side of the fence you want to be on – the one where you suffer chronically from having too little savings which causes stress, worry, and pain? Or do you want to go rogue and set up a system that works to your advantage, carving out resources to make your life easier, more manageable, and ultimately helps you attain financial health? I think the choice is obvious. Now go spend 20 minutes setting up your savings faucet so that tub starts to fill up.

General Savings Account

The difference between the emergency savings account just covered and the general savings account that we'll talk about here is actually quite simple and can be reduced to two words, *unplanned* and *planned*. In this savings universe, anything that happens that is unplanned comes out of the emergency savings account tub. Anything that you are intentionally planning and saving for should come out of the general savings account. This separation is quite stark and the metaphorical line in the sand is clear. Crystal clear – it's as clear as a fine wine glass made out of the sand in which that line has been drawn. Don't mistake the importance here of physically separating (having the two accounts themselves) and of mentally/psychologically separating them (knowing the different rationale and purpose of each type).

So what constitutes *planned* events and expenses that should be drawn from the general savings account?
I'm glad you asked.* There are several things that this account can be strategically used for: travel expenses (domestic, international, or to Neverland to visit Tinkerbell and Peter Pan #lifegoals), saving for a car purchase, a down payment on a home, or any number of larger expenses that you can reasonably anticipate happening in the near to longer term.

A good initial example, since as a nation we are entertainment obsessed,† is to think about purchasing a flat screen TV. Some simple mental gymnastics will highlight how we can think about planning for this expense. Let's say that TV costs $750 and you are

---

* Yes, I do talk to myself still. This would perhaps concern one of the more esteemed psychologists, Jean Piaget, who might say my cognitive development is still stuck in the preoperational stage. One of my life goals is to retain the creativity and inquisitiveness of a child, so maybe this is a good thing after all: https://en.wikipedia. org/wiki/Piaget%27s_theory_of_cognitive_development#Pre-operational_stage

† Americans watch over 5 hours of TV *each day*. This confounds me greatly, I just want to know who the heck you are, seriously. I just don't get it. http://www.nydailynews. com/life-style/average-american-watches-5-hours-tv-day-article-1.1711954

planning on buying it in 5 months, just in time for the Superbowl* or maybe the new season of *Orange Is the New Black* (#OITNB for life! Omgeee). Whatever your reason, you want that sucker mounted on the wall ready to view. Thus, we subtly and smartly anticipate some fringe costs of $250 for the mounting and we are really going to have an out-of-pocket $1,000 cost associated with this enterprise. We need to save $200 each month for 5 months to have this stack of 10 Benjamins.[†] Now, it's tempting to think, "Well, why don't I just get a credit card from Best Buy and buy the TV on that instead? It's got a 0% interest rate anyways." Sure, you go for it, but just remember, those cards are designed to: a) get you to spend more, and b) have you *not* pay off the card by the time the promotional period runs out (normally 12 – 18 months or so). Once this happens, many will add *all* of the back interest accumulated[‡] which can easily amount to hundreds or even thousands of dollars.

The general savings account is a dynamic place and the inflows and outflows here are going to change presumably more frequently than your emergency savings account. Similar to a Thanksgiving turkey, your general savings account has multiple distinct parts. Your TV savings goal might be the drumstick portion of the turkey. Your home down payment portion might be the breast meat, and your down payment on a car might be akin to the wings. Odd analogy notwithstanding, the general savings account, while one account, may have several subcomponents and may contain distinctly different areas that it serves. If you are wondering here about the merits of having yet more savings accounts, for example, separate accounts to cover each purchase, TV, home, and car goals, then you are spot on in your curiosity. Personally, I see no reason not to have as many different savings accounts as you

* The true form of football is of course futbol (a.k.a. soccer in America). Over 3.2 billion watched some game of the World Cup in 2014 (and 1 billion watched the final) whereas only 114 million watched the Super Bowl in 2016. A measly ~11% of the World Cup final – let the true sport be crowned!

† Stay with me people, Benjamins are $100 bills. Try beefing up on your slang if you need a little refresher: http://www.urbandictionary.com/define.php?term=Benjamin&defid=1384165

‡ As a larger point, credit card companies made $18.5 billion (yes, billion) dollars from credit cards in 2011. http://www.bcsalliance.com/creditcard_profits.html

70

have large savings goals. If your bank or credit union has a good online website – which most do these days – then opening a savings account can take under 5 minutes. On top of that, they should be free and have a reasonably small minimum opening deposit (of say $250, or even nothing at all). Once you've set up the account itself, then taking that next step of automating these savings contributions too should only take 5 or so additional minutes per account. So what, you spent a whopping total of 30 minutes to create a system to start building a strong financial foundation that millions of people have opted not to do? This is when you lean back in that chair and think, "I'm a boss."

The downside to having several savings accounts is that if you don't institute a system that helps you actually plan for and strategically save for your goals, it's really just a futile exercise. In this case, you might want to stick to one general savings account until you become more comfortable and successful saving within that one. If you plan on going this route, just be realistic about whether or not you really are serious about saving for some specific goal. For example, if you definitely want a car in 2 years to replace that rusty clunker and you want to pay cash for a $7,500 car, then you had better save $312.50 each month for 24 months to make it happen. If that sounds like a lot, maybe a cheaper car might be swirling around in the mystical crystal ball of the future instead.*

One final caveat here in terms of the savings accounts themselves is to watch out for fees and any weird features such as transaction limits on withdrawals, minimum opening amounts, monthly service charges (usually for having a balance under a certain amount), etc. Most savings accounts are pretty basic and free, but just make sure you read the fine print (as painful as that may be).

In closing, creating and actually building savings is no small task. Given competing priorities in life, savings can quickly become reduced, or worse, relegated to an afterthought. What is terribly important in thinking about yourself as a saver is looking at the

---

* I'm thinking of the creepy scene in *The Wizard of Oz* where Aunt Em is calling out for Dorothy who is subsequently overshadowed by the Wicked Witch of the West and her cackling laugh: https://www.youtube.com/watch?v=a1RvTmSf8sw

cold hard facts. Going back to the tub metaphor, ask yourself the tough questions: is my savings faucet on and calibrated to a flow rate that makes sense for me and is reasonable? Are there leaks that are allowing money to drain out of my savings account in a subtly pernicious way that slows down my overall savings goal? Finally, what is my current water level in my savings tub – is my tub empty, not full enough, or at a healthy amount? Regardless of whether you have savings or not, we all have the capacity to think about our own situation logically. As painful as it might be to look at a savings account with $50, you can start to break out of financial mediocrity and get yourself on a rogue path (a long path, admittedly) to build a much stronger financial foundation. Over the course of many years, this strategy can set you up to be much more nimble, adaptable, and prepared to accomplish your financial goals-both planned and unplanned, as we have seen. We cannot be led into the fallacious trap that millions fall into where savings are deprioritized, paused, or underfunded. This cycle can exist in people's lives for years, but you're not going to be one of them because you're ready to tackle this worthy pillar of your financial health and security.

As you build your savings, think of the Hoover Dam. One of the most famous public works efforts ever undertaken, it took 5 years to build and at its peak, over 5,000 workers worked out there day in and day out, moving earth, shaping the surrounding area, and bringing in millions and millions of pounds of materials to construct the world's largest hydroelectric dam.[*] This mega-project, like your savings, didn't happen overnight. It has so much concrete (over 4 million cubic yards) that you could pave a road from San Francisco to New York with it.[13] When you stand looking straight down the smooth concrete face to the basin over 700 feet below, it will take your breath away. All of this took planning, foresight, dedication, and an insane amount of work, but in the end, the result was dam(n) impressive and something that has had immense benefits, just as your savings account will have for you. So get going

---

[*]   It was the largest project at the time of completion in 1936 and a monumental feat of engineering, not to mention a boon to the economy as it was during the Depression: https://en.wikipedia.org/wiki/List_of_largest_hydroelectric_power_stations

with your savings and build yourself a concrete financial foundation centered around your savings.

Joe Holberg

5. DEBT

Debt Rules!

Debt rules! Right? Of all things that make us convulse financially (and maybe even physically), debt easily takes the top spot. If there is any other topic more despised than debt, I don't know of it. It's the thing that feels like a 10,000 pound* weight slowly crushing your soul and very existence at times. And it's the thing that makes you wonder if there is actually such a thing as a debt-free life or if it's just some whimsical fantasy reserved for the rich among us. If you watch *The Daily Show* with Trevor Noah, you might recall that they hosted "Third Month Mania"[14] which was a championship series like March Madness for college basketball, but instead of trying to crown an NCAA basketball champ, they sought to find the champion issue that made people angriest. The initial field of 64 "things that make you most angry" was strong and included despised items like traffic jams, slow Wi-Fi, and global warming, but had debt been in the running, I have no doubt that it would have taken the title.

While debt can be taxing and stifling, it's not all doom and gloom, per se, even if the situation looks bleak. We know it is possible to be debt free – even if it is in the seemingly distant future.-As of 2013, of all US households, 69% had debt and 31% were, therefore, debt free. It was even worse back in 2000, when 74% of households had debt and only 26% were debt free.[15] Clearly debt is pretty pervasive and is relevant to nearly all of us. (It should be fairly obvious, but also acknowledged, that even the 31% of "debt-free" households in

---

* Kudos to you if you picked up the British currency pun here ;)

2013 most likely had debt *at some point* even if they don't anymore). In sum total, we have...brace yourselves...over $12 TRILLION (a trillion, for anyone counting, is 1,000 billions) in household debt alone.* Yikes. Home loans, car loans, credit cards aplenty, that Target credit card, Gap credit card, the random furniture you bought with a store credit card, oh – and who can forget – student loans on top of student loans on top of student loans. It's a massive headache for millions and while we envision having a neat tub filled with savings, perhaps that tub feels more like it's filled with debt that is trying to drown you. This $12 trillion in combined debt is a significant amount of debt, for sure, but as we start out down this dreary and depressing debt road, I want to first ground us in a revolutionary sentiment that will defy all that we have seen for years being hyped up in the media, in conversations with family and friends, and in virtually every book, magazine, blog, or news segment that you've ever encountered regarding debt. Ready?

Debt isn't bad.

Yes, I know the cognitive explosion happening in your brain is telling you that debt *is* bad. It must be. The idea that debt is bad is so ubiquitous and time-tested an idea that few ever question it and it feels like an axiomatic truth that has no viable alternative. There are those who preach that the only way to live a successful and free life is to have no debt. While having no debt can certainly be amazing, it isn't the only way to obtain financial peace. In fact, if we fervently and blindly adhere to the preaching that debt is something to be squashed at all costs, we will run the risk of buying into an antiquated view that doesn't allow us to fully take advantage of financial opportunities (think college, buying a house, owning a car, etc.). So let me repeat this fact:

Debt isn't bad.

---

* For the economists out there, this does *not* include business/corporate debt nor does it include our US government's debt, which is an entirely different beast that perhaps someday I'll tackle (or at least try to).

And to further clarify the mental fissure happening as you read this:

Debt isn't good, either.

Now, with such a bold claim as to the neutrality of debt, I must necessarily justify to you this rogue way of thinking. Fortunately, it only takes one sentence, even though the explanation is a little more detailed: debt is a *tool* that is *neutral* and inherently is neither *good* nor *bad*. There, I said it. Jump on board and I'll show you why this is true.

The easiest way to approach thinking about debt more critically is to think of it as a tool rather than an insidious dark cloud hovering over your head. To hash this view out, we'll make a simple list of the implications of *not* having the ability to use debt for the main categories of debt out there. In asking ourselves "What would happen if I did *not* have this type of debt?" it will become apparent that debt gives us lots more choices, options, and helps us to achieve many goals much sooner than had we not had debt, even if the debt itself is a tough pill to swallow. We'll also start our exploration with debt that is generally *the most expensive* and proceed to debt that is generally the *least expensive*. Here, and later in this chapter, we'll cover, in this order from high interest rate (a.k.a. Annual Percentage Return (APR)) to lowest interest rate: credit cards, retail cards (think specific retail outlets like Banana Republic, Best Buy, etc.), personal loans, student loans, mortgages, and car loans. Let's answer our hypothetical question about what would happen if each of the categories of debt didn't even exist:

Type of Debt	What would happen if this debt didn't exist?
Credit Cards	Any larger expense that you've ever had, that you didn't have cash for immediately, you wouldn't be able to purchase. When you get paid on Friday, but your cell phone bill is due Tuesday, credit can make it possible not to fall behind on bills or expenses like gas, food, or other necessities.

Retail Cards	Clothes and furniture that you might have needed, perhaps in the case of a new job or a new home/apartment, couldn't be purchased. This might leave you underdressed on day 1 of your job (not so good) or you might be sitting, eating, and sleeping on the floor for several months if you've recently moved (or shoot, you might not have been able to afford to move in the first place without the credit cards listed above).
Personal Loans	People use these to start businesses, invest in their homes, and so many other things that it's hard to encapsulate. Millions of Americans have used personal loans to bring about millions of jobs. Hardly a good thing if this didn't exist.
Student Loans	Say goodbye to your education. No student loans means you have to pay for that education in cash and last time I checked, very few 18-year-olds had $15,640 laying around to pay for school *each year.**

---

* Assumption here is that this is the average cost for public institutions. Want to go to a private school? You'll need more than that $15k each year. Want to go out of state? Forget about it. If you're thinking you'd just get more federal grants if there were no student loans, you're sorely mistaken, virtually everyone would qualify for government support in our new system that have no student loans so you might eek out a thousand or two in support, leaving you with the vast majority of the expense on your own dime. https://nces.ed.gov/fastfacts/display.asp?id=76

Mortgages	The modern economy is built on access to mortgages. Take this away and our economy would shut down. Seriously though, if we didn't have mortgages, the vast majority of us would pay rent forever more to the ultra-wealthy who would have an outsized ability to further monopolize property. If you did ever have the ability to own a home, you'd have to buy it with cash and you'd most likely be at least 50 or 60 before you'd be able to do so. Oh, and toss in the fact that banks wouldn't exist, so we'd be reduced to using cash and storing it under our mattresses and in boxes buried in the back yard.**
Car Loans	No cash, no car. Sure, we overbuy cars in America like no other nation in human history, but without car loans, millions of us would be walking to work right now. Hardly a good thing for the individual or the economy at large. Don't fool yourself about leases, though – I'll have my time to slander them later.

Far from being a debt-free nirvana in this alternative universe, it would be a much less dynamic, much smaller economy where options would be constrained to whatever you could afford with the cash you had in your wallet or bank account. Individuals would have much less choice, purchasing power, and overall we wouldn't be able to achieve as much as we've been able to with debt. As a country, we most likely (almost certainly) wouldn't even exist without debt. We started our country by using debt. When the American Revolution

---

** It's worth noting here that the abuse of the mortgage system by private companies like Countrywide Financial, AIG, Wall Street in general, coupled with the poor oversight and practices of government institutions like Fannie Mae and Freddie Mac are what made the economy come crumbling down during the Great Recession of 2007 - 2009. Mortgages themselves didn't cause this, but the predatory and speculative nature were the causes (and we'll toss in lack of solid judgement and understanding for good measure). This is an area of particular interest of mine and if you are at all inclined to read up on what is essentially the equivalent of the Great Depression for our generation, start with *On the Brink* by Former Secretary of the Treasury Henry Paulson, who I had the pleasure to meet and have lunch with in 2012, or *The Big Short* by Michael Lewis.

began and Britain was pummeling us into near submission, debt saved us and paved the way for us to buy much needed supplies and keep our still unborn nation afloat. Without loans and debt from various European countries such as Holland and France as well as local loans from domestic individuals and the extension of credit from businesses, we would almost certainly have collapsed and lost the war and the opportunity to build the United States. The ripple effect of this is immense. The US would most likely not have created the best university system in the world, manufacturing and engineering would have stalled or grown much more slowly (we might still be in Model T's and using telegraph lines for communication). Forget the Internet and your smart phone. The amount of progress that we've made as individuals and as a country (and in fact, as a globe) are due in large part to financial products in the form of debt, like those in our table above.

Personally, my life has been shaped by debt, and yours has too, whether you know it or not. My debt journey started in college while I was at the University of Michigan. I remember very clearly wandering into the Michigan Bookstore during Summer Orientation in 2006. The World Cup final game was on and I stood there watching an epic battle between France and Italy. Zinadine Zidane, one of the world's best players, head-butted an Italian player and received a red card – a stunning shift in the game that left my jaw dropped to what felt like the floor. The protracted match went into overtime and then into penalty kicks on the shoulders of Buffon, the Italian goalie, who had the game of his life. Italy emerged victorious and I cheered amidst textbooks and school supplies. I came back to earth and remembered my original intent for visiting the store: to buy said textbooks. Thirty minutes later, I had dropped $500 or so onto a credit card to pay for my first semester's reading. I'm glad I had credit at that point and throughout college, it was a pattern I repeated for 4 years and the $4,000 in credit card debt that I graduated college with was not only necessary for survival, but it was just above the $3,000 average amount that all college graduates have in *just* credit card debt upon getting a degree.[16]

Sometimes I had enough cash to pay them off over the semester, sometimes I didn't. But because of being able to acquire debt via my credit cards to buy books, I was able to learn and obtain an education. That's a pretty solid trade, I'd say. In an ideal world, I'd have a benefactor who would sponsor me and pay for all my studies like Alexander Hamilton had, but hey, I can thank Discover for letting me buy books with their credit cards instead.*

I think of the plethora of endeavors which I could not have undertaken had it not been for debt. And I'll give you a quick list while simultaneously challenging you to think about what you have been able to do because of debt in its various forms.

For me, debt has allowed me to:

- Buy textbooks in college
- Use student loans for tuition, fees, room and board, ultimately resulting in getting a degree
- Pay for moving to Rhode Island for my first job after college
- Travel to California 3 times in one year (2012), giving me greater exposure and appreciation for the diversity in our country (as well as fantastically fresh seafood)
- Get a car loan to buy a (used) car to get to work.
- Start Holberg Financial to change (hopefully) millions of lives for the better
- Buy ample amounts of coffee while writing this book for you...

And that's a short list. I could go on, yet the truncation is welcomed, I assume. You can see, if through my own example only, just how

---

* Hamilton's chief sponsor, Hugh Knox, helped put together a fund that allowed him to go to America from St. Croix following a massive hurricane that devastated the island. He ended up studying at King's College (now Columbia University) and helped to shape America into what it is today. We can appropriately thank Knox and other donors. Interestingly enough, Hamilton was one of the primary people who understood the power of both national and private debt as a means to increasing prosperity and financial well being. Page 37 - 38, *Hamilton* by Ron Chernow.

debt can be wielded to pursue and accomplish various life events and goals. Clearly, debt isn't perfect, nor is it good or bad. It is something to be approached with zealous caution, mature thought, and used with an intentional purpose. What has debt allowed you to do? Your list might be similar to mine, but a list exists for all of us, either directly with your own anecdotes or indirectly by being part of a system that is governed by debt.

Now that we've established that debt is really a *tool* and something that can be ultra-useful with untold benefits, we have to dive into the nitty-gritty. We will quickly see that not all debt is created equal. Some of it turns out to be safe, stable, and useful while other types are volatile, dangerous, and intentionally designed to hang out in the gray area between legal and usurious. One of the main goals in looking at debt is to make sure you have the proper information and understanding of debt. In pouring over the intricacies, I can show you the expensive debt traps and the myriad of tricky subtleties that can leave us debt-ridden and feeling like we're stuck in the financial muck and mud. I will also you how to leverage and strategically employ debt to work for you, not against you.

In thinking about debt, think about how you can go from having debt rule you to a much better space where you rule debt. In terms of this tool, debt is like a screwdriver. You can either use it to screw a bunch of things together to build an item from your imagination (or maybe just an Ikea chair) or you can use it to disassemble something that you worked so hard to build and ultimately be left with a sad pile of raw materials that would leave a fervent Bauhaus student in a state of depression.* I want you to learn how to use your debt screwdriver to build an awesome financial foundation and life instead of using it to screw up in a dark hole of oblivion and oppression.

In closing, debt rules! It's either a system where you are ruling it

---

* The Bauhaus school achieved critical acclaim in the 1920's and 1930's in Germany. It was closed by the Nazi's in 1933 for being too intellectually liberal, but its influence has radiated across the world and across time influencing many subsequent modernist design philosophies and architecture schools of thought.

or it is ruling you, and in order to figure out which side of the coin you're on and how to become better at paying down and leveraging your debt, we will first have to look at the "rule of debt" itself . We will then proceed logically through each of the major forms of debt in the U.S. and how they relate to you. I'll implore you with a caveat here: even if you don't currently have much debt or a specific type of debt, read the section anyways. Just because you don't have it now doesn't mean you might not need to use the concepts later. Learning about them now can help you in the long run and better prepare you to make more informed decisions.

The One Rule of Debt

It's time for a math lesson. Do. Not. Freak. Out. This is a math lesson that I have taught to 7th and 8th grade students, so you can hang. Trust me. Once you grasp this simple concept, debt will be carved up neatly into two main camps of expensive and inexpensive. My hope is that, over time, you'll be able to view your debt rain cloud more as a necessary weather pattern that has its uses such as bringing water back to earth, rather than as a perpetual ominous dark cloud that exists solely to blot out the sun and keep you from enjoying taking in the sun's rays and some Vitamin D.

Before we look at the One Rule of Debt, I want to take a short digression, down a path almost never travelled in personal financial books (or hardly any book for that matter) that will prove helpful in your financial journey. Ask yourself, "How did I react to the first sentence in this section when I read 'it's time for a math lesson?'" Did you firmly put yourself in the "I'm bad at math" or "I don't like math" camp? Were you thinking, "yes, finally, some math!"? Why do we respond the way we do? In the U.S., from a very early age, we are taught and socialized to think of math in very different ways, primarily depending on gender. Essentially, if you are a boy, you should like math, you are expected to do well, and you are encouraged to do more of it. If you are a girl, you are taught that it's ok not to be good at math, that there are other things like reading and art that might be better for you, and that you are generally encouraged much less to persist in math as the years go on.* As jacked up and backwards as this is, this inequality isn't just seen in math. Our entire system is set up this way related to science, technology, engineering, and math (known as the STEM field). We put males into the STEM bucket and we put women into the non-STEM bucket.†

If you don't believe me, you don't have to look far to see that this is true. In 2014, Google was the first major tech company to honestly and publicly present their diversity numbers and the gulf is staggering: 70% of Google's employees are males and only 30% are women.[17] This prompted other companies to release equally dismal numbers about their own gender diversity, which has helped to bring the discrepancy towards the forefront of our national consciousness and conversation. How we talk about gender and STEM is a major issue that needs to be further addressed and while it will take a while on the national stage, we can at least address it right here, right now, on the individual level.

First, regardless of which view you have of yourself related to "math," it is important to realize that our belief about our math abilities has implications on how we interact with finances. If you

---

* It boils down to teacher bias in that teachers expect more mathematically out of male students. I know that I'm not exempt from bias, and as a former teacher, one way I tried to combat this was by covering up students' names when I scored my tests. Further, I would be remiss to not point out that it isn't only teachers who perpetuate this bias. It includes the school systems, textbook manufacturers, our national discourse and policy, the media, marketing, parents, TV shows, and the list could literally go on. We are quite susceptible to this bias and a landmark book written in 1792, far ahead of its time, imparts the imperative to guard against this trap (among others). *A Vindication on the Rights of Women* by Mary Wollstonecraft does well to point out the unreasonable historical roots of this suppression of the education of women and how any society based on reason and virtue must seek to eradicate inequalities among the sexes. She is perhaps one of the first universal suffragists and I can't help thinking just how well she and Sheryl Sandberg would get along if time were not a limiting factor. http://www. slate.com/blogs/xx_factor/2015/02/10/teacher_bias_in_math_new_study_finds_ teachers_grade_boys_more_generously.html

† This gender binary exists in the societal conversation around STEM, unfortunately it is not only deleterious in its own right, but further trivializes those in the LGBT community.

are less confident in math, you are more likely to be less confident when presented with numerical financial information. Think of how many times situations require you to think about and process financially numerical information: 25% off sales at the store (sounds like a good deal, right, but how much is it exactly?), checking a receipt, looking over your bank account statement, vetting options for credit cards with various interest rates (is 18% vs. 24% really that big of a deal? Hint: yes), checking out your retirement portfolio performance (meh, it's probably doing alright, right?). These are just a handful of examples where math and finances intersect and there are numbers everywhere related to your finances! Your underlying belief about your math abilities exposes you financially. It can open you up to susceptibility in decision making or vulnerabilities in how you process financial information. On the flip side, having confidence or a healthy belief in your math and financial knowledge can be empowering and this allows you to overcome financial hurdles.

In taking a detour and talking about how we think of ourselves mathematically, it's my hope that you will be able to combat your feelings and gut responses not only to topics in this book, but more importantly, in the real, ever-changing world around you. If you are able to break this huge societal rule and go mentally rogue here, you'll find that a more informed, cognitive approach to numbers, math, and finances can lead to much better results – and that, after all, is the whole point.

Obviously there isn't a hard line here. There exist plenty of women who are mathematical geniuses and women who are rock solid when it comes to confidence and financial abilities. There are men who struggle with adding and shy away from anything related to numbers or finances. The point isn't to categorize people exclusively; it is to bring our level of awareness up so that we can properly identify potential mindsets that we all have and how that has the potential to play out in our financial lives. If you think back to the beginning of the book and breaking rules, going rogue, and becoming un-average, this is it. Do it. Stop buying into the idea that you suck at math – you can definitely learn and become better at both math and finances. Doing a little self-analysis in this area can help us process information better and orient us to how we think about money. This in turn can give us the necessary confidence and resiliency to deal with something as burdensome as debt, that discussion to which we will now return. #tiradeover

Now that we are less apt to succumb to our mindsets around math and numbers, we are on the same page, so let's figure out what this one rule of debt is. At its core, our debt rule is all about ranking our debt from most expensive to least expensive based on the interest rate (a.k.a. the annual percentage rate or APR – I'll use APR and interest rate interchangeably henceforth). Once your debt is ranked according to interest rate and *not* the overall balance, you will note whether the APR is higher than or lower than 8%. We'll talk more about why 8% in a minute, but first, I want you to understand how to rank your debt.

At the heart of all borrowing is the idea of interest. When you borrow money, it means that someone else lends it to you (i.e., they are a creditor). When that lender lets you use their money, they incur a cost and a risk since they are unable to use that money for other purposes. Further, they are taking a calculated risk (or not so calculated, depending on who they loan to) since they are expecting you to pay them back. But any number of things could prevent that from happening such as becoming ill (or dead) and you could be unable to pay or have too many other debts outstanding that makes theirs deprioritized. Since the creditors are taking a risk on you as a borrower (debtor), they expect to be compensated. In order to be compensated, the lender will charge you interest so that they can make money in exchange for taking the risk.

The technical details notwithstanding, the amount of interest you pay is mainly dependent on two facets: time and risk. In terms of time, the longer you hold debt, the more expensive it is. This is easily enough highlighted by thinking of a simple scenario in which we ask which event is more probable. Is it more probable that your house burns down sometime in the next week or is it more probable that your house burns down sometime in the next 10 years? Clearly, it is more probable that your house or apartment burns down within a much longer time frame rather than a shorter one. There is, therefore, more risk in longer time horizons than short ones, and as such, the interest rate will be higher for debt that lasts longer. As a second comparison, 15-year mortgages have lower interest rates than 30 year mortgages, all else being equal.* It's easy to see that if a bank gives you a mortgage and you have 15 years to pay it off, that means the other person who gets a 30-year mortgage has twice as long to have things happen whereby they are unable to make payments. Thus it is more risky and the lender will want a higher interest rate to compensate.

Secondly, risk itself comes in many forms, not just embedded within time horizons, as discussed previously. A mortgage is relatively low risk compared to a credit card, because if you stop making payments on a mortgage, the lender can repossess your home (your home is the asset, so your mortgage is "asset backed") and resell it to offset the lost payments. On the other hand, if you don't pay your credit card company, it is much harder for them to get you to pay (credit cards and the like are thus "not-asset backed"). There isn't anything they can immediately take from you and so it is harder to recover any losses. There are still many negative consequences for you if you don't pay, such as your credit score being lowered, fewer companies willing to lend to you, etc. So not paying is almost never a good strategy even if it seems like you'll come out ahead. This, then, is one reason why credit cards are more risky to issue than say, a mortgage. As a consumer, you will face higher interest rates on credit cards than you will with mortgages. (I'm ignoring those oh-so-tempting credit card 0% APR introductory deals and all that jazz for now, so hold your horses†).

---

* Alternatively, *ceteris paribus* would have sufficed and duly paid homage to economics, business, and law professors the world over. One nuance that I always found enjoyable is that the "c" is pronounced as a "k" sound and not an "s," as its etymology stems from Latin.

† I can honestly say I've never held a horse...I've held the reins and I've sat on a horse, but never have I held one nor do I think I could if I tried. They look heavy.

We could go on and on all day comparing different types of credit, but this is not a risk analysis book, so I'll spare you. A final thing to note on the rationale behind interest rates (i.e., APRs) is that when you combine both the time and the risk considerations, you will get a whole range of APRs that vary widely. So some debt that has more risk than another type might may still have a lower APR because of the relative time associated with it. It's complex for sure, but at the same time, presenting a brief overview is designed to show you in part how lenders think about risk and to equip you to tackle your debt in the most strategic and advantageous way.

Let's conjure up a pretty typical and realistic example to see how we can go about ranking our debt from high to low APR. The only thing that makes this atypical is that our fictitious friend's name is Imogene. She wakes up not only with some debt, but some antlers that have magically grown on her head overnight.* Fortunately, she creatively navigates both her new world of antlers and her ongoing world of having to manage debt.

Imogene graduated from college a couple of years ago and has $15,000 in student loans at 5.5% APR. She also bought a used car and has $8,000 left to pay, but she got a decent deal of 2.5% since her credit score was solid (~700-720). While her antlers might cause an issue on the upcoming plane trip she is taking to see her non-antlered friends in San Diego, California, she still has to figure out how to pay down her credit card of $1,800 at 24% APR that she used to book the trip, the hotel, and the rental car. Like in *Imogene's Antlers*, she lives at home with her antler-friendly parents so she doesn't have a mortgage quite yet. And finally, she spent $1,500 to outfit her professional wardrobe once she landed her new job. She put this on a retail credit card and got a decent rate of 10%. (Pause: there were a lot of numbers in that last paragraph. Do a quick self-

---

* As a child, I loved reading *Imogene's Antlers* by David Small, a Detroit based children's author who I met twice after writing short stories of my own. The second time around in 1998 he thought I was trying to get a second signature on the same day, but as I piped up that he had signed my copy first in 1993, he obliged by writing, "You're still Joseph and I'm still David Small!" His kindness and outreach to local school children was anything but "small." To learn more: http://www.davidsmallbooks.com/

assessment: How are you feeling? Flustered? Confident? If you felt a little anxious or skimmed over it to hurry past the numbers, after taking a deep breath or two, or five, go read the paragraph again.).

In ranking Imogene's debt according to interest rate, we are going to look at the highest to lowest APR and go from there.

- Credit card – 24%
- Retail credit card (clothes) – 10%
- Student Loans – 5.5%
- Car loan – 2.5%

If you notice, we did *not* take into account her current balances. Even though the student loans have the highest balance, they rank lower because the interest rate is lower and therefore, over time, the credit card will become the most expensive one to hold on to. What does it mean to be the "most expensive" on our debt list? It means that the amount of interest you are paying relative to both the balance and the time frame is the highest. Numerically, if we think about $1,000 of debt in the course of 1 year for each of the interest rates, it will become clear that the credit card is the most expensive. For illustrative purposes, we are making some assumptions,* but it will make our math a little clearer. So how much interest will you have to pay for each one if you have $1,000 in debt in each of the categories?

- Credit Card – $240
- Retail Credit Card – $100
- Student Loans – $55
- Car Loan – $25

Yikes! just the interest from one year, and you still have to pay back the original $1,000...it doesn't take a wizard to figure out that having debt year after year can really add up.

---

* Namely, that no payments are made, there are no fees/penalties for non payments, and that the compounding period is of 1 year's length.

Since the name of the game is creating a much more financially healthy and secure life, then we have to figure out how to manage our debt load in a way that helps to achieve our goals. This is the point at which our 8% returns as an important number. It is important because it is the "break-even" point that you can achieve with your money given the choice of what to do with it. Let's say you have a dollar. Just a single George Washington and you have to decide where you want it to go. It can go back in your pocket and just sit there, but you know that if you deploy it into the universe to work for you, it might be better off. Your choices are numerous, but you decide that you either want to pay off some debt or you want to invest it in the stock market. Good choices, but which will be the most advantageous? It's exciting to think that you might buy a stock that explodes in value and turns your dollar into $10 in a year. That would be awesome, but unlikely. On average, the stock market, over a long period of time, has returned right around 8% per year since way back in the day. Year in and year out, this has been the approximate average return stretching back all the way to 1926.* Sure, there were "hot" years where growth was contagious (37.6% return in 1995 at the beginning of the first Internet Bubble) and there were "cool" years of slow or negative growth (-1.43% in 1939 towards the end of the Great Depression). While not a perfect measurement, this is the statistical average that can guide our thinking. We won't go into depth here regarding the stock market as we will later, but for now, we need it as a comparison point to our debt situation.

To complete our "One Rule of Debt," we will compare our current APRs to that of the average stock market return, 8%. The way it works is that if your current APR on a given debt is *higher* than 8%, then you should prioritize and pay off that debt most rapidly. If your debt cost

---

* The most recent update of this work is *Stocks, Bonds, Bills, and Inflation: 2006 Yearbook™* by Roger Ibbotson and Rex Sinquefield. Here, they find that the average stock market excess return for large stocks in the S&P 500 is 8.5% (that return is the amount after subtracting the risk-free return of government backed Treasury Bills, or T-Bills. In this case 12.3% - 3.8% = 8.5%, but I'll round down because we won't always be able to completely capture the inherent market diversification, you'll almost always face some fractional amount of fees in transacting, and because, well, 8% is just neater and easier to remember).

is exactly 8% APR, then you are on the fence, technically, but since there is risk and volatility in the stock market, you are most likely still better off paying your debt instead of investing. Finally, and this is the most counterintuitive position, if your debt is below 8%, then you should *deprioritize* this debt and only make minimum payments in favor of investing extra money in the stock market. (Don't worry if you don't know how to invest yet, more to come later!).

If you're screaming bloody murder at this point, you aren't the only one. But remember, debt isn't inherently good or bad. This is the textbook case that explains why it's true. Going back to breaking society's rules, this is it. You have been taught that holding debt is a terrible thing and it should be avoided at all costs. Books say it, it's on TV, financial "pros" teach you to pay it off as quickly as possible – and now I'm telling you that you should keep some certain types of your debt and only pay the minimums? Yes.

Essentially, if you do have the choice between paying off some cheap debt (something like a student loan at say 6%) and investing it in the stock market (gaining, on average, 8%), you are going to be 2% better off each year if you invest your money in the stock market than paying off your student loans. Why is this? Because paying your student loan debt means you're not incurring 6% interest in the future, so you've effectively decreased your liabilities by $1.06 by making that payment. Alternatively, if you invest, you will walk away with an asset increase of $1.08. Since a liability *decrease* and an asset *increase* both move your net worth in the positive direction (which is good), we simply have to see which had the greater effect. You can see now that investing made us 8 cents (or 8%) better off, while paying extra on our student loans made us 6 cents (or 6%) better off. If you're like most people, you'd rather get 8 cents for every dollar than 6 cents, unless I'm living in some crazy backwards universe, which I don't believe is the case (as much as it may seem plausible at times).

One massive caveat here is that this does *not* mean you shouldn't pay your debts in favor of investing as much as possible. On the contrary, you should *always* make at least your bare minimum ment each month. The most obvious reason for doing so is that you borrowed money and made a legal commitment to making payments. Secondly, if you miss payments, you can severely damage your credit report and score (more on this later), which can make life exponentially more difficult. When discussing where to allocate your money, we are talking about the *extra* money after all of your mandatory obligations have been satisfied.

Looking back at Imogene, she has debts with a wide range of interest rates. So we'll use our new One Rule of Debt to figure out which ones she should prioritize and which she should deprioritize when tackling her debt:

Prioritize (make larger than minimum payments when possible):

- Credit card – 24%
- Retail credit card – 10%

-----Break-even point – 8%

Deprioritize (make at least minimum payments, always):

- Student loans – 5.5%
- Car loan – 2.5%

Remember, Imogene should still be paying the minimum on the student loans and on the car loan, but if she really wants to become more financially secure, she needs to make larger payments on her most expensive debt first, in this case the credit card, in order to drive down her debt load. Once she pays off her credit card and her retail credit card, the next best thing she can do is set up the proper investment accounts (more on that later; see the retirement and investment chapters). She can then start to invest in her future and in the long run. Yes, there are lots of mitigating circumstances and competing priorities that extend beyond the One Rule of Debt discussion, like trying to buy a house, absolutely fearing student loans, etc. But from a strict comparison of debt versus investing and thinking about "how can I be better off" financially, this is what will build your net worth, dollar for dollar, in the most strategic way. I know it is tough to think about *voluntarily* holding a debt such as your student loans, but as you can see, it may often be more advantageous to *keep your student loans*. Now how's that for becoming un-average? Maybe now you can finally sleep at night without thinking that debt is crushing your hopes and dreams.

"Snowballing" Your Debt

Now that we've identified our break-even point and how to rank our debt according to interest rate, we're ready to get to the practical step of what to do about it. You may have heard of it already, but the time-tested technique of "snowballing" your debt is the way to go in terms of tackling and accelerating your debt payments. The snowballing closely resembles the adage "a rolling stone gathers no moss," except in this case the moss of your debt is that slimy and pesky interest that is accumulating. So let's get this metaphorical stone rolling and shed some moss while we're at it.

Looking back at Imogene's debt profile, we know that her credit card has the highest interest rate. As a reminder, here is her debt ranked highest to lowest by interest rate, but this time, we've put in the minimum payment for each as well.

Item	APR	Minimum Payment
Credit Card	24%	$72
Retail Card	10%	$60
Student Loans	5.5%	$163
Car Loan	2.5%	$142

Now, Imogene is a hard-working person and she usually ends up with a couple of hundred bucks a month that she can save, invest, pay down debt with, or use for tickets to a concert.* She definitely lives her life and makes sure she's saving a little bit, but she knows she can make some serious headway if she starts making additional payments on her credit card debt. So she decides to always make a $150 payment on her credit card each month instead of the $72 minimum. She also knows the One Rule of Debt, so she is going to only make minimum payments on her retail card, student loans, and car loan. Even though the sheer quantity of her balances makes her want to pay more on her student loans, she resists since the credit card interest is more costly to hold.

As her snowball payments of $150 begin to take effect, so too does her momentum in crushing that credit card debt. To see the difference it makes, let's check out the comparison and see what would happen if she only paid the minimum payment ($72) versus making some larger payments ($150). We'll see that she not only saves on *interest*, but she'll save lots of *time*.

Credit Card	Minimum Payment Scenario	Larger Payment Scenario	Amount Saved
Payment	$72	$150	--
Total Interest Paid	$1,575	$279	$1,296
Total Time to Pay Off	9 years and 5 months.	1 year and 2 months.	8 years, 3 months of your life.
How Imogene Feels	I feel sad. :(	I'm awesome! :)	Woohoo!

These are *real* numbers and this is the *actual* difference. Don't believe me? There is a great tool out there to test this yourself and you can use it for any of your debt. It's on www.bankrate.com, click calculators (at the top), then click "Debt Payoff Calculator."[18]

---

* Probably a Beyoncé concert, if I had to guess.

Take a minute to digest the information in the table. It's actually quite striking. First, let's talk about the huge difference between the amount of interest paid. Making minimum payments lands you with an extra $1,575 in interest. That's insane. If you recall, her original balance was only $1,800 so she is, in effect, paying almost *double* for whatever she bought. Think about it this way – if she used her credit card to buy a TV, that TV would have cost her a grand total, with the interest, of $3,375. Now if you were standing in Best Buy and the TV had that sticker price on it, would you have purchased it? I can't imagine you would. It would be so expensive! Well, it turns out if you only make minimum payments on your credit cards, then it really does turn out to be that expensive.

On top of that, look at the time difference. It will take you over 9 freaking years to pay it off (and that's assuming you never make another purchase on the credit card again!). Where are you going to be in 9 years? I have no idea where I'm going to be, but that's almost a decade of my life and if I make minimum payments, wherever I end up, that credit card bill is clearly going with me. Comparing it to the larger payment of $150, we shed the burden of having this credit card balance in just over 1 year. One year, people. Not only did you just save the difference between the interest, a whopping $1,296, you also now have an extra 8 years and 3 months where you *do not* have to make a credit card payment at all. Pretty sweet right?

One additional insight we can glean from this credit card analysis is this: whatever your balance is on your really expensive debt, you can estimate what you will pay in total when you only make minimum payments. It's an estimate, but at least you can get a sense of how costly it can become. All you have to do is take the balance and *double* it. Going back to my own personal example, those college textbooks that I bought for $4,000? Well, if I made minimum payments only on them (which I did for years), I could expect to pay roughly *double* or roughly $8,000. I mean, that's disturbing for several reasons, not least among them is that is a crap load of money spent on textbooks! Try it yourself and see how much your high interest debt is costing you. It might be quite a surprise (and quite a scare).

Distilling this first portion of the debt snowball section, we've uncovered several simple facts. First, we only focused on the highest interest rate item. All other line items, we essentially ignored and said "make the minimum payment." You can do this too. You don't need to obsessively think of ways to pay off your car loan (low interest), for example, if you have a credit card balance (high interest). So get your stuff in order (literally) and take care of the highest priority item first. Further, we realized that if we only make the minimum payments, then our debt snowball is going to look a lot like the feared and fanged Abominable Snowman in the 1964 classic *Rudolph the Red Nosed Reindeer* movie. Yikes!

Your Debt Snowball On a Roll

Now that our highest priority item is sufficiently taken care of, what happens next? Your snowball is sufficiently gaining speed and momentum and now it's time to take advantage of it. If you look back at the next item, it is Imogene's retail credit card with an interest rate of 10%. Taking aim at that, we have to combine two numbers to get our new monthly payment on the retail card. This is truly where the power of the debt snowball becomes more visible. We will not only continue to make the minimum payment ($60), but we will now add the *entirety* of the payments that we were making on the credit card ($150) for a new monthly payment of $210 on the retail credit card. It's important to note here that we aren't simply making a subtle increase in payments by combining the two minimum amounts ($60 and $72, respectively for a total of $132), we are committing the full $150 from the credit card payments and now just shifting it to the retail card. While making a $132 payment is surely better than making a $60 payment, the snowball grows bigger and fast if you keep up with it by making a $210 payment as we can see below.

Retail Card	Minimum Payment Scenario	Larger Payment Scenario	Amount Saved
Payment	$60	$210	--
Total Interest Paid	$143	$41	$102
Total Time to Pay Off	2 years and 1 month	7 months	1 year and 4 months
How Imogene Feels	Meh :-/	Snowball on a roll!	More time and money? Sign me up!

Once again, Imogene comes out on top and while the savings don't look as glamourous, it's mainly because the initial balance on the account was relatively low. But as you can see, Imogene saves quite a bit of time and some extra cash and is now ready to tackle the major balance beast: her student loans. As you might have guessed already, she is in the position to make an additional $270 payment on top of her minimum payment of $163 for a new student loan payment of $433. If you take a step back and look at where she's come from, she was barely making an extra payment amount on her credit cards a mere 1 year and 9 months ago and now she is in the position to make 3x the monthly minimum payment on her student loans *and* she doesn't have any credit card or retail card debt. This rolling stone is shedding its moss faster than Richard Simmons and his crazy 1990's aerobic workout disciples could shed weight.*

Imogene's student loans and car loan, at 5.5% and 2.5% interest respectively, are below the 8% break-even threshold. According to the One Rule of Debt, she should continue to make minimum student loan payments and increase her retirement and

---

* I remember my mom working out to the ebullient Richard Simmons VHS tapes back in the day. Those 90's jumpsuits and workout outfits are permanently seared into my mind. Check them out here: https://www.youtube.com/watch?v=H7B2VMCHXpA (be warned: you might become healthier by laughing so much after Googling Richard Simmons and his workout regiment).

investment savings if she'd like. She knows that investing can impact her net worth more positively than making additional student loan payments, but she really doesn't like having student loans. So she at least wants to see what would happen if she increases her monthly student loan payments according to the debt snowball technique. This is a tough choice for a lot of people, including Imogene. If you want to *maximize* your net worth, you would take the new extra $270 and put it in a retirement account such as a 401k or IRA instead of beefing up on additional debt payments.

For a lot of people, emotion definitely enters into the equation at this point. Even though they know they can maximize the actual monetary side of the equation by allocating money to investing once they hit the 8% break-even point in their debt list, many still want to pursue an aggressive debt pay-down plan so they can wipe out their debt faster, even if this means delaying investing and building long term savings for retirement or other financial goals. This would be akin to maximizing your *"emotional net worth"* if there were such a thing. The decision is not black and white even though it can be summarized on paper. The heart and the brain have to work together in determining what to do at this juncture, but now that you know the tradeoffs, you can make an informed decision about whether or not you want to minimize debt or attempt to maximize net worth (remember the 8% is an annual *average* and isn't guaranteed).

In Imogene's scenario, we can at least look at what would happen if she continues an ultra-aggressive debt payoff plan by tackling her student loans next with a $433 monthly payment. It's still great that she is tackling debt aggressively, so she should still feel quite positive about her financial progress and trajectory, regardless of her decision.

Student Loans	Minimum Payment Scenario	Larger Payment Scenario	Amount Saved
Payment	$163	$433	--
Total Interest Paid	$2,937	$939	$1,998
Total Time to Pay Off	7 years and 11 months	2 years and 8 months	5 years and 3 months
How Imogene Feels	Ewwww.........	I can see the light at the end of the tunnel.	No way?! I can't believe it!

This might be one of the best tables in the book and I bet you never thought you'd actually like looking at a table with some financial scenarios in it. (Pat yourself on the back if you found it at least a tiny bit intriguing. Go on, it's ok to admit you liked it). I mean, look at it! Imogene is crushing it. Just to put it in perspective, the vast majority of student loans are meant to be paid back over 10 years (120 payments) and Imogene, by snowballing her debt was able to take care of it in just 4 years and 7 months. That's pretty awesome and the great thing for her is even though the $433 payment might seem super high compared to the minimum, she slowly but surely worked her way up to this by tackling her higher interest debt first. She is not in fact actually using more of her income to make these payments. She is just using the money that she is now *not* using to pay off her credit card and retail card. She is literally ahead of the curve now and the last thing to do is wipe out her car loan payment by applying the $433 to her minimum payment of $142 for a new payment of $575. Fortunately for Imogene, and to really reinforce the awesomeness of the debt snowball, she has spent the last 4 years and 7 months to get to this point and her car loan balance is now down to $516 since she has been making her regular minimum payments on it for the life of the loan (most car loans are 5 years). So she would only have 5 months left of $142 payments anyway, but now that she has a total of $575 to make payments on her car loan, she gets to pay off her car loan *only one month after she pays off her student loans!* I mean, that snowball has reached max speed and size and takes out its last two targets almost simultaneously as it reaches a snowy crescendo that eliminates her debt. Total time: 4 years 8 months. Total saved: just over $3,396! Well played, Imogene. And to think that the tiny snowball started almost five years ago with only an extra $78 going towards her credit card each month...

The credit card debt is gone. No more retail cards weighing her down. She's happily one of the few of her friends without student loan debt, and now she wholly owns her car and there is no more car loan hovering over her head. She's debt free and she did it by being patient, calculating, and methodical. She was thinking about using some of her extra money to get top of the line antler removal, but now, she's pretty happy with herself and decides that antlers aren't so bad after all now – after all, there are antler ornaments, gloves, and all kinds of other antler opportunities out there for her. On top of this, now she has an extra, unrestricted $575 in dough each month and is thinking of either saving for a down payment for a home of her own or adding more each month to her retirement savings. You go, Imogene!

In closing out the debt snowball section, Imogene has one question for you, "What would you do with something like an extra $500+ each month in your pocket?" It's a tantalizing question and one you can find the answer to after getting your debt snowball moving down the hill in your own life. Even though she made more than the minimum payments on debt that had interest rates lower than 8%, she still committed to a great debt snowball plan that left her debt free. Whether she follows the debt snowball all the way to the end or strategically beefs up on investing once hitting the 8% break-even mark, there is no doubt that having a plan is better than not having a plan at all. Selecting exactly which course you pursue is up to you, and the journey itself is complicated and long enough as it is. So give yourself credit for formulating a plan in the first place as you work towards your ultimate debt objective.

Diving Deep on Debt

Let's not be fooled by how tough this journey is. Setting out on this journey to pay down your debt is more or less the same as Frodo and the Fellowship of the Ring taking off from Rivendell with the noble and risky venture to destroy the Ring. Unless you've been hiding under a rock for the past 10 years, you know that Frodo & Friends have to go to the end of the Earth (quite literally, they are traveling to Mount Doom in the far reaches of Middle Earth) to achieve their mission – a formidable task on the very best of days. The burden is heavy, it's taxing, and there is both internal debate about the right and wrong ways to proceed, with everyone chipping in their opinion about what to do next as well as the looming and ominous threat of the great eye of Sauron that searches endlessly to regain control of the Ring of Power. Facing off with blood-thirsty, murderous Orcs, bringing on the Ents as allies (they are a living tree species whose lifestyle pace is slower than ice melting in the Arctic), and wrestling with the almost-but-not-really-lovable Gollum are but a few of the arduous tasks that the Fellowship has to dexterously and nimbly adapt to and deal with along the way towards their ultimate pursuit.

As the quest draws to a fateful close, Frodo climbs the scorching mountainside to destroy the ring by casting it deep into the lava from when the Ring was created. Going back to the source and taking it on face to face is, of course, the only way to truly save all those that he cares about back in his quaint and innocent home village of the Shire and Middle Earth at large. Pain, failure, missteps, creativity, resiliency, friendship, force of will, strength, and perseverance are but a few of the traits and attributes that Frodo & Friends demonstrate along the way, and their sacrifice pays off with the great reward of peace and freedom from the dark forces that used to shroud their safety, livelihood, and existence. Essentially Frodo = YOLO.

When it comes to the journey of tackling your debt, you *must* embrace your inner Frodo.

In our day and age, it is tempting to think that our debt situation is going to just get better if we keep on keeping on, but what we need is a plan of action, just like the nine in the Fellowship had in seeking to destroy the Ring. They sat around Rivendell with the Elven leader, Elrond, and Gandalf (The Grey, at the time) and said, "*This* is what we want to accomplish and *here* is the best way we can conceive of achieving it at the present time." They certainly didn't know exactly what was going to happen once they set out. (Remember Shelob, the freaking giant spider? Yeah, you didn't see that coming). But they always knew where they wanted to end up even if the course changed along the way.

It is the exact same situation with your debt. You know where you are currently (some amount of debt, small or large), where you want to get to (much less debt, most likely debt-free), and you know how you want to get there (using the Debt Snowball method described above). What you should be equally aware of, and planning for, are the crazy, unforeseen, and straight-up distracting challenges that blindside you and take you so far off track that you will seriously question whether or not you will be able to make it to a debt-free life in the next decade, or perhaps ever. If there weren't challenges in The Lord of the Rings, then the story would have gone like this:

Bilbo brings Ring to Shire. Frodo takes Ring to Rivendell. Fellowship decides to destroy Ring. Fellowship waltzes into Mordor. Most evil and powerful enemy, Sauron, smiles as Frodo daintily drops Ring into fire. Middle Earth saved. Happy ending.

That's a pretty sucky story, btw, and my literary prowess compared to the intellectual giant J.R.R. Tolkien is like a toddler running against Usain Bolt in the 100-meter dash. We know that stories and life don't just unfold in simplistic and ideal ways, but we have to be willing to take them in stride anyway and do the best we can.

In the subsequent couple of sections, we are going to dive deep into specific types of debt, with the aim of learning more about them so that when you are on your own debt reduction journey and crap hits the fan, you have solid information upon which you can rely. We'll cover, in order: credit cards, retail cards, personal loans, student loans, mortgages, and car loans. You need to beef up on the types of debt that are out there floating around the financial atmosphere, the intricacies that each type has, the way each works and the way each doesn't work, and how each impacts your financial life. This is a critical step in your debt journey and reading and learning about them is akin to the adage "practice makes perfect." Think about the difference between Michael Jordan and Allen Iverson. Jordan practiced harder than almost any player of his generation (and perhaps of all time) and Iverson stated annoyingly in a press conference in 2002 about the merits of practice, "I mean, listen, we're talking about *practice*, not a game, not a game, not a game, we talking about *practice*...[19]" And do you know what the differences between the two are? Championships: Jordan: 6, Iverson: 0. Enough said. Everyone wants to be the Air Jordan or the Frodo of their debt, so get out there and practice by reading up on and getting acquainted with the major types of debt out there. Whether you currently have them or not, read on, so that you're ready for whatever life throws your way.

Credit Cards

There is a thing I like to call the "credit card conundrum" out there affecting millions of people each and every day. It's subtle and it plays to the weakest and most impulsive characteristics of humans. This credit card conundrum boils down to the phrase, "to use or not to use, that is the question."* Our rational, thinking selves know that we should not carry a credit card balance and that we are paying lots in interest. We know that we shouldn't use it as much as we do, but our raw desires in the moment often hijack our ability to delay and stop ourselves when we're in the store or buying things online. This

---

* While no Thespian, I do feel like I can appropriate at least one or two of the immortal Shakespearian lines with at least a modicum of dexterity.

compulsive, erratic, and natural behavior undermines and undoes all of our "textbook knowledge" about the negatives and drawbacks of using credit cards prolifically and the "shopping experience" starts playing on the harpsichord of our emotions, luring us in, compelling us to buy more stuff and to buy it more frequently. With a credit card in hand, it's so much easier to toss that extra dark chocolate bar into the cart, grab an extra beer at dinner, or get the slightly nicer (and more expensive) pair of shoes.

In fact, it's been observed repeatedly that you spend more with that plastic than with cash. But by how much? Quite a bit actually. You spend, on average, 12 – 18% more even if you pay off your balance in full each month. McDonald's found out that their sales went up even more than 18% from $4.50 to $7.00 when people used credit cards instead of cash (which is a Whoppering 55% increase!*). That might not seem like too much, but put another way, imagine getting a salary raise from $45,000 a year to $70,000 a year. Yikes. That might be the sweetest thing to ever happen and it would make a huge difference in your life just like it does for the bottom line at the Golden Arches. Not only were they consuming more calories, but customers were ever so subtly falling into the trap of buying more than they needed by the swipey swipey phenomenon going on inside their head. This happens *everywhere*. It's not just restricted to fast food purchases. Essentially anywhere you can make a purchase, you are subject to this effect.

The credit card conundrum and desire to consume reduces to a simple evolutionary observation: we want resources now and we have a hard time justifying not consuming stuff right now (and not just in the eating sense, but consuming more broadly). After all, running around the African, European, and Asian terraforma 10,000 years ago, our ancestors were always on a razor's edge trying to eat, find shelter, and stave off both the elements and predators. Life was rough and if you had the ability to eat, you did. And you ate as much as you could stomach because you never knew what was next. Same thing for shelter; you found a cave or a covered alcove, you took a nap for sure or at least took refuge from the rain or heat at midday. Back then,

---

* Does this made up word make me the Burger King of Puns?

it just made sense to consume when available and the relative scarcity kept our biological systems in check.

Now however, in the modern era in developed countries like the U.S., we have stuff, we have food, and we are fortunate enough not to need to run around hunting and gathering on a regular basis. This then takes away the immediate need to consume everything now, like our ancestors needed to, because we know, with relative certainty, that there's more where all that stuff came from. As such, if we were to evolve more quickly with the times, we wouldn't allow our brains to scream at us to buy, buy, buy (a.k.a. consume, consume, consume) every time we rolled through the drive-through, found great clothes online, or saw the biggest and best deal ever. We'd pause, think about tomorrow, and we'd most likely override our in-the-moment temptations and think about the bigger picture. And we'd resist. The use of credit cards compounds this innate consumerism by removing us one more degree and essentially outsources the feeling of losing cash. When you spend cash, you experience a high degree of loss aversion, which makes you more conscious of your spending and thus can temper your impulses and lower your average expenditure. But once you slip that credit card into your pocket, the degree of loss aversion goes down. After all, you aren't giving away your cash right away. You are just committing to give away your cash sometime in the future when your credit card bill is due. That makes it a lot harder to check your spending in the moment like the use of cash does.

Let's make that 12 – 18% more tangible, since it might not seem like that much on the surface. Let's imagine that you spend $1,000 a month on things where you are able to choose a credit card as your payment option. This implies that if you use your credit card instead of cash, you'll spend between $1,120 and $1,180 a month instead of the $1,000 you would have spent had you used cash. Probably doesn't sound all that bad, but if you add that up over the course of the year, that means you would spend an additional $1,440 to $2,160. That's a nice chunk of change that could be used to fund your savings account or finally take that vacation that you haven't been able to do for years. Start dreaming of what you can do with that extra money. On top of the amount saved, we haven't even taken into account the additional amount you'll save in interest by avoiding credit cards. You can see how quickly it adds up year after year...

A lot of times people think of the solution to the "credit card conundrum" (should I trademark that phrase?) in overtly simplistic terms like "pay more than the minimum" or "pay off the balance each month." While the nuances – and the fine print – can be really intimidating or even something we gloss over in its entirety, most people generally understand the concept that credit card debt is expensive and "not good." This conundrum really centers around needing the credit card to cover expenses, then paying off some/ all of your balance later. You look in your checking account and see $250 left and you know you need groceries for the week. So instead of swiping your debit card and having your checking account balance go down to $200 (or less), you swipe your credit card and plan to pay it off once your next paycheck clears. Same thing goes when you're at the pump: swipe credit card now, pay off later. Ohhh and that book* or shirt off of Amazon – it's soooo easy to click (quite literally, you can use the "one click checkout") and it magically shows up in two days. Again and again, round and round we go. Shop, swipe, new item obtained, look at credit card bill, sigh because you spent more than you thought, pay off some/all of it. Rinse. Repeat.

We're not doing so hot as consumers. On average, we have $8,392 in credit card debt *per person*[20] and a total amount of credit card debt alone standing at a massive $747 billion – just shy of a trillion dollars.[21] Ouch.

If we hark back to the opening discussion of the neutrality of debt, we have to remember that even credit card debt isn't inherently bad. However, having a lot of it for even a short amount of time can have severely negative consequences on your financial life. On the

---

* In my case, it would be better phrased as "those books" since I can hardly help myself from buying *all the books* out there. I jokingly say that "buying books is my only vice" even though it generally elicits eye rolls due to my continued corniness.

flip side, credit cards can put you into financial beast mode if you use them right and you can get lots of cash back, free gas, miles, hotels, rental car insurance, concierge service, etc. The commercials and ads tout these benefits and they are certainly real benefits. But if you're incurring the borrowing cost (i.e., paying interest), then you most likely are paying more in interest than you get in benefits, no matter how many free flights or cash back rewards you get. Just ask yourself, "Why would the credit card companies want to give you more money than they earn?" They wouldn't, they wouldn't make money, and if it wasn't worth it to them, they wouldn't do it. Therefore, for the vast majority of credit card users, the price you pay (annual fee, interest charges, and finance charges) almost always adds up to *more* than the benefits you receive. This *is* the way credit card companies make more money. Just remember that the next time you think you're coming out on top.

Credit Card Camps: Which Are You In?

Let's look more practically at credit card *usage*. In the credit world, you are in one of three camps. These camps are like summer camps. Some are cooler than others. And unlike childhood camps, you have the option to upgrade to a better credit card camp. Let's look at these three camps:

You can only go to Camp 1 if *all* of your credit cards carry no balance, meaning you pay them off in *full* each and every month. Camp 1 is by invite only.

Camp 1 is a sweet place to be, with a zip line, a clear blue lake, s'mores galore, and some great friends that are akin to long lost siblings. Everyone wants to be at Camp 1 and if you aren't there yet, don't worry – your invitation will be dropped off by owl soon.*

Camp 2 is for people who are *not* actively spending

---

* While I didn't get my invitation via owl to attend Hogwarts when I was 11, I am still holding out hope that there is some exception in the Wizarding World that allows for late admits.

using their credit cards. They are consciously working on paying off previous balances that exist on their credit cards.

Camp 2 is the strategic middle ground between Camp 1 and Camp 3. It's sort of like a summer sports camp where you attend to practice and improve your skills so that when the season comes around, you've got a leg up on your competition.

People in Camp 2 have intentionally moved out of Camp 3 and they are on their way to gaining admittance to Camp 1 once they pay off their balances. The beautiful thing about Camp 2 is that it is a necessary intermediary between the two juxtaposed camps *and* that anyone who wants to go is automatically accepted. Essentially, when you show up, you have committed to not using your credit cards and to paying them off (even if it takes a year or two). It's more about your commitment to Camp 2 than it is about your current state of affairs. You might have $1,234 in credit card debt and you only need to be at Camp 2 for six months, or you might have $43,210 (it's possible) and you might need to be there for 60 months. No matter where you are, you get to *choose* to be at Camp 2. The drawback here is that you can leave at any time, and a lot of people do. The average person will walk away and head back to Camp 3 while the few rogue, un-average, status quo flouting, I'll-do-whatever-it-takes people will bust it at Camp 2 with their eyes on the prize: Camp 1.

Camp 3 is for people who carry credit card balances forward month to month and are still using their credit cards on an ongoing basis.

Camp 3 is the camp that your parents made you go to. There might have been a friend or two that you liked, but you were definitely still counting down the days until you got to go home. The showers are moldy, there's no air conditioning, and the camp counselors just informed you that there is no swimming in the lake because of a recent sewer spill that made it a toxic refuse rather than a gleaming reprieve from the hot summer heat.

Which camp are you in?

There are about 167 million people with at least one credit card and given what we know about the average credit card balance in the U.S., that puts most people squarely in Camp 3 at the given moment. Welcome to Camp 3. It's ok if you're in Camp 3; the great thing about Camp 3 is that they forget to close the gates at night and you can leave any time. You just have to make some hard choices. Many people are perfectly content in Camp 3 and will opt to go there for years on end. If Camp 3 is your jam, you're welcome to it, but it costs a lot to attend Camp 3 and you don't really get as much in return as you might think.

For those people who are both actively using their credit cards *and* have a balance that carries over from month to month, my goal is to get you to Camp 2 as quickly as possible. (Remember, you have to go to Camp 2 before being ready for Camp 1). This is both really easy and really hard. A lot of other books, blogs, financial people, etc. gloss over this point. They prescribe some generic advice about paying off your highest interest rate card first, then working your way down to a $0 balance and voilà! You are now credit card debt free. Yet it feels like a hocus pocus trick where no matter how hard you try to emulate that debt magician, you just can't pull the rabbit out of the hat.

Fortunately, the secret to the trick isn't mere optics, it's a real, conscious choice and this is where it gets tough. You have to do something that is going to make your life harder at first, even though you know it will pay off (quite literally) in the long run. If you want to get to Camp 2, you have to *stop* using your credit cards. Period. I know the alarm bells are going off in your head, but that's it. You just have to stop using them. It's unnerving – *how am I going to eat food? But my birthday is coming up. I have a trip planned in a month and I always use my credit card when I travel. But it's my card that I use for gas. I get so many points though and I can't live without my points!* Is it even possible?

The questions that are raging now will subside, but if you aren't willing to take this first step, you might as well close this book and throw it away just like the New Year's Resolution you made to exercise daily.

The beautiful thing about taking this first step is that you are automatically upgraded to Camp 2 if you decide to take your credit cards out of your wallet/purse/murse* and put them into your dresser drawer next to your socks (sock 'em away!). You don't need to go nuts here and cut them up, have some garbage can burning ritual, and definitely *do not* call and cancel your credit cards (more on this later, but this can actually hurt your credit score). To stop using them do the following:

- Put all of them somewhere you won't be tempted to use them. One of my favorite pun tricks here is to freeze my credit cards. Fill up a cup of water. Drop in cards. Put in freezer. Leave. Not feeling punny? Put them in your sock drawer if you believe that you can actually leave them there and not yank them out each time you're feeling the itch to buy something.
- Unlink all of your accounts online. In the modern era, this is a new domain and if you can still get online and buy all of your stuff, then you won't technically be eligible for Camp 2. There are tons of sites that remember our payment info, even if you don't: Zappos, Amazon, the pizza place, the online pet shop, Uber/Lyft, Grubhub, Uber Eats, etc. Unlink them. On top of that, recurring subscriptions like magazine subscriptions, Netflix, the N.Y.Times, Tie Bar, Trunk Club, etc. should all be switched to your *debit card* if you really, really, really need them.

It's important to realize here that you aren't about to disconnect

---

* Man + purse = murse. It's a real thing, Google it. If you've ever seen Veep, just think of Gary's murse, the "Leviathan."

from the world and go "off grid" per se. You aren't resigning yourself to a life of nothingness and ultra-austerity here. What you are doing is prioritizing your areas of spending and consciously deciding if it is something you should spend cold hard cash on (if it's online, it will route through your debit card now instead of your credit card). Camp 2 has lots of advantages over Camp 3. Here is a short list:

- Your credit card payments will now be decreasing your overall balance instead of keeping you on the continual mouse wheel where you take one step forward and one (or more) steps back.
- You will be accumulating less interest as you make more payments.
- You have selected the most important things to spend money on and have "trimmed the fat" off your financial spending. Statistically, you will spend 12-18% less.
- You actually have a viable pathway out of credit card debt rather than sticking to the "credit card conundrum" and its vicious cycle of spending.
- You will hopefully see your credit score begin to improve.

That list is pretty solid, but one more reason why you need to get the heck out of Camp 3 is because the average American (that means you, me, your mom, and Uncle Crazy) pays $2,630 in interest *each and every year*.[22] I want you to put that money back in your pocket and I know you do, too. If this feels brash and painfully truthful, it is. I made a promise to tell the hard truth at the beginning of the book and this is it, so take it or leave it.

Adding that insane $2,630 in avoided interest payments to the extra 12 – 18% saved by not using your cards and now all of a sudden you have the opportunity to have between an extra $4,070 and $4,790 *per year*. People, these aren't fake numbers. They are real. If you have a $40,000 salary, that means you are paying an extra 10% of your entire salary just for the ability to use your credit cards. If you're making $80,000, that's still 5% of your salary, which I'm sure you'd prefer to have instead of giving it to "Financial Company ABC."* Turns out that piece of plastic is way more expensive than it looks.

A Pathway to Camp 1

If you are in Camp 3, get to Camp 2 as quickly as possible by stopping your credit card usage. That's the ticket to Camp 2. Once you are at Camp 2, keep those cards in the drawer as you make payments as large as possible so you can drive down your credit card debt. Once it is paid off in full, you get a first class upgrade to Camp 1, which is not only the most awesome camp, but it is the least expensive camp to actually attend. On top of that, once you get to Camp 1, you can even reinstate your credit card usage so long as you continue to always make your payments in full each month!

On paper, this sounds easy, but don't sell it short. This can be a brutal, time-consuming process whereby you are moving back and forth between camps so much that you forget whether or not the camp's lake was toxic or safe to swim in. By keeping your head above water, giving yourself regular, honest assessments about which camp you're in, it's easy to think you are making progress when in reality you are actually static or even worse, making backwards progress. A system like mint.com can be a really powerful tool to track your overall balances over time and there's nothing like data to help clarify an often confusing situation. In terms of a pay down strategy for paying off your credit card debt, go back and check out the Debt Snowball section to formulate a plan for getting to Camp 1.

Credit Card Haters In the Building

A lot of financial people hate on credit cards. There is sure a lot to hate, but I believe they mistakenly tell you to rip them up, close your accounts, and never look back. This advice might have been appropriate 25 years ago and given you peace of mind, but it is ludicrous in the 21st Century. Today establishing and maintaining credit is extremely important, especially as you move towards other financial goals that require credit

---

* For Mr. Robot fans out there, this might sound eerily similar to "E Corp."

scores like buying a house, a car, or starting a business. If you take away anything from this section it should be that: a) paying off your credit card debt is tremendously valuable and important, especially to your long term prospects for achieving financial health, and b) credit cards are a powerful tool, that if used right, can be really advantageous and beneficial, so discarding them entirely is impractical and ill-advised.

In terms of being a judicious consumer, you should be wary of people who endorse the idea that you should never use credit cards. They will say things like "cut them up" or "cancel them" or "they should be avoided at all costs." Sometimes this is decent advice, but too stark and extreme a viewpoint is dangerous, just as it is in politics, business, and in thought in general. There might be a compelling reason to espouse this view since credit card debt can cost people thousands of dollars each year, as we've seen, but we shouldn't throw away a tool just because it is dangerous. If we held true to that logic, we would shun the use of all kinds of useful things like compressed oxygen tanks to help the elderly breathe even though they are highly explosive if heated or punctured. Even cars would be subject to banishment since 30,000+ people a year die in traffic accidents. When it comes to credit cards, be honest with yourself about where you're at, realize that it isn't going to be easy to dig yourself out, it will take time (more time than you probably estimate), and you'll no doubt face setbacks. But eventually, one hard choice at a time, you will come out the other side and you can confidently stay in Camp 1 while still using them to rack up those points, miles, and all the fancy rewards that will finally be worth more to you than they cost. Until then, get your butt in Camp 2 and stop getting the short end of the financial stick in Camp 3. Deal? Thought so.

Retooling with Balance Transfers: Is It Worth It?

Bombardment. That's the best word to use when it comes to balance transfer offers from credit card companies. Transferring a balance from one card to another in order to achieve a "better deal" like getting a 0% APR for 12, 18, or 24 months is a form of refinancing. Refinancing with a balance transfer is the most common form of refinancing in the credit card industry and we'll take a quick peek at what it's all about and how to assess the pros and cons since these companies send real physical mail pretty much every other day with offers to refinance. Most of these offers go directly into the recycling bin even if the deal feels more like trash. Every time you log on to your online credit card account, you probably see the same type of offers. Then there are the emails and the ads everywhere. These "extra" features abound in the credit card world and they can be confusing, dense, and even downright deceptive as the Consumer Financial Protection Bureau just proved by uncovering exploitative schemes that the National Bank of Omaha was engaged in. They had duped customers for years and it cost them a cool $35 million for their shady credit card practices.[23] It's so easy to discredit and distrust them and we discard them in the moment, but every once in a while, the thought is there, "should I refinance and do a balance transfer?" Then the question becomes, "If I do, what does it actually mean and how do I do it?"

Refinancing as a general concept is quite the powerful tool, but like anything powerful, it can be dangerous and unwieldy if not properly understood. Refinancing and doing a balance transfer is sort of like harnessing uranium for the creation of energy via nuclear power plants. It can power homes, factories, and cities with tremendous capacity that makes life easier, more sustainable, and cheaper with what feels like an unbounded amount of electricity. Once a nuclear power facility is up and running, the lifespan is quite high and it can provide benefits for decades. However, while extremely safe in concept, they are vulnerable, as we saw during Three Mile Island, Chernobyl, and others. Massive quantities of radiation were released into the atmosphere eventually killing thousands. Three Mile Island and Chernobyl will be haunting reminders just as a credit card meltdown could be for those that don't use it right. Financially speaking, this might seem like a dramatic analogy, but it will help us realize that refinancing is not something to be taken lightly and it can either be used for immense good or it can cause immense harm. We should seriously consider whether or not it is a tool that we want to use in our financial lives.

Essentially the mechanism for a balance transfer is quite simple: you have a balance on Card A and you haven't been able to pay it off as quickly as you thought or you might be approaching your credit limit. This strain makes a balance transfer look appealing. So you do a balance transfer where your balance (all or some) shifts from Card A to Card B. Boom, done. You can do a balance transfer in less than 5 minutes online in a lot of situations and it can be so quick that we miss the finer points of the tool that underlie its power and potential volatility.

First, the upside to refinancing. Most balance transfers will charge you 3% of your transferred balance. As an example, if you transfer $3,000 from Card A to Card B, it costs you $90. This $90 is a real cost, but it might actually be worth it if you play your cards right. If Card A was crushing you with interest each month, you could potentially save hundreds of bucks quite quickly by doing this balance transfer since you can now avoid Card A's interest. Let's say Card A had an APR of 24% (pretty common for credit cards to charge this much interest, remember). The way they calculate the interest gets a little complex, but we can use an estimation that is easy to apply to credit cards. Essentially all we have to do is find the monthly APR. So if 24% is for the year, then each month you will face an interest amount that is roughly 2% of your balance (since 24/12 = 2). The balance is $3,000 so 2% of that is $60. Extrapolating that *approximate* amount out over the year you would pay roughly $720 in interest. This $90 balance transfer fee helps you avoid that $720 in just one year and you are thus $630 better off ($720-$90). Not a bad move, you financial wizard!*

---

* I really should say "you financial goblin" like those that keep the books and treasure safe at Gringots in Harry Potter. The muggle vault equivalents are actually quite fascinating. The ultra-rich store their treasures in what are called "freeports" and since they link the warehouses to airports, the art, riches, and treasures stored there are technically "in transit" and their minions of financial advisors can find special tax loopholes that make them even richer. http://www.economist. com/news/briefing/21590353-ever-more-wealth-being-parked-fancy-storage-facilities-some-customers-they-are

But, there's a catch, right? The easiest answer to that is *maybe*. This is where you have to really pay attention. There are things you have to do to pull this off correctly in order to avoid a credit card nuclear meltdown. Card A, the one whose new balance is quite a bit lower, and maybe even $0 if you transferred the full amount, is looking pretty fresh. I mean, now that the balance is lower you can feel better about grabbing lunch, gas, that mini-weekend getaway, or that pair of shoes online that you've been eyeing for a couple of months. Right?

Wrong. Completely wrong. The trick here is that when you transfer your balance, most people shift their focus to Card B and lose site of the reason they did the balance transfer in the first place: to get rid of debt. Once you balance transfer, Card A needs to disappear. Recall Camp 3? When you balance transfer, you are using the footbridge to Camp 2. You can only actually move to Camp 2 if are willing to *stop* using Card A. Otherwise there is no point and you've just lost the credit card battle. It's worth repeating: if you do a credit card balance transfer, you *must* stop using the card itself. Why? Because once you swipe Card A again, that balance is going to slowly climb once more and now instead of just having Card A to pay off, you're stuck with Card A and Card B, a higher balance, more interest paid, more debt, less progress. Bad. Very bad. It should be clear that you have to ditch Card A once you transfer to Card B.

Further, you have to stop using Card B and focus on paying down the debt itself. Both Card A and Card B are off limits for transactions. In fact, the credit card companies are salivating harder than Pavlov's dogs[*] at the idea that you will continue to use both of your cards. Card A gets to continue to charge you interest and now Card B has the additional advantage of having you build up a higher balance *and* have a transferred balance that might make them money once your promotional APR expires.

---

[*] Just as Pavlov's dogs were conditioned to respond to the sound of a bell, so too are credit cards conditioned to see balance transfers as a sign of opportunity to engage you with more of their debt services and products so that they can make more dough. Some of these offerings can be really useful, but some aren't.

So how can you use this tool for your gain? It's actually pretty simple: just pay it off before the promotional rate expires. The observation can help you save yourself from, well, yourself. Understand how much you need to pay each month. In our example, let's just say, for mathematical simplicity (you're welcome, btw) that your promotional 0% APR is for 30 months and recall that your transferred balance was $3,000. This means that in order to pay it all off before the rate expires (this should absolutely be your goal), you would need to make monthly payments of $100 for each of those 30 months ($3,000/30 = $100). You should be well aware of the fact that the credit card companies don't really want you to do this. They are expecting and hoping that you don't pay it off in full so they can charge you interest and your minimum monthly payment will be lower than the actual amount that you should pay in order to achieve your goal. Your monthly payment will be something like 1 – 2% of your balance so it might be in the range of $30 – $60 in this example. Making that minimum payment *will not* help you pay it all off in 30 months. On top of that, most intro APRs are not as generous; you might get a 12, 18, or 24-month 0% APR deal, so you might need to pay much more than $100/month, per our example, in order to have the full balance paid off before the intro APR expires.

In closing, being forthright about your ability to put in place the discipline and diligence around a plan to pay off your credit card by using a balance transfer is essential. If you truly feel like you can get to *and* stay in Camp 2, then go for it. But if you are the type of person who is going to do a transfer and refinance just to shift debt from one card to another without a clear plan around paying it down while removing the temptation to use the old card (Card A), think twice. No, maybe think three or four times about what the risks versus rewards are. The last thing you are trying to achieve by refinancing via a transfer is to make *less* or *slower* progress towards your financial security and stability so think about whether or not you are ready to exploit the opportunity or if you are going to get exploited. This isn't meant to seem all doom and gloom or strike a fearful chord in your heart, but it is meant to make sure that you are fully informed and prepared so that you can be the rogue balance transfer user who actually benefits from it.

As you can see, you can get royally ahead by refinancing, but you can also get royally screwed too. In determining whether or not this makes sense for you, keep in mind the following points:

- Never balance transfer unless you are willing to stop using *both* Card A and Card B (a.k.a. commit to staying in Camp 2).
- Read the fine print. It is dry and boring, but essential to understand. Call the credit card company and talk to someone if you have questions.
- Take your balance transferred amount and divide it by the length of the promotional rate to find your *optimal* minimum monthly payment.
- Commit to paying the necessary amount to pay off your balance by the time your promotional rate expires.
- Do not transfer a balance onto a card that has an existing balance as it can cost you even more.*
- Remember, with great power comes great responsibility. ;)

Retail Cards

Retail cards, in their most basic form, are essentially credit cards. The main difference is that the retail card itself is usually associated with only one merchant (or one company). They're all over the place and you encounter them mostly at the point of sale (POS, a.k.a. the cash register or checkout). If you've gone to Target, Best Buy, Amazon, TJ Max, J Crew, Gap, or any number of retail stores, you know the drill: shop around for a while, go to checkout, smile, say hi, and bam! Right as you're about to pay, the cashier says, "Would

---

* When transferring to a card with a balance already allows the company to prioritize where your payments go. So for example, they can take your $50 monthly payment and apply it to the lowest APR "tranche" (the balance transfer portion) and not the higher interest tranche (the previous balance) that was most likely at your original rate. This means more money for them, harder for you to pay off.

you like to save 20% off your purchase today, it's free, and it comes with all these bells and whistles: blah, blah, blah." You think (or do you?). You ponder about that 20% savings – it sure would be nice. You don't realize it, but it's a person asking so you don't want to say no or disappoint them.* Plus it's free anyway so you say, "Yeah, sure." Five minutes later, as you are driving home you wonder, "What just happened?" A recent study showed that a full 21% of Americans had signed up in the last two years just for the immediate in store discount and fully 45% didn't consider the impact on their credit score.[24] Presumably you sign up in part just to get the heck out of there faster. You didn't want the card, you didn't really need it, but now you have it and sure, you saved a little bit. Without going into the details around how the entire setup is designed to do precisely what it just did to you, we now have to deal with it.

First, they can actually have lots of benefits. You have the opportunity to build your credit score if you use it and pay it off on time. Not bad. Further, you can capture some of those bell and whistle perks like extra cashback or special promo offers that are only available to card holders.

On the other side of the coin are the cons. Chief among them, thinking about temptation and spending amounts, you could wind up much more likely to actually go to say, Target, more frequently than if you didn't have your shiny new Target card. Once there, going back to what we know about swiping cards, you will, on average, spend 12 – 18% more just because you have the card (and maybe even more than that). So now, you shop more and spend more, but do you need more? Only you can answer that, but most likely you don't need it, no matter how cute that throw pillow or random kitchen hot pad is (even if you already have three of them). Anyone who actually knows me knows I don't need five more monochromatic t-shirts (even though they're so cheap) since that's practically all I wear!

---

* There are a lot of social psychological components going on here in order to break down your mental faculties to get you to sign up. Conformity, group norms, public social pressures, authoritativeness, etc.

A final, very subtle drawback is that most retail cards give you a credit limit that is relatively low. A lot are around the $500 – $1,000 point which means you could theoretically go nuts one day at Banana Republic and wind up with a new wardrobe. The risk here, and we'll get into more detail in the credit score section, is that your *utilization rate* could exceed the recommended 30% mark. To figure out how to avoid this, and thus protect your credit score, to make sure the balance on your retail card is always lower than 30% of your credit limit. If your limit is $1,000, then keep your balance below $300 even though that extra $700 spending ability is staring you in the face.

Enough on retail cards though. At this point in your journey to become financially un-average, you can see the similarities to the already discussed credit cards and now that you are aware of retail cards as a subset of credit cards, you can simply make a better decision at the POS so you don't walk away feeling like a POS.

Personal Loans

Personal loans might be less common, but the most important thing to dissect when considering one for yourself is the reason *why* you are getting a personal loan in the first place. Some of the more common reasons why people get personal loans are to pay for a vacation, refinance and consolidate credit card debt, or to pay for a bigger ticket item like a motorcycle or home improvement project. The major red flag here has to center around whether or not you can delay getting a personal loan in favor of using cash savings. You want to take a vacation this summer? Sure, I get that, but if you're going to borrow $2,400 now, you might be much better off saving $200 a month for a year and taking that vacation next summer instead. It's not simply about delaying gratification here; it's about making sure you are not living a lifestyle above your means. The best litmus test here is to realize that when you're tempted to get a personal loan, the better option would be to save for a while and pay in cash. That way you can avoid the cost associated with the personal loans.

Personal loans will do two things to your financial life for the foreseeable future: first, whatever amount you borrow, you'll end up paying more. Since personal loans are generally in the interest rate neighborhood of 6 – 14%, you can expect that $2,400 vacation, for example, to actually end up costing $400 more than planned bringing your European excursion to around $2,800.* The interest, as we've seen, can add up quickly, especially if you're making lower monthly payments. Which brings us to our second point. Unlike credit cards whose monthly minimum payments are generally lower and relatively easy to squeeze into our budget ($25 – $80 for a lot of folks), personal loans can put a much higher stress on your budget. The personal loans are treated as *installment loans* meaning they have a fixed timeline for paying them off as well as a fixed per month payment. We'll look at two main use cases for personal loans. As you'll see, the first case might not be the best way to go and the second is useful, if used correctly.

Use Case 1: Discretionary Spending

Lots of people use personal loans to buy stuff, that is, to make discretionary spending purchases. You can get a personal loan and buy virtually anything, so if you did bring home that Harley last week or retrofit the bathroom that looked like it was hip in the 1950's, you can expect your budget to look a little different going forward now that you have to pay off those upgrades. Let's assume either one of them costs $9,000 (pretend it's the Price is Right and you get to pick one, although you still have to pay for it in our example. Bob Barker sincerely apologizes for this). If your personal loan is for five years, then your monthly payment will be $191, which means for the next five years, you don't have that amount available to save, to pay down other debt, or to invest in your retirement (it will also cost you almost $2,500 in interest to boot†). It's tempting to get so fixated on the purchase itself and forget that personal loans really do extend far into the future.

---

*   Assumes a 10% APR and a 3 year term.

†   Again, assumes 10% APR.

Anecdotally to shamefully highlight this, I bought some furniture during college and it was awesome. I got going early on the Bachelor Pad and it beat sitting around in creaky wood chairs any day. My friends and I got our use out of it for two years. Then I graduated, moved, and sold the furniture. The funny thing was, I paid for it with a personal loan and the term was for 5 years. I was still paying for furniture that I couldn't even sit or sleep on (it did have a 0% APR though). Fortunately, it didn't take me the full five years to pay it off, but making a monthly payment long after the excitement of the purchase had dwindled away was like swallowing a bitter pill each time I made a payment. The new bathroom, the motorcycle, or my furniture are good examples of how most people wind up with personal loans: there is something so tempting *right now* egging you on. Do it. Do it. But take a step back, a breather, and think about whether or not you actually want to pay for it over the long run. Is it going to have value in your life in one year, five years, 10 years? This type of thinking can help you decide whether or not it's right for you.

Use Case 2: Consolidation

One mega-opportunity with personal loans is *consolidation*. Consolidation simply means taking various other debt and lumping it together into one new loan. You've probably heard of this as it relates to student loans, but in this case, we'll look at consolidating debt more generally. The quick and dirty, just like balance transfers, is that consolidation is both potentially really powerful and potentially painful. It can be really awesome in pursuit of paying down debt and accelerating the debt snowball down the hill if you are able to take really high interest debt and consolidate it into a lower personal loan. But note that you shouldn't consolidate *lower* interest debt (like a student loan of say 6.5%) into a *higher* personal loan amount (in this example, 10%) as this would be disadvantageous to you overall.

The first thing to do is rank your debt and find the debt with higher amounts than the new interest rate of the personal loan. Just like

Imogene from before, we know how to rank debt according to the interest rate. We'll make the example simplistic. Let's assume you have 3 credit cards, each with a balance of $3,000 and each with a 20% interest rate. The personal loan rate will be at 10%. Knowing this, you realize you can save the difference in the two interest rates, which comes out neatly to 10% (20% – 10% = 10%). You decide to pull the trigger on the personal loan deal that you saw advertised. Once approved, you get a check in the mail for $9,000 (banks, credit unions, credit card companies and consolidation companies all offer personal loans). You use this $9K to pay off the 3 credit cards immediately, and being a wise, rogue person, you have committed to not using the credit cards until the loan is paid off (high five!). So how sweet a move was this? Well, you have lowered your overall interest rate substantially by consolidating so you just saved yourself a whopping $3,801. This amount is the difference that you would have paid had you continued to pay 20% on your credit cards compared to the new total interest paid via the personal loan. There are tons of calculators online, like bankrate.com, that can help you figure this amount out. The personal loans that are out there can really do some damage to your outstanding debt (in a good way!) even if they are relatively expensive forms of debt themselves.

A final thing to be aware of is that you might have found it easy to skirt by with those low credit card monthly minimums, so just get ready for (and ask beforehand) about the new, most likely higher, personal loan payment. Being aware and informed can help you figure out not only how much you can save by consolidating, but also how it will affect your budget each month throughout the course of the loan.

If we compare the two use cases for personal loans here, we have more discretionary use highlighted by buying things, whether they be vacations, motorcycles, home upgrades, etc., versus the strategic use case of using a personal loan in an effort to consolidate higher interest debt. While both are certainly justifiable along many lines, the pros and cons are at least a little more elucidated now. If at all possible, try to set a longer term saving goal for the first use case of making a larger purchase. It'll cost less to take a trip using cash to pay for it rather than personal loans (or credit cards for that matter). Yes, you most likely have to wait longer, but you can travel feeling that much better knowing that when you come home you can focus on looking at all of the beautiful vacation photos (unless you put them on Snapchat*) instead of looking at the payment due at the end of each month. In terms of consolidation, you've got to be ready for the long haul and be ready to match the consolidation process with an equal level of dedication to stop incurring debt in other forms. Once you consolidate, you're in Camp 2 for quite a while and the grass is going to look greener back at Camp 3 where you can keep using your credit cards and retail cards. But we both know you don't want to head back there.

Lions, Tigers, and Student Loans

Lions, Tigers, and Student Loans, oh my! The mounting accumulation of student loans that individuals have, many of whom are just getting started with college or a career, makes Dorothy's adventures in Oz look like a cakewalk. The Wicked Witch of the West has nothing on the $1,260,000,000,000 in outstanding student loan balances held by Americans (that's $1.26 Trillion)[25] and if that amount doesn't make you melt faster than water on a witch, I don't know what will. Outside of housing debt, this is the largest monstrosity of debt, and being saddled with it in increasing amounts at a young age can set the entire populace back many years – even decades – as each of us searches for economic and financial independence.

As you go throughout your college years, most people think about what classes and student organizations they are going to join rather than the technical jargon that surrounds student loans such as subsidized vs. unsubsidized, cosigners, income-based repayment, forbearance, and deferment. Who cares? I don't have class on Fridays and I'm lovin' it! If you were like me, you were more concerned about football games on Saturday and choosing the best

---

* Snapchat summary: I just don't get it. Am I really that old already? I love technology, but can't figure this one out.

house party to go to with your friends on the weekend while still getting your homework turned in on Tuesday. Student loans didn't make the list of top concerns, even though they reared their ugly head too often.

A quick story to highlight this point: I was so naive when I first started school (and not focused on student loans) that I very seriously said to a group of guy friends one night that I was thinking about joining a sorority. They laughed and thought it was a great joke because what hormonal 19-year-old male wouldn't want to infiltrate a sorority? They invited me to join their fraternity, at which point I realized the difference between the two (neither of my parents went to college so I was flying blind and devouring the new, mysterious world of college life). So there I was, figuring out the social landscape as a juvenile tenderfoot, and yet I was apparently already "informed" enough about college to have accepted $10,000 worth of loans (for my first year alone) prior to learning the basic difference between frats and sororities. While most people might not make silly social blunders like I did (and still do), there are plenty of financial blunders to make along the way even if the years at school are more focused on academics, meeting people, and being exposed to new ideas raining down from the Ivory Tower than they are about managing and understanding your student loan accumulation.

Once done with school, the other side of the equation, also known as "the real world," isn't filled with roses and frolicking in the fields of learning and academia. If you're someone with student loan debt or if you've turned the TV on in the last 5 years, you know what's happening with the crazy amount of student loan debt out there. But as a refresher course (this one is free, I promise): The amount of student loan debt has ballooned recently, especially since the turn of the century. In the last eight years alone – since the Great Recession – it's gotten pretty nasty out there and the price of school is expected to continue to rise for the foreseeable future. No, I take that back, when you blow up a balloon, you can watch it expand slowly. Student loan debt has *blown up*. It has *more than doubled* in the eight years since 2008. That's insane. Imagine if food prices had doubled in the last eight years. Every time you went to your grocery store instead of walking out of there with a $2.00 loaf of bread it would cost you $4.00 and the $200 monthly food budget now crushes you at around $400. This wouldn't be sustainable. It wouldn't be reasonable. So too with the student loan debt: it's not sustainable nor is it reasonable. In the same period that the total outstanding student loan debt has doubled, from 2008 to 2016, the National Center for Education Statistics has estimated that the total undergraduate enrollment will only increase by a measly 7%.[26] So clearly it's not like there is some massive increase in demand for school that would realistically drive up the price to so high a level (and in turn, the student loan burden). What the heck is going on here?

What is clear and undeniable is that someone is getting the shaft and quite honestly, it is almost always the students themselves who end up with piles of loans since the onus of price increase in college is shifting to students. Consider the following two facts. First, the price of college has increased at a wicked rate. From 2001 to 2016, the average price of tuition, fees, and room and board have gone up an astronomical 67% from $11,655 in 2001 to a ghastly $19,548 in 2016. Remember too, that this is just for *one year of school*.[27] The second fact, alluded to earlier, is that the amount of student loans held per graduate is skyrocketing. Nationally recognized student loan expert, Mark Kantrowitz, has calculated that the average 2016 graduate has $37,172 in student loan debt.[28] Ouch. We are paying more for school than ever, getting an education, and walking away with way more debt before most of us have spent 25 years on the Third Rock from the Sun.

Millennials across the U.S. of A. who are saddled with student loan debt are having to make bigger and bigger sacrifices as they enter their twenties and thirties. The tradeoffs are real and loans can stifle all types of lifestyle choices, alter your living situation, and change your long term financial health prospects – they invade every conceivable portion of your life and a couple of these impacts in the Citizen's Bank *Millennial Graduates in Debt* survey[29] are highlighted to show just how many millions of people are finding it more challenging to cope:

- 40 percent have limited the amount they can spend on rent or mortgage payments.
- 46 percent have limited their spending on entertainment and social events.
- 50 percent have limited their shopping for clothes, shoes and accessories.
- 45 percent have limited their spending on eating out.
- 54 percent have limited their travel.

Before you shed an ironic tear for people who can't spend as much on clothes, shoes, and eating out, I'll point out that this impacts more than just those with debt – it makes the economy worse off. Our economy is based on consumption, housing, and various other facets such as tourism and investing. When people have large student loan debt burdens, they are "servicing debt" which simply means that they are paying debt. At the macroeconomic level, debt servicing is less beneficial and productive for an economy's growth than when people invest in housing and real estate, consume goods, and have money left over to invest. Since millions of millennials are spending lots on debt servicing rather than on living life, the economy suffers. This shows up in a variety of ways, one of which is that millennials saddled with debt are not as actively able to help build the economy through spending and purchasing. They are subsequently paying less in taxes through decreased retail and sales tax (i.e., excise taxes). When you have less money, you spend less, which makes the amount of taxes you pay less, which hurts state and federal budgets.

Another subtle way student loans hurt America is through the tax break to those who pay student loan interest since it is a deductible line item. Yes, the tax break is initially good for people who pay student loan interest since you can deduct the amount when paying your taxes. But a group of individuals led by George Schultz from Stanford's renowned think tank, the Hoover Institute, pointed out that these types of "tax-expenditures...severely erode the tax base and reduce tax revenue by over $1 trillion per year."[30] Short term: good for people with student loans. Long term: bad for people with student loans *and* for the government and economy at large. We don't need to go further into tax, economic, or public policy measures, but the overwhelming directionality of our compass continues to point out that the increase of student loans is deleterious, burdensome, and harmful for individuals as well as the economy at large.

Obviously the whole scenario can't be entirely bad and oppressive, because people are still getting the best education in the world at American colleges and universities. In fact, 17 out of the top 25 schools in the world are right here in between the Atlantic and Pacific Oceans.[31] While our schools and universities are still amazing and people are better educated because of it, the student loan issue is bubbling up as faster and with more force than people can handle. Yes, your future earning potential increases as does your knowledge, but the complexity and scope of this issue is massive and problematic. It can't be waved away with simple clichés like, "You're investing in yourself" or "It'll pay off in the long run," because these sentiments are more strained than ever given the burden of loans that even Atlas might find tough to shoulder.[*]

This issue deserves the full attention of legislators, policy advocates, consumers, government officials, and many others if a well-designed and expedient solution is to be reached that will lessen the burden on student loan holders and help them once again obtain an education with a reasonable price tag. After all, this has been a national priority that has allowed us to build the world's largest economy, advance all types of research, and spur innovation and technological improvements in every sector, industry, and virtually

---

[*] While science has long since rendered the Greek god Atlas as only figuratively holding the earth on his shoulders keeping us from falling to the bottom of space, I'm still holding out for him to be useful in shouldering some of our nation's student loan debt.

all corners of the globe. It's an issue we probably don't want to screw up as badly as we're on track to as we speak. While it's tempting to go into further details to look at the reasons why this outrageous inflation in the cost of education and the subsequent shift and burden placed on individuals via student loans has happened, it's far too detailed and complex to be included within the scope of the book. Furthermore, this book is about equipping you with the tools and knowledge to deal with your loans rather than wax poetic about legislative and policy issues. So let's refocus on what you can do right now to deal with your pesky student loans.

Student Loans for Life? Heck No!

Remember how you are becoming un-average? This is a time to do just that. Before we tackle the student loan beast, it's a perfect time to do a spot check and think back to our debt prioritization concept. Look at your debt profile and recall that you need to deal with your *highest interest* rate debt *first*. I say this because if you are at all, in any shape or form, holding credit card debt, you should focus extra funds on making larger than minimum credit card payments rather than increasing student loan payments. Lots of people will be in this very common situation: holding some credit card debt and holding student loans. After all, it's already been pointed out that students graduate with between $3,000 and $4,000 in credit card debt alone to go along with the student loan debt. The quick answer to which to focus on first, is to continue to deal with your credit card debt and *potentially* think about other student loan repayment options. It's worth noting that you can still act as it relates to your student loans even if you aren't quite ready to make larger than minimum payments. There are several income-based repayment options as well as public service loan forgiveness that might be appropriate and useful. More on these in a bit. Just don't lose sight of your credit card or even personal loan debt that is higher on your Debt Snowball list, as this is most likely a main area to continue to focus on.

This is the first thing I bring up because, psychologically, the sheer size of your student loans can feel downright oppressive. It can be super tempting to want to apply extra funds that you might have in a given month to your student loans and lose sight of the fact that your higher interest debt is more important to tackle. Think about it, if you've got $1,000 in credit card debt and $37,000 in student loan debt – that $37k seems like a way more massive item to deal with. While it is a way bigger amount, granted, it is also going to be much less expensive due to the interest rate being lower (probably ~6% versus ~20%+). The $1,000 credit card balance seems like a small thing, but remember, dollar for dollar, credit card debt costs way more to hold, so go deal with it. Then come back once that is gone (revisit the Debt Snowball section if you doubt me).

As time goes on, we have a tendency to look at the largest balance items instead of the largest APR. I certainly have the tendency to do this – and have to fight the temptation – because I know that I really want my student loans to go away for good (I still have about $7,000 to pay off as of September 2016 and if you recall, Barack Obama didn't even pay off his loans until 2004, the same year he ran for Senator of the United States[32]). Like me, I'm sure you've sat there and thought, "I'm going to make huge payments on my student loans this month. It's no match for my will or my wallet!" This can be awesome and by no means am I saying don't do that. I'm just saying that you should make a huge credit card payment (or other higher interest debt payment) if you have it. Then once that's gone, be my guest and crush your student loan debt with big payments. Until then, break out of the psychological trap of focusing on student loans. It goes without saying, if you're currently working down the Debt Snowball list and you're appropriately at the place where making big payments on your student loans makes sense, then by all means, carry on!

For the most part, as we discuss your student loans, we will talk in terms of *federal loans* since more than 90% of all student loan debt is in the form of federal loans.[33] A quick note on private loans is that they act like regular installment debt (like an auto loan or mortgage) so you don't really have as many refinancing or special opportunities to lower your monthly payments since they are held by private lenders that are generally less willing and able to offer alternative repayment options. If you do have private loans, include them in your debt prioritization list as you look to snowball your debt and take them on when appropriate (while still maintaining at least the minimum payment each month). An interesting note here on private loans is that they can actually have lower interest rates than federal loans which are generally in the 5% – 9% range, but private student loans can vary drastically, from around 2% to as high as 11%+. So make sure you are aware of your terms and interest rate before committing to a course of action.

As with all debt, it's important to know what you owe. Sounds simple, in concept, but a survey conducted by Citizen's Bank found that 59% of millennials had no idea when their student loans would be paid off,[34] and a full 50% have not even explored the idea of lowering their monthly payments.[35] So first things first, do a quick survey and double check what your outstanding balances are. The sure fire way to see how much you owe is to check out the federal student loan database, National Student Loan Data System (NSLDS),[36] to see a list of your loans and balances. The NSLDS is designed so that you can easily and quickly access a list of all of your federal loan information in one place, even if you have different lenders. It is a useful tool to use to make sure that your loan information looks correct and to find your aggregate outstanding amount. Once here you can see your various loan packages, interest rates, what type of loan they are, and so forth. A platform like the NSLDS is great, but sometimes you need more information like your payment history, current status, etc. If you do need this, you can always log on to your student loan lender's website to see statements, account information, payment history, etc. and if that isn't clear enough, pick up the phone and call your student loan servicer. Yes, really, picking up the phone and actually speaking to a person is still a thing, even though it might seem like a historic relic of the 90's, like Britney Spears and N*SYNC.*

---

* The lyrics from "Sometimes" by Britney Spears might be more suited for relationship advice, but don't apply the mentality of "sometimes I run, sometimes I hide" to your student loans. Running and hiding never works out. Face them head on so that you can eventually say "Bye, bye, bye." And yes, I do hope these songs are now stuck in your head for at least a week.

The Big Tradeoff

Regardless of your situation, there are lots of things you can do now to deal with your student loans. We're treading into interesting territory here. While there are lots of new options regarding student loans, the tradeoffs can be quite staggering and should be fully understood before seeking them as alternatives to help pay off your loans. The quick and dirty is that the main tradeoff boils down to "monthly payment amount" vs. "total amount of interest paid." The relationship is an *inverse* relationship meaning that as one goes up, the other goes down, and vice versa. If you decide to sign up for one of the many programs that allows for your monthly payment to go down (presumably because you need less pressure on your monthly budget), then your total amount of interest will be higher in the long run. Doing this can greatly increase your ability to make payments and live a little more comfortably month to month, but just be aware that this type of move can cost you thousands of dollars in extra interest paid. Conversely, if you make larger monthly payments, then your total amount of interest paid will be lower, but you will have less disposable money left over in months where you make big payments. If you're able to make larger than required payments, it often makes tons of sense, especially if you are really keen on getting your loans taken care of and putting them in the rearview mirror of your life.

As a quick example to show how serious a trade-off this can be, let's look at an example: Patricia gets her communications degree (hot off the press) and is offered a job as a Marketing Associate at a small advertising company right out of school. They've offered her a starting salary of $35,000. It's not as much as she'd like, but it's a start and it helps her move to the city of her dreams (obviously Chicago because the Cubs are finally starting a baseball dynasty after a dry spell of over 100 years of championship-less baseball. She's a huge sports fan, btw). She moves to the city with her $20,000 in student loan debt, finds a cute apartment even though the rent is a little high. To buffer this cost, she found a roommate, but even after the dust settles, her monthly budget is a little strained. As she's thinking of creative ways to lessen her overall monthly expenses, she thinks maybe there's a way to lower her student loan bill. She hops online to studentloans.gov and finds the incredibly useful Repayment Estimator tool[37] to see what choices she has to lessen the burden of paying her student loans. After she plugs in her information, she gets super excited about the new potential monthly payments – they are so much less than now! Patricia is pumped and she's only a couple of clicks away from having some extra dough in her pocket each month. Score!

Not so fast...the table she is looking at looks all fine and dandy in Column One where the monthly payment is located, but her eyes scan across the page and she sees two other columns that are more concerning: the total amount paid and the repayment period columns don't look so hot.

Repayment Plan	First Monthly Payment	Last Monthly Payment	Total Amount Paid	Repayment Period
Standard	$232	$232	$27,866	120 months
Graduated	$134	$403	$30,051	120 months
Revised Pay as You Earn (REPAYE)	$143	$308	$31,270	144 months
Pay as You Earn (PAYE)	$143	$232	$31,633	155 months
Income-Based Repayment (IBR)	$215	$232	$28,066	122 months
IBR for New Borrowers	$143	$232	$31,633	155 months
Income-Contingent Repayment (ICR)	$166	$199	$33,118	184 months

Repayment Estimator from Studentloans.gov for Patricia.

We can see as quickly as Patricia that lowering her monthly payments (even if only temporarily) *always* increases the total amount paid. Assuming you always make the minimum payment, this will *always* be the case. That's not always bad though, especially when we look at the standard plan (if Patricia does nothing) compared to the next cheapest option, Income-Based Repayment (IBR). She gets a reduced monthly payment of $17 ($204 per year), which isn't a terrible amount necessarily, but it's something (comparatively, you could just pack your lunch two times more a month to capture this savings instead of opting for IBR). If she does choose IBR she'll end up paying an extra $200 over the course of the loan and she'll make payments for 10 years and 2 months instead of 10 years under the standard plan. The two months extra isn't all that much.

However, Patricia's move to Chicago has left her wanting more than just a $17 decrease in her student loan payments and she's thinking

---

* Accessed on 9/2/2016. Assumes Patricia has $20,000 in student loans at a fixed interest rate of 7%, she is filing her taxes as Single, and that her annual income is $35,000, the site makes additional assumptions as well.

that the Revised Pay as You Earn (REPAYE) option would be best for her right now. $143 payment is looking mighty awesome. The tradeoff here is a little more Draconian. Yes, her new monthly payment is $89 lower, but there are three big trade-offs she's now making:

1. She's going to pay $3,404 more in interest. That is a significant price to pay.
2. She's going to make payments for 35 extra months. That's almost 3 extra years of payments beyond the original 10.
3. She will eventually pay *more per month* than her original $232 payment. Her last payment, as we can see, will be $308, which is $76 more than the $232.

For each of these plans, a strange way to think about the choice set and the trade-off between monthly payment and total interest accumulated is to think about getting punched in the arm. Your choice is that you can get punched by your best friend (or worst enemy) "medium hard" right now or delay it. It's not a light punch by any means, so you know it's going to hurt. Before your friend winds up, she offers you a deal: instead of punching you medium hard today, she will let you choose to be punched really lightly today, but a few years from now, she gets to punch you *really hard*. As you consider it, much like the loan repayment options, this "new deal" is tempting because you can escape today with little to no consequences and that "really hard" punch isn't something that seems all too real since it's hovering in the unknown future. Being smart about it, you realize that if you know that hard punch is coming, you can hop over to the gym or the boxing ring to get stronger and train for that punch. Like Rocky running the steps in Philadelphia and eating raw eggs, you've got time to get promotions, pay raises, and continue to climb the ladder so that your finances are way more buff when your friend comes knocking at your door to deliver the hard punch. By then, the idea both physically and financially is that you are going to be more equipped to receive the punch and it will hurt less because of what you were able to do in between your really light punch a couple of years ago and the blast to your right shoulder today.

So which deal would you take? It's ultimately up to you. They all come with pros and cons and even though Patricia's cons seemed pretty high, she (or you) might really need a temporary amelioration in the form of a reduced monthly payment. Life happens, and budgets get pinched. The proverbial money tree isn't bearing fruit, and funds aren't always readily available – that's why the government has created so many repayment options for borrowers. At the end of the day, what I care about is that you make a decision that works for you and that you are able to fully weigh the trade-offs because they are serious and significant. You've already borrowed thousands of dollars and carelessly opting in to paying a couple thousand more isn't something to take lightly. No one wants to wake up in the ring with Mike Tyson, who's ready to do whatever it takes to get those loan payments made, even if it means taking a bite out of your financial ear.

Gettin' Nitty-Gritty With Student Loans

Now that you get the gist of how to evaluate your options and the subsequent tradeoffs, we are going to roll up our sleeves like Rosie the Riveter and get to work learning about the options out there to manage your student loans, optimize your personal circumstances, and even potentially lower the total amount of interest paid over the life of your loans. The brief history of student loans started in its current "accessible" format when college attendance increased substantially in the post-World War II era first with the "G.I. Bill" in 1944 for returning war veterans.* It occurred again in the Sixties as part of Lyndon B. Johnson's "Great Society" initiative that included massive funding increases to students as well as colleges and universities via the Higher Education Act of 1965.[38] In this period of American education history, there was an increased expansion of enrollees as well as those who were taking on student loan debt.

But two mitigating factors made it a relative non-issue for those who attended. First, higher education was not as equitable; it was still generally limited to those who had means or were able to utilize the

---

* The actual name, which is much less memorable, is the Servicemen's Readjustment Act of 1944.

G.I. Bill. Secondly, the sticker price on college was much cheaper and the jobs that people attained afterwards were generally well-paid. This lower debt load and greater job certainty, coupled with increasing, but still limited access, made college a sure fire way to the middle class and beyond. Everything ran more or less smoothly and college even became more equitable for the last 30 years of the 20th Century as more women, minorities, and low-income students were able to access higher education. By 1979, women constituted the majority of students on campus for the first time in history.[39]

The equation was pretty simple for those that went to college: enroll, receive grants and/or loans, learn, and finance the rest with part-time work, graduate, pay off a small amount of loans, live life unencumbered. Achievement Unlocked: Live the American Dream. This rosy formulaic process, while admittedly not perfect or limited in its accessibility, hummed along for decades. One of the triumphs of this was that people had very little to no student loan debt upon exiting college or were able to pay it off in a reasonable time frame without too heavy a burden. Check out this stat from the Center for Economic and Policy Research: only 46.2% of students graduating in 1990 took out student loans. Further, they graduated with far less than half of today's amount of student loan debt, $12,482.[40]

The past situation as it relates to student loan debt is a neat and quaint picture compared to the new unknown and unexplored Martian-like landscape of student loans in the 21st Century that has allowed companies (as well as the government) to spring up offering all types of financial tools, refinancing, deals, and discounts. They know that people are being weighed down by student loans, and while some are offering genuinely decent options for people with student loans, many aren't constructed so nobly. These options are popping up and expanding at an insane rate as they each try to take a bite out of your financial key-lime pie.

No joke though, these companies are out to make money and while their offerings are seductive and potentially beneficial, just remember they have skin in the game. Each one of them, just like the government repayment options (which we'll explore in more detail now), can help. But per your increasing awareness and rogue ability to think critically about financial situations, you know you've got to do just as much homework when it comes to student loan repayment options as you did for that brutal Organic Chemistry course.* We'll look first at government refinancing options. (Newly graduated Patricia's scenario started that discussion.) These options generally tend to be the most favorable, flexible, and financially sound. Next we'll look at alternatives in the private sector. Banks and credit card companies like PNC, Wells Fargo, Discover, and others are getting in the game with deals for transferring your loans to them as well as companies that are primarily focused on student loan refinancing. You might have heard of these companies such as Credible, SoFi, and Earnest – they are the new kids on the block, relatively speaking. Finally, for the "do-gooders" or "bleeding hearts" of the world that wind up working in government, non-profits, hospitals, schools, and other service related positions, you just might be in luck if you're able to get thousands of dollars' worth of your loans forgiven via the Public Service Loan Forgiveness (PSLF) program. Hold on tight as we roll through the riveting world of student loan repayment options!

Consolidation Definition

In the upcoming sections, we'll use the term *consolidation* a couple of times. To consolidate your student loans means to gather them into one big student loan heap and subsequently only have one new loan from your various disparate student loans. A couple of things to note:

- You generally can consolidate your loans at any time.
- You can consolidate all of your loans or only some of your loans into a new consolidated loan.

---

* About the only thing, other than analyzing the chemical and structural composition of cocaine on my Organic Chemistry final, that I remember is that my teacher would fill six giant chalkboards per lecture and my hand would hurt from copying it all down. In fairness, she was a great lecturer even if my brain matter wasn't too keen on remembering chemical reactants and reagents. I did get an A+ in the lab though, probably because I liked playing with fire and Bunsen burners so much.

- Your new consolidated loan interest rate will most likely change.
- Your new consolidated loan monthly payment will most likely change.
- Your new consolidated loan term (length to payoff) may change.
- Consolidating your government loans can be advantageous, but you may lose some benefits such as counting the number of qualified payments you've made to date towards various programs like the Public Service Loan Forgiveness (more on this later).
- You can consolidate federal loans with private loans, but they will no longer be considered federal loans. This might be beneficial, but you will lose all of the federal loan repayment options that can be useful, as we shall see.

This short list is more of a reference point, it's not exhaustive, nor do you need to necessarily memorize it, per se. Just check back here if you need to as we get going with the various refinancing methods below. While consolidation is done for many reasons, consolidation can be more advantageous to do immediately upon exiting school for a variety of reasons. However, it can be pursued at any time. At this point, you will not be surprised, and you may even have anticipated that consolidation comes with a whole host of tradeoffs just like refinancing, so do your homework. Consolidation itself has become much less of a necessary move in recent years as it is becoming easier and easier to manage your student loan repayments online via the various lender websites. Back in the day when you had to send in paper checks, it wouldn't be out of the question that you'd have to write 5 – 15 checks just for your student loans. Now, even if your student loans are split out by lender and by semester, you generally don't have as large a concern in making the payment transactions themselves. For example, while I make two student loan payments per month, one of them technically pays 8 separate student loans, but I don't have to make each of these line item payments, fortunately! This commentary only scratches the surface and if you think you'd benefit from a more streamlined payment each month, then check out the link below. Of course, there are more rules, options, and things to know about this and one of the best resources out there to learn more is at: https://studentaid.ed.gov/sa/repay-loans/consolidation.

Government Refinancing

This is a thorny beast, no doubt. As alluded to before, if you are able to make your payments, even if a little tight on that monthly budget, your best bet is going to be to do nothing as it relates to alternative repayment plans (i.e., refinancing). As we saw with Patricia, the short term alleviation of monthly payment requirements always results in higher overall amounts paid back, so pursue this option only in the case where the strain due to student loans is super high or you're slipping in other areas of your financial life (like not being able to pay all of your bills, having to rack up more expensive debt to cover life and expenses, etc.).

This portion is not intended to rehash the various litany of details surrounding each of the main repayment options – you can look that up online in a million places. This information and system falls under the government's purview, so you guessed it: it's overwhelming, complicated, and the information is extensive (fortunately), but they offer virtually no advice or strategy that relates to you (unfortunately). This leaves you saturated with information, but in a state of paralysis – essentially how I feel after Thanksgiving dinner each year, no matter how many times I try not to go back for a second serving.* We need a way to both synthesize the information *and* to take any necessary actions (even if the best course of action is inaction).

In this vein, instead of contributing to the information excess, we'll pinpoint and flesh out a more useable strategy that you can implement to see which alternative payment plan is best for you, should you need to utilize one. First things first, unlike most government websites, https://studentaid.ed.gov is pretty legit and understandable. It's going to be home base for our operations and familiarizing yourself with it will make decision-making that

---

* Who am I kidding? I meant thirds...cough cough: fourths.

much easier. The site has almost everything you'll need for your own analysis and they have actually developed a comprehensive Repayment Estimator.[41] This is a great tool for analyzing the various options at your fingertips and subsequent tradeoffs. Assuming you are ready to look at specifics, you have eight main options to choose from. I've included a simplified overview of each with a column describing examples of "who might use" as a way to put a more realistic face on each of the plans. There are of course many types of people who might use each plan, but describing them in a broad sense will hopefully elucidate the technical details so you can start to get a sense of common personal situations and circumstances that would make each plan desirable or amenable.

Repayment Option Breakdown

Repayment Plan Name	Overview	Who Might Use
Standard Repayment Plan	10 year fixed monthly payment and is the default student loan plan. By default, all borrowers are eligible for this plan.	People comfortable making monthly payments who want to minimize both time to pay off and total interest paid.
Graduated Repayment Plan	Still 10 years (or less), but monthly payments are low at first and increase over time. All borrowers are eligible for this plan.	People who might have lower initial incomes that expect to have more or less steady income increases.
Extended Repayment Plan	Up to 25 years* and payments can be fixed or graduated.	Generally, you must have quite a large student loan balance ($30,000 or more in federal loans). Borrowers needing reprieve for an extended amount of time.
Revised Pay as You Earn Repayment Plan (REPAYE)	Monthly payments will be 10% of your discretionary income and payments are recalculated each year. Loan term extends to 20 – 25 years.*	Someone who doesn't expect income to rise significantly during loan payback period or is strategically using this because they are seeking Public Service Loan Forgiveness (PSLF).

<u>Pay as You Earn Repayment Plan (PAYE)</u>	Monthly payments are capped at 10% of discretionary income, but could be less and will never be more than the standard 10-year monthly payment amount. Payments are recalculated each year. Loan term extends to 20 years.* Must have a Direct Loan disbursed after Oct. 1, 2011.	Someone who doesn't expect income to rise significantly during loan payback period and has a high debt relative to income. Also good for someone who is strategically seeking Public Service Loan Forgiveness (PSLF).
Income-Based Repayment Plan (IBR)	Monthly payments are capped at 10% or 15% of discretionary income and will never be more than the standard 10-year monthly payment amount. Payments are recalculated each year. Loan term extends to 20 – 25 years.*	Someone who doesn't expect income to rise significantly during loan payback period and has a high debt relative to income. Student borrowers of PLUS Loans. Also good for someone who is strategically seeking Public Service Loan Forgiveness (PSLF).
Income-Contingent Repayment Plan (ICR)	Monthly payments are capped at the lesser of 20% of discretionary income or amount paid on a fixed 12-year loan. Payments could be more than the standard 10-year monthly payment amount. Payments are recalculated each year. Loan term extends to 25 years.*	Someone who doesn't expect income to rise significantly during loan payback period, needs temporarily lower payments, or are parent borrowers of PLUS Loans. Also good for someone who is strategically seeking Public Service Loan Forgiveness (PSLF).
Income-Sensitive Repayment Plan	Monthly payments based on annual income and loan term extends to up to 15 years. Repayment amount varies by lender as the formula for calculating can change.	Someone who doesn't expect income to rise significantly during loan payback period, needs temporarily lower payments, or are borrowers of FFEL PLUS Loans or have FFEL Consolidated Loans.

More complete descriptions here:
https://studentaid.ed.gov/sa/repay-loans/understand/plans
* signifies that any outstanding loan balance will be forgiven at the end of the loan repayment period.

Importantly, the above options are *specifically* regarding Direct Loans and Federal Family Education Loans (FFEL) Program Loans. PLUS loans are also included under the umbrella of Direct Loans, even though they will not be eligible for all of the repayment options. Further, the above table does not cover Federal Perkins Loans,[42] which are a smaller subset of student loans for students who demonstrate exceptional financial need. There are still repayment and consolidation options here, but since school institutions themselves manage the loans, you will need to get in touch with them to see what specific options they have and these will vary by school since each school administers them slightly differently.

As you can see, the eight options are quite varied and each has a nuance that can make them either advantageous or potentially that much more deleterious. The variables here too are large and range from simple questions such as much do you want your payments to be each month to the much more uncertain and complex questions such as what do you expect your income to be in 5, 10, 15, 25 years from now, are you or will you be married, and how will you file your taxes? Oh, and P.S., what is your current debt to income situation? The questions, assumptions, and considerations are quite vast. In helping you to arrive at a decision, one of the best ways to sort through the information is to ask three broad questions to help narrow down your list:

1. **Am I eligible for the given repayment option?** You might be able to eliminate several options just by asking this question first, making the choice much easier. Many people will find that they are not eligible for *all* repayment options.
2. **What do I think about the relative tradeoffs?** If you are really trying to lower your monthly payments and aren't too concerned about the total amount paid, then many of the plans will be suitable, but if you aren't keen on paying more in the long run, then some of the options where you pay more now might be your best shot.

3. **What life and financial situations do I think might change in the future?** While this is virtually impossible to answer with certainty, it does provide a valuable perspective. For example, you'll notice many of the plans are good options if you are seeking Public Service Loan Forgiveness (PSLF). If you think you are for sure going to be in a position that is eligible for PSLF, then getting a lower monthly payment now can yield a *massive* windfall through the public service loan forgiveness program that can amount to thousands or even tens of thousands of dollars. However, if you think you just need a small break on payments for a couple of years while you tide yourself over before launching into a career or job where you could make serious money, then opting into the REPAYE or PAYE options could mean significantly larger monthly payments in the future, which might be hard to stomach and handle. It's not about finding absolute certainty with this question, it is more of a mental exercise around the *reasonable expectation* of certain life events happening. Plot out a couple of realistic future scenarios, and see if any of them point you towards a repayment plan. Then, if there are future scenarios that are pointing towards a given repayment plan, this one might be best in that it has a higher probability of coming true compared to, say, becoming a millionaire (although if this does happen, student loans will become a moot point!)

While these questions are guides in determining the answer to an important question, there is one failsafe built into the decision-making process around student loans: you can change your repayment plan at any time (obviously pending eligibility) *and* it's free. This design is ultra-reassuring in that it empowers you to make a decision *now*, test it out, and see if it works for you. And if you need to change it or your financial and life circumstances change in the future, your repayment plan can change with you. Other debt, such as mortgages and auto loans or leases, aren't this flexible and the inherent flexibility built into federal student loans is extremely valuable as it can allow you to continue to opt in to a plan that is best for you at a given time.

In closing, it might seem like overkill to discuss federal student loans in this much detail, but on an individual level it can amount to thousands of dollars staying in your pocket and allocated to your other financial goals. It can also provide you with much needed relief in the form of lower monthly payments, making life much more bearable and less stressful. Both of these end results justify the attention given and since student loans compose over $1 Trillion in debt in our economy, we have solid grounds to focus on them with a discerning eye. After all, millions of people, myself included, are working to find best repayment option for their own, unique situation.

Private Refinancing

Private refinancing is an option. But is it a good one? Some of the hottest new, flashy companies are putting an age-old refinancing scheme in some new clothes (primarily through slick technology, websites, and alluring marketing campaigns). So how do you decide whether or not refinancing your student loans with a private, for-profit company is a good idea? You need to know three trade-offs that you're making.

Federal versus private terms

Your federal loans have tons of advantageous options such as lowering your monthly payment through the previously mentioned income-driven repayment options. Federal loans also have economic hardship, forbearance, and deferment options. Private loans don't have these traits. If you're switching to private loans, you will lose these options forever.

Interest rates versus monthly payments

Lots of people consider private student loan refinancing because they are searching for ways to make lower monthly payments. A primary way that many refinancing companies will lower your monthly payments is by extending the length of time that you have to pay back your loans. Further, while many "teaser" interest rates will be lower than your federal loans, they often increase to higher rates once you apply and enter your personal information. Both of these dimensions can increase the overall amount you pay back, which can amount to thousands of extra dollars in cost to you.

Fixed versus variable interest rates

Fixed rates are generally higher than variable interest rates, which makes them look disadvantageous up front. But variable interest rates are allowed to go up or down and if yours go up, they might end up being significantly more costly in the long run. Even if your interest rate is fixed, at least you have the guarantee that your monthly payment and the amount you pay back in total is going to be the same no matter what.

Each one of these dimensions is inherently a pro and a con – they shouldn't be seen in a "good" versus "bad" light. Rather they should be evaluated along objective lines depending on your situation. Private loan refinancing might be the best, worst, or neutral move so try to think along these variables so that you can craft as complete an analysis of your situation as possible.

Public Service Loan Forgiveness & Other Forgiveness Options

If you are engaged in any type of public service or in one of the various fields that are geared towards benefitting others, listen up. This section is for you. What exactly does it mean to be in one of these positions? The definition is actually pretty broad and if you think you might be doing it, then check out the section on studentaid.ed.gov that deals with forgiveness, cancellation, and discharge.[43] Some quick examples of public service and positions eligible for forgiveness or cancellation, as defined by the Department of Education:

- Teacher
- Employee at a not-for-profit

- Nurse or medical technician
- Serving in the Armed Forces
- Law enforcement or corrections officer
- Government employee at federal, state, local or tribal
- Attorney working for federal or community public defender organization

The details themselves get nuanced pretty quickly, but the larger point is to make sure that these programs exist to alleviate the potential student loan burden for those who wish to work in positions that are more directly geared towards the general welfare of individuals and of the country. The government has wisely created loan forgiveness and cancellation options so that positions that might pay less on average still have an alluring financial upside in loan forgiveness for employees.

Some of the programs for cancellation are more advantageous than others, but if you can utilize any of them, you could save a bundle and be compensated for your heart of gold. A lot of the forgiveness is centered around the Public Service Loan Forgiveness (PSLF) program. In essence, you can get 100% of your remaining Direct Loan balance forgiven after 10 years.[44] This is really appealing for people that know they are going to work full-time in government or nonprofit work. If you are even remotely wondering if you qualify, go research your options. The nuances, rules, and sub-rules get tricky so read up to make sure you are actually eligible. The first technicality that people usually get hung up on, for example, is the 10-year thing. It's actually "120 qualifying payments" which in its consecutive, uninterrupted sense, is 10 years. Fortunately, if you take a break from work, or have a gap in employment, you could still be eligible provided you make those payments over a longer time. For example, you might work for 6 years (counts towards your PSLF qualifying payments), take a 3-year break for something like traveling or child rearing (doesn't count towards PSLF), and then rejoin the labor force for 4 years (does count). Since you worked 10 years and presumably made 120 qualifying payments over that 13-year period, you would be eligible for PSLF. As a counter-example, the Teacher Loan Forgiveness program requires you to teach for 5 consecutive years in order to get up to $5,000 forgiven (or $17,500 depending on what you teach, again, another nuance). No breaks allowed.

To share a personal story with you, I got Perkins loans when I went to school (thanks again, Uncle Sam) and while I didn't end up teaching for 5 consecutive years and therefore was not eligible for the Teacher Loan Forgiveness program, I was still eligible for a partial cancellation of my Perkins Loan. I about lost my mind when I found this gem of a piece of information. I had somewhere in the neighborhood of $8,000 in Perkins Loans and since I taught for two years, I was eligible for 15% cancellation each year (it is a tiered cancellation system), so I effectively got 30% of my balance completely *erased*. That amounted to around $2,400 or so. I literally just had to print off a single piece of paper, get it signed by the administrator of the school, and send it in and boom, a couple of grand was gone. Awesome.[45]

The bigger issue is two-fold when it comes to all the people out there who could qualify for some type of cancellation or forgiveness: first, lots of people don't even know it exists. I remember the time I was standing on the corner of a not-so-busy intersection with some friends in Chicago and we were waiting for a cab. Naturally, no cab came. Then, one of the guys I was with said, "Oh, let's just use Uber and it'll come pick us up." I was just like, "Huh? What's Uber? You mean someone knows we're here *and* that we want a ride?" Game changer. You don't know what you don't know, but when you do find something out, whether it's Uber or about student loan forgiveness, it can rock your world, and in the case of student loans, it can literally save you thousands of dollars.

The second issue is that once you do know it exists and you start to do research, you can quickly become overwhelmed by the inundation and deluge of information and options. I mean, shoot, there are around 10 viable *repayment options* that we just covered and now I'm telling you that there are something like 50 different qualifying ways that you can get your loans *forgiven or cancelled?* It's mind-numbing and dizzying once you start diving into the links, the sites, the information, and the options. In terms of finding a solution and capitalizing on programs that were designed for you to benefit from, it is really about taking a methodical approach to sorting it all out. As such, be patient, take your time, and if you feel overwhelmed or disheartened, take a break and come back to it later (but not too much later). It can also be really helpful to ask friends, family, or coworkers who might have been in a similar situation or to get a second set of eyes on the actual documentation since it is written in quite a lawyerly fashion and isn't always that clear.

Finally, there is strategy angle to take when it comes to addressing student loan cancellation and forgiveness since many of them take years to actually complete (5 – 10 years for lots of the teaching and public service loan programs). Essentially, you want to ask yourself whether or not you are going to fulfill the eligibility and time requirements. This is a really tough question to answer and takes on a gender dimension as well since women are more likely to take extended breaks or leave the workforce entirely.[46] In order to simplify and give more concrete scenarios on making this choice, I will leave you with three examples that hit the entirety of the spectrum for those who are currently in eligible positions to get cancellation or forgiveness:

Certain Susan

Susan is an attorney and she is working as a public defender. She is eligible for PSLF and has $100,000 in student loans from law school. She thinks she will get married and that it's probable that she'll have kids at some point. She is committed to her career so she knows she isn't going to leave it or change it down the road. She has aspirations to become a district attorney at some point as well.

Outcome

Susan would be best suited to 1) enroll in a repayment program that minimizes her monthly payments and 2) to submit relevant paperwork as she works towards making her 120 qualifying payments.* Since she is super certain about her career pathway, she has relatively little risk of not meeting the requirements for PSLF and just needs to get her "ducks in a row" by filing the correct paperwork along the way. Once she does that, she can bust it to be the best attorney she can be and focus on her clients' needs and her own professional development.

This "one-two punch" allows Susan to pay *as little as possible* over the next 10 years so that once she completes her 120 qualifying payments, she can get *as much as possible* forgiven. Her one-two punch strategy is a perfect example of how to use PSLF most advantageously. Even though the total amount of interest paid looks higher on paper, she still opts for the plan that minimizes her monthly payments because she knows that the remaining balance will be forgiven so she will be off the hook for the increased interest amounts. Depending on her salary, this strategy could add up to well past $10,000 in loans forgiven.

Oscillating Oscar

Oscar is currently at a nonprofit and he loves working at the after-school community center in his neighborhood. He has created lots of programs and activities that allow the kids to blow off extra steam from the school day and he's always working on ways to keep them engaged in learning. It's a tricky balance, but he's getting the hang of it. Oscar can see himself staying in the nonprofit realm for a long time, but he worries about sustainability, both from a financial perspective and an energy perspective (he voluntarily stays late several times a week and gets roped into weekend activities frequently). He's got $30,000 in student loans and would love to get them forgiven, but he has a knack for design and might want to pursue this at a technology or advertising company. The thought of

---

* It's important to note that you are *not* automatically granted forgiveness or cancellation just because you are eligible. You need to file paperwork both during and at the completion of your 120 payments. Stay on top of your paperwork! It's best to periodically file the Employment Certification for PSLF form, which can be found here: https://studentaid.ed.gov/sa/sites/default/files/public-service-employment-certification-form.pdf

trying it out in a year or two is appealing even if it's generally on the back burner in his mind. He's pretty open to either scenario (and others that might spring up).

Outcome

Like millions of people, Oscar ultimately is driven by his actual work and career prospects and values purpose rather than just focusing on which financial scenario leaves him "best off." Yes, Oscar could simply pick the pathway that minimized his student loan burden and/or maximized his overall financial picture, but he is going to most likely make a decision that best suits his lifestyle and bigger life goals of finding meaningful and sustainable work. Currently, his scenario is pretty typical in that he doesn't know precisely what the future holds so he has only one simple action item regarding his student loans: file the Public Service Employment Certification Form. It's a quick clerical step that he needs to do so that he's set up to earn PSLF if he ends up working in the nonprofit space for 120 qualifying payments (10 years provided he is continuously eligible). If he decides to leave to pursue other options, no big deal; he just will forego the final paperwork submission after 120 qualifying payments so it's no skin off his back. He can always switch back to a PSLF eligible position and pick up where he left off in terms of making qualifying payments.

Shifting Sam

Sam is all over the place in terms of interests, career prospects, and places that seem interesting to live and to work. Sam is like millions of people who want to make the world a better place through her work and Sam is someone who goes with the wind, seizing opportunities as they arise. Working hard in all scenarios and trying to think of creative ways to impact the world are Sam's hallmarks, both personally and professionally. Sam is currently dedicated to working in government or in the not-for-profit space, both of which qualify her for PSLF. Interestingly, Sam has Perkins loans, but isn't in a position where they are eligible for Perkins loan cancellation. While Sam is young and career-focused now, it is a real possibility in Sam's mind that raising a family might pop up, soon so she isn't sure if 10 years of working in positions that will allow for student loan forgiveness is going to come to fruition. Sam often plays the "what-if game" at night before falling asleep by asking questions like, "What if I change careers?" "What if I go back to school?" "What if I get married and decide not to work once kids come into the picture?" Alas, Sam is figuring it out and is comfortable playing the what-if game knowing there doesn't have to be a perfect answer right now.

Outcome

Sam's ability to remain pliable and flexible as it relates to work, career, and lifestyle are impressive and she will definitely be able to leverage that openness to opportunity along the way. But the student loan forgiveness question is a little tricky since we can say that there is a relatively high probability that Sam won't end up completing 120 qualifying payments while working in PSLF-eligible positions. This is something that happens to millions of people for one of two primary reasons: first, some people just switch jobs into non-PSLF eligible positions. Wages are generally higher in the private sector compared to government and nonprofit positions and the temptation to go after them is real. Sam might end up in the private sector after all. Who knows? Secondly, there is a family dimension where Sam might leave the workforce to raise a family with a partner/significant other/spouse. Many young people at the outset of their careers are certain they will continue working and will stay the course in PSLF-eligible positions regardless of family and baby developments, but life happens right? You get married, a new baby pops out, and all of the sudden you're thinking it might be better for one of you to stay home to raise the cute new baby instead of both working. This leaves you in an extended position where you aren't making qualifying payments towards PSLF (even if you are making payments, they are only qualifying provided you are in full-time employment).

Sam's scenario is common and also takes on a subtle-yet-important gender dimension as well in that women comprise a larger fraction of education, health, and nonprofit jobs;[47] they are more likely to leave the workforce than men;[48] and they still face a leadership gap[49] as well as a wage gap.[50] This doesn't mean that men don't also leave the workforce to raise families, it just means women do so more often. In either case, Sam and millions of others are in this type of scenario and it needs a solution. Fortunately, like Oscar, it is relatively simple: just file the paperwork while you're in PSLF eligible positions. One caveat here is that if you are planning on either moving to the private sector or leaving the workforce, your repayment options are a little more complex. If you are headed to the private sector and expect your income to increase later, then options that aren't tied to income might be better choices for you so you don't have a significant increase in student loan payments later. Similarly, if you might leave the workforce, be careful to choose a repayment plan that you'll be able to continue to pay even if your income goes to zero. The most probable scenario here is that you leave the workforce and said partner/significant other/spouse is the "breadwinner." You'll use that single income to pay for your joint student loans if you both have them. In this case, if you are married, your joint income will be used to calculate your repayment amount for REPAYE, PAYE, IBR, and ICR plans. The big thing to consider here is the tradeoff between lower payments now versus the probability of making a life decision that moves you away from PSLF. Sam's scenario implies that this future probability is higher than say Oscar or Susan, so if it is at all possible, making standard payments on student loans would be preferable. The reason for this is so Sam can make a bigger dent now and drive down the student loan balance before leaving the workforce which will lower the overall amount of interest paid and potentially the total amount of time needed to pay off the loans themselves. It's worth repeating that this scenario is definitely complex, but bringing it back to the overall point of weighing student loan repayment options: if you can afford to stay in the standard, 10-year repayment plan, you should do that since it minimizes the total amount paid and the time in which you have to pay back those pesky loans to begin with.

This is of course provided you aren't going to be eligible for PSLF or other forgiveness options.

In closing, your life situation is going to be unique to you and while the future is certainly uncertain, it shouldn't stop you from making sound decisions now. You can and should weigh the likelihood of various scenarios playing out and make an informed decision based on the available information. This type of uncertainty plagues people, companies, and institutions the world over and it complicates decision-making, but if you ask leaders the world over, they will all agree with one underlying core fact: that making no decision is always worse than making a decision. So get out there, do your research, and make a decision that works for you.

Deferment & Forbearance

Deferment and Forbearance can be powerful opportunities to temporarily pause payments on your student loans. In many situations, you will not only be granted the ability to stop payments, but if you have certain types of loans, you will be able to get your accumulated interest paid off once you exit your deferment or forbearance period. As you might have guessed, this can be a significant sum of money and is quite the perk. People who do Peace Corps, AmeriCorps, and certain military or health care positions are eligible for deferment and/or forbearance.

One of the most common deferment scenarios is when people pursue college or graduate school. If you're enrolled at least half time in school, you are eligible for deferment. Almost none of the schools or positions in which you find yourself will automatically enroll you in deferment or forbearance so it's important to identify if you're eligible and then to *opt in*.

Now, with most systems online, you can generally find forms to file for deferment and forbearance electronically. It will take a little digging since these are less used features of given institutions, but you should be able to find them once you log on to your student loan provider's website or your current institution (AmeriCorps in particular has an excellent, streamlined site that facilitates forbearance requests).

One quick story to highlight the perils of inaction in this domain. I was talking to a medical student about his loans and he was telling me that he was not opted in to deferment. He had undergraduate loans and instead of opting in to deferment, he was using his graduate loans to make payments on his undergraduate loans. Now, in his defense, this might have been advantageous had his grad loans been at a lower interest rate than his undergrad loans, but in fact, they weren't. His grad loans were at 6.5% and his undergrad loans were at 4.5% meaning he was essentially transferring his student debt burden from a relatively *cheap* option to a higher cost option (namely, 2% more expensive). I don't know exactly how much undergrad student loan debt he had, but let's assume that his payments were $300 a month and he did this for 4 years. This means that not only would he have transferred $14,400 from low cost undergrad loans to high cost grad loans, but he would not have been eligible to get the accumulated interest during that period paid for. The math on this is pretty devastating:

- He missed out on getting $2,772 in interest payments (just for the $14,400, not even counting the other portion of his loans that he might have had).
- He now will pay $1,713 more in interest since he used his grad loans to pay for his undergrad loans, if he does a standard 10-year payment plan once he's done with med school.

Yikes. At a bare minimum, this is a $2,772 mistake and at max, but since he also used grad loans to pay for undergrad loans, it's a $4,485 mistake. Moral of the story: check yourself before you wreck yourself. This is an avoidable situation with a little extra knowledge and now that you have it, go use it and look up the resources below if you even remotely think you might be eligible for deferment or forbearance. One caveat here is that when you are in deferment or forbearance, you are often not making progress towards other types of forgiveness or cancellation programs such as PSLF since they are not deemed "qualifying payments." So take note of those peculiarities in particular. The PSLF program in particular does not count any payments as qualifying payments if you are in forbearance, deferment, have in-school status, or are in default. Read and reread the fine print, as annoying and tedious as that can be! Even if it causes a minor headache now, it can save you a bundle and help you avoid massive migraines down the road.

Check out this Studentaid.ed.gov guide for more information about deferment and forbearance:

https://studentaid.ed.gov/sa/repay-loans/deferment-forbearance

Check out this AmeriCorps guide to forbearance:

http://www.nationalservice.gov/programs/americorps/segal-americorps-education-award/using-your-segal-education-award/postponing

Be Warned: For-Profit Colleges and Universities

I will take one direct shot across the bow of the higher education landscape that is intended to hit an exploitative, deceptive, and downright unethical target: for-profit colleges and universities. Almost all of these "higher education" organizations do not deserve recognition as a college or university because of the sheer manipulation and extortion they are exacting on the government, the taxpayer, and on the students who are sucked into the black hole of their orbit. These raiders and bandits have surged in popularity recently, and the number of students who are falling victim to their "programs" and "degrees" has sadly skyrocketed by 217% since the beginning of the millennium, from 2000 to 2014. You've heard their ads, seen their flyers and marketing campaigns everywhere scattered across your Internet browser. This massive industry is taking off and the largest 15 of these "educational" giants comprise 60% of all students that go to for-profit colleges, the majority of which are enrolling in online degree programs. While these institutions are disastrously underperforming and harmful to those that attend, I won't deny that there are a select few whose students do come out on top after completing the dangerous labyrinth of a private for-profit college.

If you are someone who has gone to a for-profit school, graduated, felt like you left with a reasonable amount of student loans, and you got a better job than you could have without the degree, then the highest amount of kudos to you, for sure, but you are the rare exception to the rule. In fact, given the likelihood of getting duped or swindled or simply ignored at a for-profit money-making factory, we owe you *additional* congratulations because you were able to achieve the double accomplishment of graduating *and* avoiding getting screwed by the school that you thought was a place geared towards actually educating people. The fact of the matter is that most people attending for-profit colleges emerge with massive amounts of debt, degrees that don't raise their income trajectory that much, and far too often many have nothing to show for it at all because they function like "dropout factories" where rates of degree attainment and completion are abysmal. Peculiarly, this heinous act and system is somehow still legal. Let's take a quick peek at the amazing "benefits" that you get by going to a for-profit college or university:

The "benefits" of private for-profit colleges:[51, 52]

- Outrageously high dropout rates. 78% of students at for-profit 4 year programs don't finish,[53] compared to 35% for private non-profit and 45% for public non-profit colleges. That's a "failure rate" 173% higher than public non-profits and 223% higher than private nonprofit colleges. May the odds be ever in your favor #hungergames.
- More expensive. For-profit colleges cost, on average *at minimum*, 2.5 times as much and *at maximum*, 5 times as

much. Saddle up cowboy, because you're going to have way more debt for way longer.[54]

- Lower earning potential compared to not-for-profit schools (if you somehow manage to graduate). You can expect 8 – 9% less in earnings per year.[55] That's like getting a pay cut each year. Ouch.
- Higher default rates on student loans at 19.1%. That means almost 1 in 5 students will default.

I think that's enough for now. If for some reason you're considering a for-profit college, I'd think severely on the above facts. Are you ready for an overpriced school, higher than usual debt, an underability to pay them back, and a general shafting of their students at every step of the way? Probably not even, though what they do is still somehow legal. Scary. A true time to say, *CAVEAT EMPTOR (buyer beware)*.

Become a Mortgage Master

It was Saturday, March 2nd, 2013. A cold spring day in Chicago even though the sun was out and not a cloud was to be seen. I walked East down Randolph Street with beautiful Lake Michigan in front of me, the brilliantly green Millennium and soon-to-be-finished Maggie Daley Park to my right, and glistening skyscrapers where the city's most well-to-do hole up high above the city to my left. I don't get nervous. I like meeting new people. Public speaking is actually fun for me, and it's a rare occasion for a quite extreme extrovert like me to do anything other than bluster my way into a social situation. This time was different.

When I walked into the main entrance of the skyscraper, I thought the doorman was going to turn me away since the vast majority of the residents dressed way better than I did and I was far too young to be waltzing around a place such as this. Fortunately, I was granted access to the vault-like elevator and was quickly whizzed up over 30 floors to meet someone whose books, papers, and articles I had not only read, but revered due to their command, insight, and gravity. I was literally standing on the brink of the doorstep of the man who had stood "on the brink" of the economic collapse of 2007 and 2008 – now known oh-so-affectionately as the Great Recession – and lived to tell the story.

I knocked and a very tall woman opened the door. Quickly all pretense about where we were faded away as she greeted me warmly and ushered me into the main room where I was struck by the austere, but intentionally chosen objects from across the globe that conveyed an appreciation for experiences rather than materialism. The floor-to-ceiling windows let in all of the natural light of the sunny day and our lunch group of about eight serenely shifted from acclimating to our host's high rise condo to discussions about education, policy, socio-economic stratification in the U.S. and comparisons to China and other nations across the world.

There I was, sitting in a comfy chair chatting it up on a normal Saturday afternoon with Henry and Wendy Paulson, two very accomplished, yet obviously humble and kind individuals. This lunch with these two was different than most because Henry Paulson is essentially someone who I consider among my financial superheroes* and I relished the time conversing with a man who had previously run the second largest investment bank, Goldman Sachs, and with a masterfully calm stroke, guided the economy as the Secretary of the Treasury from calamitous ruin during the Great Recession with the design and implementation of TARP.† Yes, TARP is that thorny $700 billion[56] "bailout" package that the Treasury put together to help buy toxic assets at banks so the world economy didn't fail and take us back to the Great Depression era or worse. Admittedly I'm being a little hyperbolic here, but given the economic recovery since TARP and the Great Recession, almost all economists agree, regardless of political views, that TARP was a significant component in why the U.S. economy was able to rebound during the next decade even if bailing out big banks wasn't a perfect long run solution.

---

* Other notables are Janet Yellen, Thomas Friedman, Joseph Stiglitz, Alexander Hamilton, and Adam Smith.

† Troubled Asset Relief Program

Our lunch volleyed back and forth between big ideas and anecdotes and the hour and a half or so too quickly passed given the laundry list of questions I had for Henry. How do you think the average American will fare in the coming years as it relates to interacting with more regulated banks? How bad would it have been if we let AIG fail? How much strain can the economy now tolerate? How do you feel about the racial and gender inequities in the housing market that have now been exacerbated because of legislation designed to "protect" consumers? Do you want to have lunch again sometime? A lot of these questions are unanswered, but I left that day wondering more about our economy and ultimately, thinking a lot more about the housing market, real estate, and mortgages that make up the world's largest asset class of over $26 Trillion dollars. This is larger than the entirety of the American stock market combined.[57] While there were tons of underlying reasons why the economy got rocked starting in late 2007, the backbone of the issue was centered around mortgages and the housing market. The overall strength and health of the U.S. economy in general has historically centered around real estate and subsequently mortgages as a mainstay for Americans to pursue the American Dream. I mean, no one wants the proverbial white picket fence if there isn't a house on the other side. Mortgages are the beating heart of the economy and they matter both to individuals and to the country as we saw play out in the decade long housing drama that changed the course of the world's history (which is still being written).

In the wake of the Great Recession, for many of us young professionals, we experienced the effects in a substantially different way than older and younger Americans did. For older Americans, they saw roughly 25% of their entire household wealth erased in just over a year[58] and over 9 million people went through foreclosure and lost their homes between 2006 and 2014.[59] This was a disastrous number that left many families living in shaky situations renting or even living out of motels – like thousands in Florida, to the point where school buses would swing by the motel to pick up distressed children whose parents had lost their homes. For younger Americans, like us Millennials, we had either just entered the workforce (and potentially exited quickly thereafter) or were still in school awaiting the barren and increasingly desolate workplace upon graduation.

The reality of this crazy situation was palpable. I recall sitting in a macroeconomics course in the fall of 2007 and going to class each day learning about once abstract concepts that all of a sudden had real world correlations. One day, we were talking about "market participants" and the conditions that can lead firms to "exit" (i.e. fail). Our visiting professor from Yale, in his thick, but lucid German accent, closed with a memorable quote, "...as you can see, the market can only bear a certain number of firms and if conditions change, some firms must exit, just like Lehman Brothers did this morning." Bam, mic dropped. Lehman of course was one of the largest firms to go under and this shook the foundations of Wall Street and the economy. But in reality, as most of us would be apt to say: we want to know what this means for Main Street.

All this hubbub about recessions, TARP, and Wall Street does actually impact you and even though the Great Recession is technically long since over, its lingering effects are beneath the subtle surface of the country's consciousness. This historical context plays out in various arenas both financially and non-financially in each of our lives and will be a defining event of our entire generation. The place that it will most likely impact us the most is related to mortgages, especially now that the Consumer Financial Protection Bureau (CFPB)[60] has guidelines and rules that are designed to keep a lid on the housing market so it doesn't blow up like it did during the Great Recession. This is both good and bad for you as a consumer. The good thing is that you are much more protected when it comes to getting a mortgage. This means that you won't get hoodwinked or excessively charged just to get a mortgage like in the past. Back in the day, the joke used to be that all you needed was a pulse to get a mortgage and while that certainly allowed millions to get into the homes of their dreams, it was the exact same type of underlying logic (or lack thereof) that created the housing bubble and collapse. So yes, you'll have to jump through more hoops now, but this is ultimately setting you up for a mortgage you can handle. It's sort of like studying for an exam–it sucks that you have to put in a ton of work up front to prepare, but you're ultimately glad you did when it comes back with a well-deserved grade up top that you can plaster on your refrigerator.

One of the drawbacks to this new mortgage and housing environment that we find ourselves in is the exact same thing that makes it better: it's more difficult to get a mortgage and lenders (banks, credit unions, etc.) are more stringent in their process when it comes to evaluating you as a potential borrower. It might really frustrate you in March when you are hoping to get a home by June or if you saved up for a couple of years but find that your debt is too high compared to your income. But honestly, while it will keep you out of a house for a little longer, the rules are there in a good faith attempt by the government to help us avoid another meltdown. Further, if it's any consolation prize for your frustration, the banks themselves have to adhere to a way higher bar now and the limitations and considerations on them amount to several thousands of new rules and pages to sift through. So even though getting a mortgage is tricky and complicated, just remember the banks have had to beef up their due diligence even more so than we have had to as consumers. All in all, regardless of the level of difficulty and the new regulatory environment, we still have to figure out how mortgages directly affect us and what the core pieces of information are that we should know so we can plan to take on a mortgage and handle it properly as it relates to newly acquired property.

First things first, this portion of the book is specifically about *mortgages* themselves. This is why it is included in the Debt section. Later in the book, we'll cover various "home buying strategies" that include things like creating a down payment savings plan, figuring out how much house you can afford, renting versus owning, and all things related to the house process itself. Right now though, we'll focus on mortgages as a financing tool to actually buy a house. Virtually anyone in America who wants to buy a home will get a mortgage. If you've got a trust fund or family who will help you buy a house while avoiding a mortgage, good (scratch that, great) for you, but this is very uncommon. Even families that have a lot of wealth still find that mortgages are either a) advantageous or b) necessary. Ironically, getting a mortgage is one of the greatest certainties in America and yet it is one of the most confusing and daunting endeavors out there. As an added peril, slipping up in this process can be one of the largest ways to take you off-track financially.

For millions, homeownership is the ultimate dream that can provide motivation and hope, but knowing the increasing difficulties therein can be equally stifling and depressing. This dual recognition makes thinking about mortgages long before you actually get one an absolute necessity. You can use time wisely in preparation leading up to the day the keys are handed over to you and you become an owner. This "pre-mortgage" period can and should last a while so that you are best suited to actually get a mortgage. We have too many resounding examples, including a global calamity, that shows us what can happen if we get mortgages without the proper preparation and financial stability. How long is this pre-mortgage period? It'll be different for everyone, but it should last anywhere from 1 year to 10 years, more or less, with the majority of the time dedicated to enacting a house-buying strategy, as previously mentioned, with more details on that coming later in the book. As such, your journey begins with information, so buckle up and dive in so that you can become a mortgage master.

First things first, a mortgage is literally just a huge slab of money that you use to pay for your house (or condo, town home, flat, loft, or whatever fancy names there are for your desired dwelling). You get a mortgage primarily from a bank or a credit union. There are pros and cons to going to a bank versus a credit union. Ultimately though, while there isn't a clear cut answer on which is better, it distills down to where you can get the best deal from. So shop around by calling, emailing, and walking in to talk to mortgage lenders before you decide. Most people's goals when it comes to finding the "best deal" center around closing costs, total amount approved for, and your interest rate, but there are lots of other factors to consider and you might find them in any of those places, depending on your situation and the options around you.

Even before you start looking around Zillow, Redfin, or any number of websites with dream homes, bay windows, cute breakfast nooks, kitchens with all stainless steel appliances, and the various features that make your pupils dilate, you should be sketching out your likelihood of getting approved for a mortgage to get said dream home in the first place. After all, buying a home and getting a mortgage is probably going to be the largest financial transaction of your life and getting it right can be worth tens of thousands of dollars. Making mistakes can set you back years in terms of working towards longer term financial goals. So not to turn up the pressure on you too much, but hone in on the vocabulary, the rules, and the process. It will be well worth the upfront effort now as you prepare for getting a mortgage.

Going back to Harry Potter analogies, in the first book, the Sorcerer's Stone, I like to think of mortgages as if they were Fluffy, the massive three-headed vicious dog. Fluffy guarded the trapdoor leading down into the Devil's Snare en route to the prized Sorcerer's Stone (eternal life, no big deal) and you certainly didn't want to mess with him. Somehow though, the trifecta of Ron, Hermione, and Harry had to get past this hellhound.* The thing about Fluffy, just like mortgages, is that it can rip you apart faster than you can say boo, but if you have the proper knowledge on how to soothe Fluffy, you can avoid impending death. In Fluffy's case, all you have to do is play the right tune via a harp or flute in order to lull Fluffy back to sleep and ultimately control a potentially vicious beast. You definitely want to control your mortgage so that it is a tool for you to leverage to get a house rather than allowing it to run wild and eat you alive, just like Fluffy would, given the chance. Fortunately, the Consumer Financial Protection Bureau (CFPB) has laid out a really

---

* Three-headed dogs are generally known as hellhounds in Greek mythology and the most monstrous of them all was Cerberus (probably Fluffy's great-great-great-grandfather) whose job it was to stop anyone from trying to leave the Underworld to return to the land of the living.

clear way to think about this in its Ability-To-Repay rule.[61] Lenders now must consider at least 8 key factors to determine whether or not you can reasonably be expected to repay your mortgage. From your perspective, these 8 factors are essentially like the application checklist that you had to follow carefully when applying for college or a job. Just like getting your essays, cover letters, and paperwork ready to submit to colleges or a job, you have to systematically go down the Ability-To-Repay list to make sure you are walking into the bank with your best foot forward so that you can walk out with the best mortgage possible. The considerations are:

1. Your income and/or assets.
2. Current employment status.
3. Monthly payment on the covered transaction (i.e. your monthly mortgage payment).
4. Monthly payment on any simultaneous loan.
5. Monthly payment for mortgage-related obligations.
6. Current debt obligations.
7. Monthly debt-to-income ratio or residual income.
8. Credit history.

Some of the terms in that list need some explaining so we'll look at each in turn and you can start to think of your own personal scenario and how a bank might think of you as an "applicant" for a mortgage. As someone thinking of a mortgage, your goal is to maximize your chances of success as well as the quality of your mortgage. Make sure that each of these points is touched on in your mind and in your financial life well before you sit down with a lender. This checklist gives you a great framework. It is instructive and you can actually act to exercise control over your situation. It's transparent too, which removes the ambiguity of the "black box" in that you know what banks are looking for and as such, you know what you need to do in order to get approved for a mortgage.

Points one and two, income and employment, are fairly obvious. You need to have a job and be making money to get a house. Further, most lenders want to see a *stable* income. It's not necessarily the amount you make (more is better), but stability counts too. If you made $50,000 last year, but $35,000 this year, you probably won't look as hot as if you made $40,000 each year. Steadily increasing wages and stability also help your case. If you're hourly instead of salaried, they will ask you for more details on the regularity of your hours and potentially for more paystubs to show a longer track record of the hours worked, so make sure you're saving them digitally or physically (or at least have access to 1–2 years' worth, if possible).

Related to employment, they are mainly looking for you to have a job currently (the longer the better) and they are also looking for gaps in your employment. So having as few gaps as possible is helpful. If you do have gaps, that's ok and it doesn't necessarily disqualify you, but be prepared and confident with a narrative explanation. Maybe you traveled the world or decided to re-enroll in school for part of that time. These narratives can actually help (or at least not hurt) in that you can draw out a positive story line to show the lenders why that gap actually makes you a better applicant. This is a good place to be confident and self-assured as gaps in employment are usually criticized, but if you can own it and put a positive spin on it, you're building a better case for yourself.

Three and four are worded obliquely, but really refer to the monthly amount of your mortgage and the payment on any loan made simultaneously. Lenders consider how much this is relative to the strain it will put on your income and financial situation and they can't give you unnecessarily large loans. This will be factored more in to point seven, the debt-to-income ratio. But note here that many people will also simultaneously get another loan when getting a mortgage. They may get a home improvement loan or a consolidation loan for other debts. While this is possible and potentially useful, be judicious and wary of stretching yourself too thin. The initial excitement and enthusiasm of getting a new home is justified, but getting a massive additional home improvement loan right away might not be. This scenario is the quintessential "biting off more than you can chew" situation, as being a new homeowner comes with all kinds of unforeseen opportunities as well as responsibilities. If you qualify for extra simultaneous loans at the time of applying for a mortgage, then you will most likely still be able to get another loan, like a home improvement loan in the future if you are as financially healthy as they say. So delaying and taking a smaller bite now with just a mortgage and foregoing a simultaneous loan can be a great way to keep from getting in too deep right off the bat. This is also an area where you can quickly fall into the "Target Trap." The Target Trap is one we all know: you walk into the Target store for shampoo and toothpaste and you walk out with two new shirts, coffee, a pair of shoes, oh and toothpaste (forgot shampoo though).

In this case, you walk into the bank looking for a mortgage, but you walk out with a bigger mortgage than you initially planned on, a home improvement loan to outfit the kitchen and redo the bathroom, and you figure you might as well consolidate all of your existing debt into one easier personal loan. Bam, you just fell into the Target Trap. Go in with a plan and clear limits on what you want and don't want. Saying no to other options doesn't reduce your qualifications to get a mortgage, so try to get as small a mortgage as possible. In other words, avoid the "up-sales" just like you try to avoid super-sizing that McDonald's meal: more calories = more stomach ache. More mortgage and loans = more financial headaches.

Isn't five the same as three and four? Not quite. Mortgage-related payments are those pesky and seemingly innocuous parasites hanging out on the periphery of your mortgage itself. They are things like homeowners' insurance, property taxes, homeowner association (HOA) fees, and the various other items that can quickly add up that surround your mortgage. This might be as little as $50 to a hundred dollars and it can easily be upwards of a thousand dollars or more when you live in areas that have high property taxes or HOA fees (in major urban areas, such as Chicago, the HOA fees can sometimes be *more* than the mortgage itself!).

For a lot of people, number six, current debt obligations, is where the rubber meets the road. In today's reality, having student loans, credit card debt, and a car payment, can easily stress your budget even before considering adding a mortgage on top of it. Sadly, the path to homeownership has significantly changed post-Y2K* with the corresponding explosion of personal debt that people are racking up earlier and earlier in life. Your current debt obligations are things like student loans, credit card payments, personal loans, and car payments (leases or loans). Creditors look for the minimum monthly payment for each of these items, not necessarily the amount you pay each month. Just a heads up, so you won't get penalized for being on top of things and making extra payments.

The monthly "debt-to-income" ratio, while scary sounding, brings together each of the preceding factors and calculates one number to synthesize all the numbers into one ratio, expressed as a percent. You can (and absolutely should) calculate your own DTI (as it is commonly called) to get an estimate of where you fall. The reason this number is so important is because the CFPB now restricts banks to ensure they lent to people whose DTI is at or less than 43%. Back in the wild west heyday of mortgage lending, DTI guidelines were just suggestions and they were largely ignored in millions of cases. As we now know, lack of guidelines brought the economy to its knees. The reason such a hard line in the sand now exists is so that people don't borrow more than they can afford each month.

The calculation is actually pretty straightforward and you can jot it down and figure out your rough DTI in about a minute. It's just a couple of addition problems and one division problem, so you're even closer to becoming a mortgage master once you find your DTI. First things first, let's look at the equation:

$$DTI = \frac{Total\ monthly\ payments\ of\ debts}{Total\ gross\ monthly\ income}$$

---

* Y2K was the infamous and silly idea that at when the clock struck midnight bringing in the year 2000 and the new millennium, that all the computers in the world were going to somehow malfunction and shutdown. Some even went so far as to say the world was going to end. Even as a 13 year old running around playing ping pong and foosball in my friend's basement with other acne-faced teenagers as the ball dropped that night, we knew in our infinite wisdom that Y2K was just a hoax.

Looking at the easier portion first, the denominator, we see that you should use your *gross* income, not your net (or take home) income. This is good news for you since your gross is larger than your net income. To find your gross income, simply take your annual salary and divide by 12. If you make $54,000, then your gross monthly amount is $4,500. If you don't make an annual salary, use your estimated monthly wages. For example, if you work 40 hours a week at $12/hour, then your gross is just 40 hours * $18/hour * 4 weeks/month = $2,880/month.

Next, tackling the numerator is simply writing out a list of your monthly debt obligations. Write out, then sum up each of your debt obligations. As mentioned before, this includes things like personal loans, credit card payments, student loans, and car payments. Remember to write the minimum payment due and not the actual amount you pay since that's what the bank will use. This portion does not include regular expenses like rent, cable/internet, cell phone, food bills, etc. Just include debt payments.

As an example, imagine Mortgage Mike has a $200 student loan payment, a Discover credit card payment of $30, a Chase Freedom Sapphire Ultimate Gold Rewards Plus Mumbo Jumbo credit card payment of $35, and a car payment of $325. If Mortgage Mike adds this up he winds up with $590 in total monthly debt payments.

Before dividing his debt obligations by his gross income, he needs to add in two more crucial items: first he needs to add in is his new (or expected) mortgage payment and secondly, he needs to add in his mortgage related obligations per number five from the list above.

One of the tough parts about this is that most people don't know exactly how much either of these two final values will be. But you can do a decent job estimating how much your mortgage will be with online mortgage calculators like those found at bankrate.com.[62] You just plug in how much the house costs, the type of loan (30 year fixed is the most common), and the interest rate (try different rates to see how they impact your monthly payment amount).

Let's assume Mortgage Mike is trying to get a $200,000 mortgage, a 30-year fixed mortgage, and is estimating he will get a 4.0% interest rate. Plugging that into the bankrate.com mortgage calculator, he comes up with a monthly payment of $955. Further, he assumes that he'll have to pay somewhere in the neighborhood of $300 in mortgage related obligations (taxes, insurance, etc.) so he has an additional $1,255 to add to the numerator in the DTI equation.

If we assume Mortgage Mike makes $4,500 a month in income, we now have all of the information to plug into the DTI equation:

$$DTI = \frac{Total\ monthly\ payments\ of\ debts}{Total\ gross\ monthly\ income} = \frac{\$200+\$30+\$35+\$325+\$955+\$300}{\$4,500}$$

Simplifying this, it becomes:

$$DTI = \frac{\$1,845}{\$4,500} = 0.41 = 41\%$$

Mortgage Mike is pumped because after his calculations he is pretty confident that his DTI is under 43%, even though it's pretty close. The goal here is to be under 43% so that you can put yourself in the best position possible to get a mortgage, but that doesn't mean that you have to get as close to 43% as possible. A lot of people play the "how much can I afford?" game where they figure out what the maximum amount is that they can qualify for, and then they go out shopping for houses in that price range. This is not only a backwards approach, but it can be detrimental in that you are then stressing your budget to the maximum suggested amount, which is substantiated by research. That number, 43% isn't some random number, it's like the yellow light right before it turns red as you're cruising towards an intersection. When I was in driver's training, we were approaching an intersection and the light turned yellow so, as an aggressive (and immature) young driver, I hit the gas. My driving instructor, having brakes on the passenger side to thwart bad decisions like mine, hit them quite hard and we came to an abrupt stop. She looked over at me and said, "What are you doing?" I replied excitedly, "Trying to beat the light." She tersely admonished me, "Yellow means stop." And that was that, lesson delivered.

Much like a yellow light, having a high DTI in the 40 – 43% neighborhood doesn't mean push harder for the mortgage. It is a warning that even more cautionary judgement should be applied. It's a zone where yes, you might continue on through the intersection and get the mortgage, or you might pump the brakes and come to a stop, heeding the warning so you can go forward with a mortgage later, once the light turns green.

If you aren't approaching that yellow-mortgage zone (40-43%), you are essentially driving through an intersection with a green light. Pushing the analogy just a touch further, as we know, driving has inherent risks and while you've got the green light with a DTI lower than around 40%, there are still hazards out there. Just like driving, you should continuously be evaluating your environment (which mortgage is best? What rate should I reasonably expect?), watching out for road hazards and accidents (high fees, pushy mortgage lenders, confusing language), and steering yourself towards your ultimate destination without veering off course or taking unnecessary detours (buying more house than you need, deciding to get an expensive or disadvantageous mortgage). It can be tricky to navigate, but the more you prepare and get to know the ins and outs of mortgages, the better off you will be. Taking a little extra time, tortoise-style, can really help instead of trying to blow through the process just to get the keys. After all, the goal is to keep those keys and your house; not to lose them a couple of years down the road when some unforeseen event happens that causes additional pressure on your financial life.

Wait! Don't forget number eight on the list (far) above, hanging on at the end. Your credit history and score counts too! This 3-digit score is arguably one of the most important numbers of your life and having a high credit score when applying for a mortgage can mean the difference quite literally, in tens of thousands of dollars over the course of the life of your mortgage. There are two things to note here related to getting a mortgage. First, there is the yes/no decision a bank has to make as it relates to your credit score. If you have a score below 620, you most likely won't be able to get most conventional forms of mortgages (these are the best and least expensive) that banks offer and that are backed by the government. If you don't quite have a score in that range, you can apply for a Federal Housing Administration (FHA) loan so long as your score is at or above 500.

If you are at or above either of those thresholds, good, but it's not necessarily a cake walk from there. The second point to make is that the strength of your score will determine all kinds of things including whether or not you're approved, what type of mortgage you can get, and perhaps most importantly, the interest rate you will pay on your mortgage. There isn't a set guide, but the table below should help sketch out the implication of your credit score on your interest rate:

- Boss Mode (Excellent: 760-850) – Your credit score will put you in the best position possible. You will most likely be offered the lowest rate available.
- VP of Credit (Very good: 700-760) – Your credit score might have a small impact on your interest rate. It's possible that you are offered interest rates 0.25% higher than the lowest rates available.
- Wishy Washy (Good: 660-699) – Your credit score will most likely impact on your interest rate. You could face rates up to .5% higher than the lowest available rates.
- Meh (Moderate: 620-660) – Your credit score will most likely negatively affect your interest rate. You could face rates up to 1.5% higher than the lowest available, which could result in thousands upon thousands of extra dollars paid over the life of your mortgage.
- Think Twice (Poor: 580-620) – Your credit score is going to have a huge impact. You may get rates 2-4% higher

than the lowest possible and you most likely have other financial factors that are more important to address than getting a mortgage.

- Not Your Time (Very Poor: 500-580) – You most likely won't qualify for a mortgage, and even if you do, you should seriously consider waiting until your financial picture and credit scores improve. You could face extremely high rates that could bury you in debt and interest for decades to come.

We'll have much more to say about credit scores, reports, and how to protect and build your score later, but for now, if you aren't at or above 660, you should seriously consider waiting to get a mortgage as the higher interest rate you will most likely get if your score is lower could undermine your ability to build financial security and success in the long run. Sometimes waiting is the best option and this can be the case when your score isn't super strong.

It's worth noting that lenders can approve you for a mortgage when you don't necessarily meet all of the criteria. However, it's unlikely since 65-80% of mortgages are backed by Uncle Sam,[63] and thus do meet the criteria outlined above. As a consumer, you should be ultra-wary of a lender who is willing to help you get a mortgage when you yourself aren't in the strongest position to do so. This is one of the classical examples of letting our emotions and desires trump our practical, rational selves. The main thing that pushes people to get mortgages that aren't the best for them is the desire to actually own a home, whether they are ready or not. I'll be the first one to agree that owning a home is an awesome and fundamental component of the American Dream and it is a core characteristic of our national identity, but that doesn't mean we should rush into a decision without carefully and thoughtfully thinking about and analyzing the implications.

All in all, the Ability-To-Repay framework forces Americans to be in a better financial position when applying for mortgages, even if it does limit their ability to get the mortgage itself. These are weighty aspects to consider and it can take years of hard work, dedication, and discipline to get your metaphorical ducks in a row. But if your goal is to own a home, then get cracking and keep the following tips in mind:

- Drive down your debts and try to get rid of some, such as car payments or credit cards, before applying for a mortgage.
- Get an income boost either through a promotion or by picking up extra work on the side.
- Consider getting a slightly cheaper house.
- The three items above will lower your DTI, which will make it easier to get a mortgage.
- Build your credit score and protect it like Fort Knox protects its gold reserves.
- Start saving for your down payment early and save often. A goal of 20% is a great target, but you can get a house for as little as 3.5% down. Aim for at least 10%.

Types of Mortgages

The world wide web of mortgages is vast. There are terms that even the most discerning among us struggle to comprehend. Before you know it, the house of your dreams is clouded by a flurry of mortgage, legal, and tax paperwork swirling in front of your face with so many i's to dot and t's to cross that it makes your 2nd grade cursive writing instruction look like a cake walk.* It can make your head spin faster than an Olympic figure skater doing a triple axel twist.

Not to worry. No matter how much paperwork there is, how many options there are, and how fast your mortgage lender talks, you only have two main choices among dozens – two of which are viable. All

---

* I'm pretty sure the practice and subtle art of writing in cursive is all but extinct in America circa the advent of the smartphone. Now students learn swiping and opening apps by the time they are two, mastery of basic games like Fruit Ninja and Angry Birds by four, and email proficiency by six (but who are they emailing anyways?!).

the others you should run away from faster than Usain Bolt from his competition.*

The two main mortgage options that have existed for decades and are the go-to mortgages for the vast majority of people are 30-year fixed mortgages and 15-year fixed mortgages. They are straightforward and transparent compared to the slew of alternatives. Essentially, the fixed component means that your interest rate will remain unchanged for the life of the mortgage. This is one of the best facets of the fixed rate mortgage and one that should be sought after at all costs (well, almost any cost). What it boils down to is *certainty* in that you will know exactly how much your mortgage will be each and every month for the rest of the mortgage. This level of certainty is highly prized for you as a consumer, as we'll see when we compare it to adjustable rate mortgages.

In comparing and contrasting the time element, that of 30-year versus 15-year, once again, like a good white wine sauce, it reduces to a simple observation, one that has mega financial consequences for your bank account. If you can afford the monthly payment on a 15-year fixed mortgage, you should do it. Just do it. Why? Several reasons. First and foremost, you will have your mortgage debt for only half as long as the 30-year mortgage. Duh. Less time in debt, better. Secondly, look at the rates on a site like bankrate. com (or anywhere for that matter). What do you notice? The rates on 15-year mortgages are roughly 0.7 – 0.8% less than the 30 year mortgages (3.36% vs. 2.63% for a discount of nearly three quarters of a percent[64]). This reduction in rate may seem topical and hardly worth a headline, but reductions in interest rates can be worth their weight in gold (we're talking amounts in the range of hundreds of thousands of dollars). The 15-year mortgages have lower interest rates because they represent less *time risk* from a bank's perspective.

---

* A living legend no doubt, Usain Bolt has 9 gold medals and 11 world championships. Fastest. Man. Ever. I'm actually convinced that he hasn't even run his fastest time since his competition is so unequal to his speed - he simply hasn't had to truly exert himself at max capacity. When he runs, he just looks so calm and composed. Then again, what do I know?

If they have to rely on a borrower making consistent payments for 15 years instead of 30 years, they will have less exposure to life's uncertainties. And certainty equals money back in their pockets. Do a quick (and morbid) thought experiment: are you more likely to die in the next 15 years or the next 30? The answer is painfully obvious, and it's also obvious that we are more likely (even if slightly so) to miss payments on a mortgage in a 30-year period than a 15-year period. As such, you represent less risk to the bank under a 15-year mortgage. And guess what? You actually get to capture that reduction in risk through a lower interest rate.

Going from the explanatory to an example, let's figure out just how much this is worth using the rates above. In the case where you get a $250,000 house/condo/bungalow with a 30-year mortgage at 3.36%, you will wind up with an approximate monthly payment of $1,103. Not too shabby you might think, where do I sign? But hold on...you will end up paying a whopping $147,139 in interest alone, which brings the price tag on your lovable living quarters to $397,139. A full 59% more expensive than the original purchase price. So what's the comparison situation?

Let's compare that same house with the same price except this time with a 15-year mortgage at 2.63% instead. This time around, the monthly payment goes up considerably to $1,682 per month. This is in fact, one of the primary reasons people don't go with the 15-year mortgage. The monthly payment must, by definition be more, since you are attempting to pay off the same amount in less time. If we harken back to our debt-to-income calculation, you can surmise that many people will go over their allotted 43% DTI if they opt for a 15-year mortgage instead of 30. As a result, a lot of people just fall back on the 30-year mortgage. The total amount of interest, however, is substantially less. This comes out to roughly one third of the 30-year mortgage at a blissful $52,817! That's a savings of over $94,000 compared to the 30-year mortgage. The total cost of your home with the 15-year mortgage is $302,817 which is roughly 21% more than the sticker price. I don't know about you, but being able to pay less in overall interest and for a shorter amount of time sounds like a pretty sweet deal – and it turns out it is, even if it is more challenging to make that monthly payment.

Moral of the mortgage story: it's hard to get a 15-year mortgage for a lot of people because of the higher monthly payment amount. It stresses people's budgets and therefore their DTI when applying for the mortgage. And yet, if at all possible and you're up for the challenge of racing to pay off your house faster, save 15 year's worth of time, and save a boatload of money, then you should totally go for the 15-year mortgage as it can be worth its weight in gold. Literally though, that $94,000 in savings could buy you 71.646 ounces of gold at today's market rate of gold which is just shy of 4.5 pounds of gold.[65] Only Flava Flav could rock that much gold and (sort of) pull it off.

Like most situations in life, mortgage types included, there is a laundry list of pros and cons, but this one is a pretty straightforward situation. A lot of people will initially scoff at the length of both of these loans and say to themselves and others, "But what should I do if I'm not planning on living in my place for that long a time period?" The answer isn't so much about how long you envision living in your new place, it's about the financing associated with it. Even if you are planning to be in your house for 5, 10, or 20 years, you still have the same underlying mortgage calculus to contend with and better yet, you'll probably want to live somewhere once you move out of the home you bought. So unless you're buying the next one purely in cash, you will have the same underlying mortgage analysis to conduct. As such, the information here is just as relevant for your first, second, or even third home purchase. Learn it now, save later, and pick a mortgage option that works for you.

On that note, I mentioned earlier that there were dozens of different types of mortgages. We just covered the two most solid mortgages out there, but we should at least be aware of the other options so we can be conscious consumers and avoid traps set for us just beneath the surface. Per the previous mortgages, we saw that there was a time component as well as an interest rate component. If you've deduced that these can change, then you're ahead of the game. If it's not a fixed rate mortgage, you will have a variable (aka adjustable) rate mortgage. While you will be tempted because of the initially lower rate, it's prudent to avoid adjustable rate mortgages (ARM is the common acronym you'll see).

There are all kinds of names for these variable mortgages, ranging from ARM loans, ARM (interest only), variable rate mortgages to the more complex 5/1 ARM, 7/1 ARM, Balloon mortgages, Jumbo mortgages, and Humbladoo mortgages (believe it or not, only the last one is made up). The cautionary yellow (dare I say red?) flag here is that first and foremost, if you don't understand the mortgage or exactly how it works, you should avoid getting it. Children don't drive cars precisely for the same reason you should hesitate to get a variable rate mortgage: because they are complex and take a lot of training to know how to use them properly (if at all). One of the biggest risks for people who take out an ARM loan* (from here on out, we'll just refer to all variable mortgages by the acronym ARM) is the very fact that the interest rate can change. They have very alluring and attractive rates up front that are expected to change within just a few short years. Some will change in under 3 years, leaving you exposed to 27 years' worth of potential variable interest rate changes. According to *Profitwise News and Views*, a publication of the Federal Reserve Bank of Chicago, an ARM loan's average increase (called the margin rate increase) was between 2.3% and 5.5% from 2004 to 2006.[66] Remember how much of a difference that 0.75% made on the lifetime interest paid on a fixed rate mortgage? Let's see what would happen if your mortgage jumped up by the mean value of that range, which is 3.9%, after 5 years.

That tempting ARM loan would end up costing you $442,780 dollars in *interest alone* and your quaint $250,000 purchase would set you back a total of $692,780. I'm not joking here. You are reading it right: your home would cost almost 3 times as much as you thought and you would be paying almost *half a million dollars in interest* to own your home. By the way, that is a *conservative* number in that we selected the *lowest* average mortgage origination interest rate from the same 2004 to 2006 time period.

I could drone on about ARM loans, Jumbo mumbo dumbo loans,

---

* While ARM loan is technically redundant, it's more verbally palatable and helps us to avoid confusing it with our upper bodily appendages.

variable rates, etc. until I was red in the face, but I think you get the point. The summary is this: ARM loans are extremely attractive, especially since they are specifically designed for people who are deemed the least prepared to actually take on a mortgage. Consider this: only 26.45% of prime loans (aka loans given to those who are deemed most qualified) were ARM loans and yet 73.31% of subprime loans (i.e., people with shakier finances) were ARM loans in 2004. Essentially, people who have better finances, and thus more choices in mortgages, choose ARM loans at a rate that is 300% less than people who get subprime loans. This should scream at you from the pages of history to run from ARM loans. One of the quickest pulse checks you can do for yourself is to see what you qualify for when you start talking to lenders. If they tell you that your best bet is to get an ARM loan, then it might be time to go back to the drawing board. There is more time and there are more options if you dig down and beef up your financial situation for a time before trying to get a mortgage. And yes, it can really suck to have to wait to buy the home of your dreams and yes, it can really suck having to rent year in and year out, but I think you'd rather buy your home knowing you weren't spending an extra half million in interest on it. Put that dough in your pocket and not in the bank's.

Finally, there are other options if you don't have a huge down payment, an awesome credit score, or the lowest DTI. You've probably heard of this alternative mortgage pathway muttered about in dark corners of the universe. It's called an FHA loan and it's out there for people who want to get a loan, but might need a little extra support doing so. Before we take a peek at FHA loans though, I want to leave you with an extended quote from the *Profitwise* report issued by the Federal Reserve Bank of Chicago reinforcing the implications of, and cautionary warnings attached to, ARM loans:

"When an ARM resets after the initial defined period (which may be as short as one year or as long as seven), the interest rate and, consequently, the monthly mortgage payment, may go up substantially. Higher payments may put enough stress on some families that they fall behind on their mortgages. While these loans seem attractive at first because of low introductory interest rates (and low initial payments), they expose

borrowers to additional risk if interest rates go up or if credit becomes less available in general.[67]

FHA Loans FTW!

An FHA loan is a loan that is insured by the Federal Housing Administration (FHA). This helps the lender in offering loans that have low down payment costs, low closing costs, and have lower credit qualifying requirements. Down payments can be as small as 3.5% with an FHA loan which makes it much easier to afford. Further, there are all kinds of state and local government programs that can help with your down payment. Many of these range from free counseling to grants of several thousands of dollars that you can use towards your down payment.[68]

The loans themselves are made by FHA-Approved Lenders and not the government. FHA-approved lenders will have different rates and costs, so shop around for the best rates. Additionally, you have to pay for mortgage insurance and premiums as well, which can add up. There is an upfront premium of 1.75% of the loan amount ($1,750 on a $100,000 loan, for example), which can be paid directly or financed as part of the loan. Afterwards, you are charged an annual premium of between .45% and .85% and this varies based on the loan-to-value ratio and the length of the loan.

While these costs can add up, FHA loans are alternatives to traditional mortgages and may be suitable for people who might not qualify for the more stringent traditional loans. These extra costs are offset partially by other useful FHA loan features such as the ability to borrow cash for repairs via a 203(k) loan and, in some cases, temporary forbearance or payment deferral for those in severe economic hardship.

6. Retire Like a Boss

Aren't we supposed to talk about retirement at the end of the book? You know, last, final, end of the financial story? I mean, I'm so far away from it right now that I can hardly think about 20, 30 or 40 years from now. I have time, I can deal with it later for sure. Not today. Tomorrow. Scratch that – next week, maybe next month, heck I'll definitely get to it by next year.

False. We need to talk about it now. If you recall, we are still in the "foundation" section of the book and there is good reason why I'm elevating retirement to such a prominent place in the book The reason boils down to a simple sentence: if you start working towards retirement now, you will be able to attain it, but if you wait, you're only setting yourself up for *massive* headaches and heartaches down the road.

There is this pervasive and destructive idea out there that leads millions of people not to think about retirement as something that requires immediate consideration and action because the demands and the stressors of the "now" are so high that you can't possibly sock away money for "later." The whole idea of tending to all the loud, screaming alarm bells of your daily life such as student loans, debt, buying a house, and meeting up with friends for a weekend dinner severely sabotages the fine balance needed to focus energy and effort on the "now" while still maintaining a little focus on the "later." Instead, like the caricature of a playground episode, we end up with the seesaw being way out of whack when the older brother catapults his younger sister high into the air on the other end. Just like the seesaw, we're unbalanced and we end up focusing way too much on today rather than on tomorrow.

There are lots of reasons, both internally and externally, that we find ourselves behind the "retirement 8 ball" in a precarious, seemingly no-win scenario and many of them might appear to be odds we aren't destined to overcome. We've got evolution to contend with so when food shows up, you eat it. If you don't, it will spoil or you might not get the chance to eat tomorrow. So we eat today.

Here, we can substitute a variety of words for eat that are appropriate modern-day equivalents such as spend, buy, purchase, use, etc. Rewriting that sentence in accordance with our fast-paced lives: We've got evolution to contend with so when money shows up, you spend it. From a genetic and evolutionary standpoint, we have not evolved enough to think seriously about saving for the future, whether it be food or money. It's all about today and not tomorrow.

Exacerbating the internal hardwiring for immediate consumption, think about all the external factors in society messaging you. You have to be able to keep up with the proverbial Jones family next door with their white picket fence, new car, and fancy vacations. Now you can see all this immediately on Facebook, Instagram, and Snapchat so you never have to miss a moment of your friends' consumption. You instantly see all their new shiny possessions, and pics of expensive meals at five-star restaurants.

Perhaps one of the biggest forces out there, on top of evolution and comparing your life to your friends (we all do it, be honest), is the media that dazzles us with sleek and sexy commercials, ads, and media campaigns designed to push us to spend now, rather than save for later. We're a generation that craves things and experiences now and we've even developed our own lexicon to talk about it: YOLO, Treat Yo Self, 24-hour flash sales, deals of the month, week, and even at the daily level, with things like Prime Day on Amazon. There are tons of examples across the economy that collectively pull in billions upon billions of dollars like a high-end Hoover vacuum cleaner sucking up that pesky dirt patch on the floor.

While we might seem doomed to fail when it comes to combating the internal and external forces that want us to spend it all today, there is actually a very, very easy way to mitigate our perpetual tendency to indulge and live in the moment. Not only that, but the whole goal is to get you into a position where you can retire and do the things you care about: travel the world, spend time with family, golf, knit blankets, or run a marathon in your seventies. As mentioned before, retirement is a catch-all term and I don't really care how you define it for yourself now or even in the future. What I do care about is giving you *more* choices rather than *fewer* choices, and that is precisely what I am going to provide.

A Million Dollars Is Still A Freaking Million Dollars

A couple of months ago I actually came across an article talking about how a million dollars wasn't really that much anymore and I almost had a myocardial infarction (a.k.a. heart attack). While my body didn't seize up in pain, my mind did. What a freaking preposterous article. I couldn't believe that I was actually reading about the trials and tribulations of how little you could actually do with one million dollars today compared to yesteryears. Needless to say, I wanted to reach through the screen and deliver a stern message to the author of the article. Worldwide, according to the Knight Frank Wealth Report, there were almost 18 million millionaires in 2015.[69] While that may seem like a lot at first blush, it represents less than 0.2% of the total population. This article complained and lamented that those with more money than 99.8% of the population were in a bind because they didn't really have as much anymore. Queue the ironic sympathy. A million dollars is still a freaking million dollars, folks, and to figure out how you yourself can get there (or close enough to be comfortable), let's take a journey back in time...

Do you remember the McDonald's Monopoly game from when you were a kid? I sure do. It was awesome. You'd go in to get French fries and you'd walk out with a colorful paper Monopoly board that you could put your stickers on once peeled from the fry container, the Big Mac box, and even the drinks (although you usually had to supersize to get stickers from the beverages – genius marketing, btw). I'd peel those suckers off with an uncanny certainty that today was the day that I got Boardwalk and I was going to get a million bucks. I got St. James Place, Marvin Gardens, and always 3 out of the 4 railroads – but I struggled to find my elusive Boardwalk. No joke though, I had so many Park Places sitting so tantalizingly close to Boardwalk that I could feel that million bucks buzzing in my head. (Nope, in reality that was just the unhealthy sugar buzz from the Coke that was half as big as I was). That little rectangular piece that I so craved never materialized and I'm still searching for my Golden Ticket and my million dollars (oops, mixed up Monopoly with Charlie and the Chocolate Factory, my bad).

However, all was not lost. I started thinking about it a little more when I read the fine print on the Monopoly board itself. If you were lucky enough to win the coveted prize, you had two payout options. Option One was obviously to get an immediate, full lump sum pay-out. As a curious, awkward pre-teen, I figured the taxes on that would be super high and you'd have to pay the government a crap ton of money. Didn't seem like a good deal to me. Option Two however, sounded much better. You could get a pay-out of $50,000 a year for 20 years. That sounded like a sweet deal because I knew that my parents made somewhere in that range (or so I thought). My rational was basic: I (or my parents) could pretty much not work for 20 years if we won. My prepubescent brain thought that would be amazing. Further, as a child, you are endlessly tagging along for errands, whether to the post office, the bank, or the grocery store, so when I went to the drab, boring bank with 1970s style brown walls, I always noticed this sign that said the savings account interest rate was 5%. I didn't know really what that meant, so I naturally had to relate it to the only thing I knew: McDonald's Monopoly – duh. I wanted to win that million dollars and saving the winnings sounded like a good plan, so I just figured I'd put it in this weird savings account at the bank called a "CD."*

---

* Naively, I initially thought you put your money in the bank and they gave you a physical Compact Disc back to prove your ownership of your savings. Foolish little boy... Turns out the bank CD stands for Certificate of Deposit and they still exist, albeit with lower interest rates than the glory days of the nineties.

With my limited math abilities at the time, I punched into a calculator $1,000,000 x 0.05 and got $50,000. What?! Crazy. My mind was blown and I thought the banks and McDonald's were conspiring against me. How could it be that the interest earned in this strange CD account on a million dollars was exactly the same payout as Option Two of the McDonald's payout on hitting it big with Boardwalk?! I was freaking out and life would never be the same...

Now, what the heck does this have to do with your retirement? Surely there can't be a legitimate connection. There is though, and it is this: If you can somehow, amidst all of life's uncertainties, twists, turns, and craziness, figure out how to save up to a point where you have $1,000,000, then you can theoretically never work again and always live on the interest payments alone, provided they are $50,000 per year (or equivalently, 5% APR). Talk about hitting it big! Everyone always talks about becoming a millionaire and while we believe it's possible, very few of us will actually achieve it.

At this point, you should be fairly certain that the reason most people won't become millionaires is not because it's too hard or the cards are too heavily stacked against them. It's simply because they don't have the long term vision, system, or understanding about how to achieve it. After all, it doesn't happen overnight. It literally will happen after decades and decades of diligent, thoughtful, and dedicated savings and investing. The trick though is to realize that it is also truly within your grasp if you stay the course and commit to small changes and savings today to add up to massive amounts later.

One thing I love about this realization is that a cool $50,000 per year is quite a lot of money. If we look and compare this amount to the September 2016 Census Bureau median household income data, we can see that the average household makes $56,516.[70] So, right now, the households have one, two, or maybe more people actually working to make the $56,516 per year. If you can figure out a way to save your million bucks, then you can earn only $6,516 less than the average household *and* not have to work one minute that year! That's a pretty sweet deal and it shows the ultimate point of saving for retirement, right? I mean the point is to save up so you can still have some funds in retirement and not work. Bliss achieved. Think about what you could do with that $50,000 a year. You could travel, go see kids, grandkids, friends, family, give to charity, start a side business, help mow your neighbor's lawn, cuddle with kittens for 8 hours a day – the world is your oyster.

Getting From Point A to Point ZzZzZ

Now that you're all jazzed up about becoming a millionaire, it's time to talk about how to actually put in place the structures that will help you achieve it. We'll look at some simple steps, many of which you might actually already be doing right now. We will also talk about the various routes you can take to get to Millionaire Estates at the end of our version of the Game of Life.* First though, it should quickly be noted that a million dollars as an end goal is obviously not going to be the appropriate goal for everyone. Some might need to aim for 3 times that or even half as much. It all depends on your personal situation.

But two primary reasons for focusing on a million dollars as a retirement goal are that it is both easy to grasp as an amount and that it actually has a strong bearing in reality in that the quality of life you would achieve by drawing a $50,000 salary in retirement would be sufficiently adequate for the vast majority of people to live on (social security earnings notwithstanding). You could definitely live a great retirement lifestyle on $50K and it's right around the average household income, as we've just seen. So it has additional merit as a value to strive for. I say this because it can be intimidating to think about a million dollars when your savings account has a

---

* If you played the board game Life as a child, did you retire to Millionaire Estates of Countryside Acres? You can make fun of me, but I usually chose Countryside Acres so I had more "cash" from the tiles available to me - I figured when I was old I would rather be out traveling instead of staying at a big empty house all day. That's just me though. To each their own.

couple thousand (or hundred?) dollars in it and there will surely be outside detractors who think you are wildly foolish for pursuing "such a large amount." But it will become clear why you should duly consider this as a long term retirement and life goal. Let's dive in.

What's the answer to this literal million-dollar question? It is this: save $215 per month, for the rest of your life and you'll have a million dollars. Boom, done. I'm a millionaire. Next challenge please.

Obviously this is filled with assumptions and it's not quite one size fits all, so let's explore it in more detail to see exactly what it means. Mathematically speaking, we only care about a couple of variables. The first is your age. This $215/month amount assumes that you save starting at age 22 and you save regularly and uninterruptedly until age 67 (the retirement age for those born after 1960). This 45-year time horizon gives us enough time not only to continue to add to our monthly contributions, but it also takes advantage of compounding interest via our investments. If you recall our "8% break-even point" from the debt snowballing section, this is where it relates to retirement. We will assume that you are able to get the long term stock market average of 8% and for simplicity, we will compound it annually.

The best part about this is that the math itself isn't hidden in some black box of mysterious number wizardry. It is available to you and you can play with all of these assumptions readily online with all kinds of calculators, two of which I like and will suggest checking out. First, a basic calculator can be found at investor.gov[71] which is a site maintained by the Securities and Exchange Commission (the SEC) who also keep an eye on the stock market and almost all things financial in the U.S., so you know this is a legit site. Next, one of my go-to places is bankrate.com. As mentioned before, you can click on calculators at the top of the screen, then scroll down to find the retirement income calculator.[72] This latter calculator has more assumptions that you can toy with such as taxes, interest rates during retirement, etc. Try both out and see how they compare.

One of the biggest things we need to account for is age since not everyone gets a jump start fresh out of the gate at 22.* So let's keep everything else equal (*ceteris paribus*) and just change the age at which you start saving for retirement to see what that would do to the necessary monthly savings amount to reach your goal of having a thousand thousands (a.k.a. a million):

Necessary savings amount per month to reach a million dollars by various starting ages:

Starting Age	22	28	34
Monthly Savings	$215	$349	$571
Amount at Retirement	$1,000,000	$1,000,000	$1,000,000

What does our table teach us? It shows us three things:

1. You can still reach a million dollars even if you didn't start out super early in your twenties – there's still hope and a viable pathway.
2. Starting earlier is obviously beneficial because the monthly amount is quite a bit lower.
3. The longer you wait to start, the harder it gets to "catch up." The age 34 is relatively young, but dang, you have to save almost three times as much *for the rest of your working life* in order to reach the same million-dollar goal.

The reason we see such a discrepancy in the necessary monthly savings amount based on age is because of the nature of *compound interest*. For each year your money makes 8%, the next year your money will make 8% on both the original amount, the additional savings, *and* on the previous year's earned interest. It is this latter

---

* I use this for simplicity in that it's the rough age of college graduates even though you can technically get cracking at 18 years old.

portion, the "interest earning interest" that has the most significant impact on your investment growth in the long run. Hence, this is why *time* is so essential to creating a larger pot-o-gold at the end of your retirement rainbow. Wherever you're at right now though, young, old, or in between, the moral of the story here is to *start* and do something rather than bow to the "tyranny of the urgent"* where the day-to-day demands weigh on us and distract us from exerting the necessary amount of energy, thought, and time to setting ourselves up with a plan that is designed for the long run and the future.

So how do you match up? Are you on track, behind, or perhaps even way ahead of the game? Below is a table showing you the annual *pacing* that is required to achieve the million-dollar mark. Essentially, for each given year, if you have the amount shown, you are on track. If you have less, start saving more if possible. And if you have more than the amount shown, good for you – keep it up!

Age	Current Account Value	Age	Current Account Value
22	$2,587.29	45	$172,739.56
23	$5,381.56	46	$189,146.01
24	$8,399.37	47	$206,864.98
25	$11,658.60	48	$226,001.46
26	$15,178.58	49	$246,668.87
27	$18,980.15	50	$268,989.66
28	$23,085.85	51	$293,096.12
29	$27,520.00	52	$319,131.10
30	$32,308.89	53	$347,248.87
31	$37,480.89	54	$377,616.07
32	$43,066.64	55	$410,412.64
33	$49,099.26	56	$445,832.94
34	$55,614.49	57	$484,086.86
35	$62,650.94	58	$525,401.09

---

*   I have to give credit where it is due and acknowledge my dear friend, Carly Gilson, who brought this poignant phrase to my attention. When she first said it, it was exactly what I needed to hear.

36	$70,250.30	59	$570,020.47
37	$78,457.61	60	$618,209.39
38	$87,321.50	61	$670,253.43
39	$96,894.51	62	$726,460.99
40	$107,233.36	63	$787,165.15
41	$118,399.31	64	$852,725.65
42	$130,458.54	65	$923,530.99
43	$143,482.51	66	$1,000,000.76
44	$157,548.40	67	Goal Achieved!

As we look at that table, the numbers become increasingly daunting and dizzying the higher up the age scale you go. But just like laying the foundation for a skyscraper, it is all about your strong base and the method by which you construct the building which allows you to eventually tower above the rest, whether physically or financially. Now that we have a better understanding of what the pathway to achieving our ambitious million-dollar mark, upwards is precisely where we need to go. As we discuss the actual routes to investing, it will become apparent that there really are two main mechanisms for investing for your retirement. You will either utilize some type of work-sponsored plan or you will pursue it individually.

In either case, getting the ball rolling is mandatory, as you will see if you take a quick peek at the Baby Boomers (52 – 70 year olds, as of 2016) and their current state of affairs. They are in pretty rough shape. A full 40% of boomers don't have *any* retirement savings whatsoever and a full 73% of them don't even feel confident that they will have saved enough for retirement.[73]

A Government Accountability Office analysis found that those Boomers between 55 and 64 only had $104,000 on average – sounds like a lot right? But look back at the retirement table. That's right around as much as a 40-year-old should have and a 55-year-old should realistically have around $410,000.[74] Don't believe me? That $104,000 average savings is roughly $310 per month if you convert it to an annuity.* Do you think you could live on $310 per month? That's precarious and untenable, yet that's where most boomers are headed. If this prospect isn't dismal and frightening to you, then I don't know what is (maybe clowns?).

It's not just Baby Boomers who are struggling. GoBankingRates conducted a survey on retirement savings and found a full *56% of Americans have less than $10,000 saved for retirement.* Oh. My. Gosh. It's not a nuclear meltdown, but it is worthy of a code red warning for sure! In this survey, they found that a whopping 33% (one out of three people!) have *no retirement savings at all.* Peek up from the book and look at the first two people near you. On average, one of you hasn't saved anything at all. Eek! It's worse for Millennials: 72% have saved less than $10,000 for retirement and almost half, 42.2% of us, have saved nothing at all. We need to get going!

As if that isn't bad enough, women are more likely than men to have no retirement savings or little retirement savings. A total of 38% of women said they have no retirement savings compared to 30% of men, and men are twice as likely to have saved $200,000 or more compared to women. There are lots of underlying societal reasons for this such as the wage gap and the fact that women are more likely to have gaps in employment.[75]

How are other races and ethnicities doing compared to whites? Much worse when it comes to retirement savings, unfortunately. According to a Pew Research Center paper titled *Wealth Gaps Rise to Record Highs Between Whites, Blacks and Hispanics,* black households have only 41.9% in retirement savings account value and Hispanics have 44.4% when compared to white households.[76]

---

* An annuity is essentially a perpetual stream of payments, usually monthly, based on some amount. It's a common way to conceptualize what your retirement funds can actually do for you once you retire. In this example, $104,000 could be turned into a $310 stream of monthly payments which is not very much to live on. http://www.investopedia.com/articles/personal-finance/011216/average-retirement-savings-age-2016.asp

This is definitely not a fair or equitable societal design (and it is often illegal, in the case of the wage gap). Ultimately it should heighten and refocus the awareness of people and their actions, especially women and minorities, as it relates to having a more robust retirement system in place. While there are more structural and systemic issues to contend with that hamper women and minorities, it is doubly important to address and work on these issues as they relate to retirement savings on an individual level. This is a massive and thorny issue for Americans at large. Regardless of your race, gender, ethnicity, or sexual orientation, the preceding section reinforces the need for each person to act to the best of their abilities to start to build long term savings – no one can afford to wait. Period.

Generational Views on Retirement: Old vs. New

In one of my favorite Russian novels, *Fathers and Sons* by Ivan Turgenev, the cyclicality of the old generation butting heads with the new is explored with gravitas centered around the philosophy of nihilism. The characters must contend and grapple with each other and ultimately come to a conclusion for themselves about their own role in the world and the universe. Like them, you too must now grapple with the way the old retirement world used to work and with the shifting and ever-changing landscape of the new way the financial world is evolving.

There used to be a pretty basic and industrial model for retirement as our parents and their parents knew. You showed up to work, put in your years, and upon retirement you received some type of pension whereby you were guaranteed a retirement salary and monthly payment of some amount for pretty much as long as you lived. Not a bad gig, but super expensive for employers to provide. This *defined benefit* world of pensions was pretty rock solid for a while until various economic and societal factors began to shift. Without going into details on the historical waning (and seemingly impending extinction) of pensions, suffice to say that very few employees are now participating in, or have access to, pensions. According to the Bureau of Labor Statistics, only 18% of private-sector employees participated in pensions as of 2013 and that number has been in steep decline since the early 1990s.[77] As these old school retirement plans have become rare, a new idea called *defined contribution* crept into place and is now the ubiquitous norm that almost every employer has if their workplace provides a retirement plan.

The defined contribution plans go by several names, but most common among them are the 401k, 403b and the 457b. They have wacky names because of the sections in the tax code they are named after, but the commonality between all of them is that they come with some type of tax advantage that is highly advantageous. So what's the difference between them? The 401k is a plan that is set up by private sector employers for employees whereas the 403b is generally found in schools and in the non-profit sector. The 457b is primarily for state and local government employees and the federal government now has what is called the "Thrift Savings Plan."

Each is slightly different and has a bunch of fine print, but the thing that is most important to find out is whether or not your employer offers them. Further, many offer some type of "match" given your level of contributions. A company match based on your contribution is one of the most significant and best opportunities to magnify your retirement funds. Matches themselves range widely in terms of the structure and amount, but most follow a basic prescription whereby your company will give you some fixed amount extra for every dollar you contribute to your 401k/403b/457b/TSP. Matches typically range from 3% all the way up to 150% or more. While this range is huge, it's important to remember that this is about as close to "free money" as you'll ever get since all you have to do is save your money in a retirement account that you should already have in the first place. The match itself is literally an incentive for you to not only like your compensation and employer more, but also to incentivize you to save for retirement.

For example, if your employer offers you a dollar for dollar match (i.e., a 100% match), that means if you save $2,000 a year, they will add an additional $2,000 to your retirement account. For every dollar you save, that's the equivalent of earning 100% in the stock market *immediately*. This would be insane, especially as the market on average consistently returns about 8% on average. So if you're thinking contribution matches are disgustingly awesome, you're absolutely right. You should be capitalizing on your company's match as much as humanly possible because things with this much of a "return" like it just don't exist.

Even if your match isn't as generous – let's say only a 25% match – that would mean your $2,000 contribution would still have a $500 company match for a total of $2,500 and that's a big win for sure. The moral of the story is clearly that company matches are awesome and should be sought after if they exist. As I mentioned before, there is almost no better way to grow your wealth and retirement savings than by getting as much of your company's match as possible.

Some other things to consider when talking about your defined contribution retirement plan options are limits to the match and limits to contributing to the account. First, lots of companies will offer a match, but only up to a certain amount. Companies will generally cap this either at a set percent of your salary or at some predefined amount. If you get a 100% match up to 5% of your salary and your salary is $50,000, then your company will go dollar for dollar with you up to $2,500. This means you could contribute this amount and wind up with a grand total of $5,000 each year (½ from you, ½ from them).

Alternatively, they might say, "Hey, we'll match your contributions at 50% up to $3,000. That just means if you save $6,000, they will match 50% of it, but not more. So if you saved $7,000, you'd still only get a $3,000 match. Don't feel too bad about this – you still got an extra $3,000 towards retirement in your account!

Even though your company might have some matching limit, that doesn't mean that is the *max* that you can contribute however. As of 2016, you are able to contribute all the way up to $18,000 per year in these defined contribution plans. If you think about it, not only is that a crap ton of money saved, but it is a savings amount beyond the reach of most individuals as one of the world's largest benefits and HR consultant companies, Aon Hewitt, found out. They found that only 6.5% of people were able to max out their retirement account at work.[78] So the max is generally not the issue for most people; it's really about increasing retirement savings in the first place.

In closing this brief intro to the new retirement plan landscape (more to come!) there are a couple of major points to summarize:

- If you have a retirement plan at work, it is a great way to save for retirement.
- If you have a match via said retirement plan, you should absolutely be capitalizing on it. "Free" money is awesome.
- Once you get to work, do not simply elect the "default" account, amount, and investment. You should actively learn about it, think about your goals, and select features that best reflect your needs and abilities (read the next section for more).

The Default Will Kill You

You know the drill when you get a new job. You show up on Day One and someone hands you a pen. You start signing this, that, and the other thing. Paperwork, tax forms, someone snaps a picture for your security badge, another person gives an overview of workplace safety, then you're directed to watch a quick video about company policy, health care, and retirement options. Click, click, sign, sign and boom you are at your brand spanking new desk and getting your email set up.

The first week slips by and you're learning about various job-related stuff and you want to seem like a hard worker so you're stepping up and staying focused. The retirement paperwork was signed and you know you need to look back over it, but it can wait a week until things "settle down." We've all been there. Things never really settle down and free time is cherished so revisiting your retirement paperwork and account hardly makes the Top 10 list (although Game of Thrones certainly does).

Don't fall victim to the default! It can kill you (metaphorically that is) in three big ways, which are also categorized from most to least consequential:

1. **Amount** – Simply choosing the default amount, which is generally in the 2-5% neighborhood is almost always less than optimal as it is probably a pretty low default amount. You are at risk to *under save* here. In order to fix this, all you have to do is log in to your account and adjust it to a level that will help you meet your long term goals. Reference the retirement chart several pages back if you need specific amounts.

2. **Investment Type** – Generally you are opted in to an *active* investment that is a conservative bet which assumes you are pretty risk averse. This process, unfortunately, is designed for the least common denominator in that they are playing it safe to avoid any blowback (think: good for them, bad for you). We'll get into this later, but for now look for *passive* investments such as broad based index funds, Exchange Traded Funds (ETFs), or equity investments. The *active* mutual funds and "portfolios" with fancy names might look good, but digging deeper, there are serious questions about whether or not these are as good as more *passive* investments that should also be available to you.

3. **Expenses and Fees** – Per number 2 above, the more active something is, the more it generally costs. The more passive, the less it costs. A corollary to this is the more active something is, the *worse* it generally performs compared to more passive investments. Remember: passive = good; active = bad. It's certainly simplistic, but there is a long history of people saying actively managed funds are way

better, without being able to prove that they are, so be on guard. Aim for investments that aren't costly and look for funds with costs in the neighborhood of 0.05 – 0.4%. If you're seeing expenses, expense ratios, or fees in the 0.5% – 1.5% range, then be cautious as these are most likely too expensive and can be detrimental in the long run. They slowly eat away at your savings like a nasty parasite stuck to the bottom of your foot. Even this small difference adds up to huge amounts. As an example of how important this is, the New York Times investigated teacher retirement plans and found one teacher who ended up having around $113,000 less because of excessive expenses and fees compared to if she had chosen lower-cost, passive investments.[79] So make sure you are selecting funds and investments that not only get solid returns, but don't cost a lot.

The moral of this story is simple: be *proactive* and do your homework. Once you've learned about your retirement options at work (yes, you'll have to read some paperwork printed in too small a font), select the amount and the investment that work for you while making sure you aren't paying too high a fee or expense. Not bad right? You'll feel like a boss once you do.

No Work Retirement Plan? No Problem.

Get this: over 50% of employees are not offered employer-based retirement plans and 53% of people, are in fact, subject to fending for themselves. Long term savings is tough, but for this half of the populace, it just got a lot harder since you have to be *proactive* and do it yourself. Right now, you should put yourself on one side of the fence or the other. Either you do have a retirement plan at work or you don't. If you don't have a 401k, 403b, 457b, or pension plan at work, there are still options for you (great options in fact). Even if you do have an employer-based retirement plan, you may still actually want to take advantage of non-employer-based plans anyways since they could actually be better than what's offered at your workplace.

For the majority of people, an Individual Retirement Account (IRA) is going to be your primary retirement vehicle (by vehicle I just mean "account." Fancy financial types like to use vehicle, but really it's just a place to dump money). The IRA is a blessing in disguise as it comes with really solid tax advantages, just like the employer-sponsored plans. At its core, you have two IRA choices. The first is the Traditional IRA (often shortened simply to IRA, so always clarify which type you're talking about) and the other is a Roth IRA.

It is absolutely, unequivocally imperative for you to set up an Individual Retirement Account (IRA) if you don't have another retirement account option available to you.

The primary difference is that the money you put into the Traditional IRA gets taxed *later* and the money you put into the Roth IRA gets taxed *now*. Often you'll hear it in slightly different (and more confusing) terms: The Traditional IRA is a *pre-tax* account and the Roth IRA is an *after-tax* or *post-tax* account. So as you're sorting through the terms remember that taxes *later* = *pre-tax* and taxes *now* = *after-tax*. This distinction is important and often difficult to track mentally for three reasons:

- It's tough to remember all the terminology. It's not like people chill on the weekends looking up various IRS and tax code literature.[*]
- It's tough to know what the implications are for your taxes. While saving for retirement might seem separate from your taxes, it's not. It only gets more intertwined the more complex your situation becomes. As your income increases over time, it becomes more important to be well-versed in this area.

---

[*] For better or worse, I do. One time I read the annual report of the Bureau of Engraving and Printing. It's a division of the Treasury that is responsible for printing the US currency. In the report, they summarized the delay of the printing of the new $100 bill (that I was excited about) because there was a tiny wrinkle created in each bill. They had to destroy over a billion dollars worth of money because of this defect which cost taxpayers millions of dollars and small tinges of heartache for people like me who had to wait a little longer to inspect the bills.

- It's also tough to know which IRA is best for you and how much money to put into it. This is doubly confusing because you can have both types of IRAs at the same time and actively contribute to both in varying proportions which adds yet another layer of difficulty.

Fortunately, for most of us, the current tax code actually makes the decision easier. I bet you never expected to hear that taxes make things easier, did you? The logic is pretty straightforward in terms of choosing which IRA to put money into: if you are at or below the tax level that you'll retire at, then the Roth IRA is the way to go. I would hazard a guess that the Roth IRA is going to be the right choice for anywhere between 75% and 95% of people. The Roth IRA and its awesomeness is heralded by laypeople and professionals alike and truly has tons of merit insofar as it is generally more advantageous to contribute to compared to the Traditional IRA. However, there are several situations where you might consider the Traditional IRA:

- (Moderately Probable) You are making a lot of money right now. For individuals, this means you're making roughly $91,000+ and for married folks, roughly $150,000+ as of 2016.[80]
- (Improbable) You cannot contribute to a Roth IRA because you make too much. For individuals this means you're making more than $132,000 and married folks making more than $194,000.[81]
- (Very improbable) You think you're going to be loaded out of your mind in retirement. This means that you expect to make *more* in retirement than you do *while working* and be in a higher tax bracket. This is quite rare so give yourself a serious gut check on this assumption. If you're in your 20's or 30's right now, you're probably going to make more money towards the end of your career in your 40's 50's and 60's, but the vast vast majority of people make less in retirement than they do at the end of their careers. Most people will see a 65 – 85% income level compared to their final earning year salaries. So if you

retire having made $100,000, then you should be prepared to make $65,000 to $85,000 in retirement, assuming you've saved well and are eligible for social security.

In either case, Roth or Traditional, you need to know a couple of things before getting cracking on saving:

First, you can only put in $5,500 in *total* in your IRAs each year, as of 2016 (though the limits generally increase every couple of years). This means that you cannot save more than that between the two IRAs if you have both. So, if you put $3,500 in your Roth IRA, you can only put $2,000 in your Traditional IRA. If you do over-contribute, you can be heavily penalized, so avoid this. In order to max out your IRA contribution, which is a worthy goal, you would need to put in $458.33 each month. This is a large amount for most people, so if you can do it, go for it. But if you're going to save $100, $250, or less than the max, then you'll be well under the threshold of concern for putting in too much money.

Sidebar: If you're wondering why you can put in so much more into something like a 401k or 403b ($18,000 compared to a measly $5,500 for IRAs as of 2016), you are asking a question that continues to baffle many people, including myself. Honestly, it's bogus since, as we now know, over 50% of people don't even have access to accounts where you can save more. We can thank legislators for this unfair discrepancy and quite honestly, if you're so compelled, pick up a phone and call your representatives, because this is something that needs to change even if it looks fixed for the immediate future.

Second, once you put your money into an IRA, it should stay there. A lot of people will tell you the Roth IRA is awesome because you can take out your contributions tax free, which is true. But generally that is not a good idea because you'll be tempted to use it, which can undermine your retirement savings progress. You can start taking out contributions and earnings penalty-free once you hit 59 ½ years of age.

Third, you should be opening an account at a place that allows you access to high quality investments *and* doesn't charge you a ton to manage your money. On this note, you should especially avoid companies who have management fees, account fees, or sell you investments that have high fees themselves (as discussed before). The name of the game here is to protect yourself and your money. One of the safest, surefire ways to do this is to do it yourself. Below are the basic steps that you can follow so you can avoid paying someone to do it for you (they'll promise you that they can "invest your money better," but remember, you know better now and you're not looking for their more active investment management services).

Lastly, there are some finer nuances to the IRAs themselves and you can read up on them, but for the most part if you are earning money (the IRS calls it taxable compensation) and are not over 70 and ½ years old, you should be able to open and start saving in an IRA.[82]

Before delineating the steps to opening and setting up an IRA, let's take a quick step back and ask ourselves the question, "What is the end goal here?" The end goal itself is to be able to most strategically and effectively save funds towards our long term retirement goals, whatever those may be for you. Sadly, a huge swatch of America is not on pace to achieve these goals. The median working-age couple has a paltry $5,000 saved for retirement and quite honestly, this is not going to do the trick. Even the 70th percentile was only at $50,000 in retirement savings, which may sound like a lot, but it really isn't up to snuff. As of 2014, according to an article on Marketwatch.com, the single largest source of retirement income for Americans is Social Security which pays out, on average, $12,232 which is hardly enough to live on.[83] Even summing up the various other forms of retirement income, most Americans will be living at income levels that are significantly (and arguably, dangerously) lower than during their working years. This leaves many people scraping by and supplementing their needs by continuing to work rather than actually enjoy the retirement they envisioned for themselves. The goal in bolstering your retirement savings now is not only to avoid being exposed to a severe reduction in quality of life in retirement years, but to actually get you into a position whereby you can focus more on later life goals rather than staying in survival mode. Saving for retirement truly is a core pillar in constructing your overall sense of financial health and wellness. So let's get cracking on the steps below to start your IRA account or accounts.

1. Determine which account you want to use. It's most likely a Roth IRA, but if you aren't sure, open a Roth and a Traditional account and contribute to both, making sure not to exceed $5,500 in total contributions.

2. Determine where you want to open your accounts. Everyone and their brother and sister offer IRA accounts. Just type in IRA to Google (or Bing it) and you'll be bombarded with ads offering all kinds of sign up bonuses to pick a given company's IRA. Two of the best places to look are E*TRADE and Scottrade. They are powerful, straightforward, and low-cost. Period. They offer you thousands of investment options *and* they are super cheap. Remember, IRAs themselves are like literal vehicles. You buy a car to move yourself from one place to another. You get an IRA to save and grow your money from one place (now) to another (later). The people and companies who have IRAs themselves are like car dealerships. They want you to buy your car with them, so you need to be a diligent and aware consumer in selecting where to "buy" your IRA.

3. Open your account or accounts. It should take you anywhere from 10 – 20 minutes to open an IRA and it should be something you can do right now if you haven't already (feel free to take a break – go!).

4. Once you have opened your account, fund it. There are two ways to fund your account and only one is a best practice. You can periodically put money in as you are able (definitely not encouraged) or you can set up an auto contribution on a weekly, biweekly, or monthly basis (absolutely, 100%, out of this world encouraged-do it. Just do it! #Nike*). Remember,

---

*   Nike is the Greek goddess of victory. She even had wings. You are the Nike of retirement when you set up auto contributions to your IRA account. Be like Nike. Achieve retirement victory.

$458 per month is the max at this point, but if you can't save that much, start small and work your way up. Try $25 for each paycheck, maybe $50 or $100. Push yourself and try to increase your contributions over time. This is also a good time to spot check to see how much this money will be worth in the long run by using a tool like bankrate. com. Head to the calculators, select the Retirement Income Calculator and play around with it to see where you might end up given various assumptions.

5. Invest it! The whole point here is to invest your money. If you don't do this, you are just putting cash into an IRA which is missing the whole point. Now you should be looking for low cost Exchange Traded Funds (ETFs) and other broad-based index funds. Avoid investing in expensive mutual funds since they generally have higher fees and costs compared to ETFs. Also, as tempting as it may be, avoid investing in individual stocks at first since they represent more risk and decrease your overall diversification (managing risk and diversification are two important aspects of building up your retirement account). Some of the top ETFs to look for are ones that track major indexes in the U.S. such as those that track the Dow Jones Industrial Average (DIJA), the S&P 500, and NASDAQ. This is but the tip of the iceberg and we'll cover investing more in the HF Unsexy Investment Strategy chapter, but for now, check out ETFs from top quality and lowest cost companies like Vanguard[84] (arguably the world's gold standard in investment options), iShares, and Powershares.

With this 5-point list, you are making a conscious choice to save for the future. This is a huge departure from the norm so give yourself a couple of well-deserved pats on the back. There is certainly more to consider in terms of building your retirement investments, but if you look back at the charts at the beginning of the retirement chapter, you can quickly set your sights on target goals for the future. Take aim, start funding your IRA, and start growing your money. This is definitely about becoming un-average and if you start to save regularly you'll quickly forget the days where you didn't save. If you were already saving, you can now rest assured that you are using an account that is specifically designed to bolster your long term retirement savings.

IRAs vs. 401ks and other work retirement plans

So if you have already have a work retirement plan and you're contributing to it, you're all set right? Not necessarily. Fortunately, there is a pretty easy way to figure out if you should have an IRA in addition to your employer-sponsored retirement plans (401k, 403b, etc.). Just ask yourself the following series of questions to figure out which option is best for you:

1. Does my employer offer a contribution match? If yes, then this is where you should contribute initially until you have exhausted your match. This "free money" is essentially unbeatable so focus here first.

2. Does my employer-sponsored work plan have good investment choices? Employers aren't required to offer many investment choices even though many do. Look through your investment choices to see if you have high-quality, low-cost options like ETFs, index funds, or low-cost balanced or target funds. Remember, if you see high expenses/fees for these, it might be a good time to think twice about funding them if you aren't getting a match on those funds. Go with an IRA instead. If you do have ETFs and other high quality options, then you can stick with putting money into your employer-sponsored plan and most likely won't need an IRA unless you are maxing out your work accounts.

3. Does my work retirement plan have a Roth 401k, Roth 403b, or Roth 457b? These are becoming increasingly common and are subject to the same analysis as the Roth IRA vs. Traditional IRA choice above. So if you think a Roth IRA would be your best choice, then consider using your Roth 401k/403b/etc. if it's available. If you don't have a Roth version (many companies don't offer them), then you might want to set up a Roth IRA instead of funding the traditional versions of your 401k/403b/etc.

4. Am I going to save more than $5,500 for retirement per year? If the answer is yes, then get as much matched at work as possible. If you don't have a match, watch out for fees/expenses in your work-sponsored account. If they are high, consider putting your first $5,500 into an IRA.

It's a little bit of a convoluted process, but the main thing to take from this line of questioning is that first and foremost, saving for retirement is a good thing and the vast majority of us should be saving more than we currently do. Once we start to get into the weeds, it's actually a good thing, even if it's frustrating. If you have to make these more nuanced and complicated decisions, it means that you are really stretching beyond the average saver who isn't saving enough and you are asking yourself the questions now that will start to have big, positive consequences in the future. Challenging, yes. Worth it, absolutely.

Joe Holberg

7. Financial Foundation Finale

Looking back over the previous chapters and the wealth of information contained, it is no wonder people get overwhelmed when thinking about how to apply the text from the pages of a book like this to their real lives. It makes sense in a quaint paragraph, but it can be a little too far out of the reach of the monthly budget. You might think, "The information is great, but there's little chance I'll be able to pull it off," or, "I love the idea of saving more, but right now I can't…"

These thoughts, along with tons of others, are very real thoughts and we all live constrained lives in terms of money and finances. While Ponce de Leon searched for the mythical Fountain of Youth, we too often search for the imagined Money Tree and like Ponce, we search in vain. While no panacea exists, we can make a concentrated effort to take away the lessons here and apply them to our lives. If we don't, we're throwing our hands up and resigning to being average. What I hope you take away from the Financial Foundations section in this book is that no matter what else is going on financially in your life or in the world, there are some simple, actionable takeaways that everyone can act on, no matter how big or small.

Find Your "Un-System"

Using a system is crucial, or a set of systems. For me, it's mint.com, creditkarma.com, ETRADE, and a spreadsheet of my monthly bills. The system itself varies, and I'm not here to prescribe a solution for you, but you need to find something that works for you (this may take some time, but work to find it). Did mint.

com work for you? Good, use it. If not, move on. Do you like your bank's rounding up the change program for each purchase you make? Good, use it. If not, move on. Do you live and breathe spreadsheets and feel at home in Microsoft Excel? Good, use it. If not, move on. Like licking envelopes to save money? Lick away. Are you the Master Couponer of the Universe? Coupon away.

The possibilities are near endless in terms of creating a financial system in your life that helps you pursue your goals and objectives. Based on the major topics in this first section, you can hark back to these questions to see if your system is purring like a happy, content cat curled up in a sunny window sill or if it is roaming around chilly and lost like a Neanderthal in search of a comfy cave.

- Am I working on becoming un-average and financially rogue?
- Am I aware of and trying to capitalize on the portions of Life's Formula that I can control?
- Am I saving consistently and automatically each month and is my savings generally increasing in size (even if there are infrequent setbacks)?
- Do I have a prioritized debt pay-down strategy and am I acting on it?
- Am I working to control and wipe out expensive debt like my credit cards?
- Do I have the optimal retirement accounts and am I actively saving at least some amount for my long term financial goals?

At the most topical level, these six questions and perhaps a couple of others, given your own circumstance, should suffice to root you in a place that you can come back to relatively frequently to do a "self-check." The Financial Foundations are certainly nuanced, as we've seen, but there is no reason why they have to remain shrouded in mystery or be obscenely complicated.

Arguably, even the questions above are more complicated than they need to be insofar as we can conduct a mental exercise in further reducing them to even more simple conclusions:

- Work to develop healthy financial mindsets.
- Save consistently.
- Pay off debt.
- Create long term savings.

Four points. Not bad. Play with them in your own mind, recreate the questions, re-distill the major points. Which are most important to you? Which are the most challenging to enact? Why? Drill down into your own brain and behavior to find these answers and continue to ask yourself the tough questions so that you can continue to meet your financial goals and bring about that awesome vision for your future.

Summary of Part 2

Life's formula is much simpler than you probably thought, right? If we recap the entire first section in one sentence it breaks down to: *go earn some money, save some of that money, use some of the money to pay off debt, and use some to save for retirement.* A huge financial fallacy that is promoted in society is that "if I am responsible and save now, I can't do anything fun." I believe this is outrageously and ludicrously *wrong.* You can have your cake and you can definitely eat it too. Literally though, if you save some and spend some, you can still meet your financial goals.

I don't have many pet peeves, but one that really sets me off is when people pretend like they can't go out to eat anymore or can't travel anymore if they start saving money in a diligent way. The ironic thing is that if you believe you can't have fun and save, then you are pigeonholing yourself into that exact situation. The trick is to realize this is a fallacious idea that we promote in society and if you break the rules and go rogue here, you are setting yourself up for two awesome things: enjoying life now and being able to achieve your goals tomorrow and beyond.

While this section is the core foundation that can take you quite far in terms of establishing a greater sense of financial health and wellness, the next section will go further and talk about how to create a much stronger roadmap to get you to a place where you become more financially fit in many domains beyond just the foundational core.

In closing, I'll share a quick story. Almost every year for the last five years, I've gone out to spend time in San Diego with one of my best friends and his family around the holiday and New Year season. It's a welcome and warm reprieve in the midst of cold, windy Midwest winters. Each year we drive across the high-arching bridge leading out to Coronado Island with the stunningly unique Hotel del Coronado that attracts locals and visitors alike with its magnificent red-roofed rotunda and sprawling asymmetrical shapes and grounds – your eyes can't quite capture it entirely in one view.

After dinner just past sunset we walk out onto the beach, the same beach where Dr. Seuss viewed the hotel which subsequently inspired a classic Seussian rendition of the building in "I Dreamed I Was A Doorman at the Hotel del Coronado." On this beach, each year, several sand sculpting artists flock to amass great mounds of sand that start out as raw, plain piles no different than any child could build with a pail and some patience. Yet, these artists have a vision for what that mound is about to become. Not only do they have the vision, but they have a plan for how they are going to ever so slowly mold and shape the fine grains into something beautiful. They have their tools. Each artists brings a slightly different set of tools, and each sets out to work early in the day.

As the day progresses, more and more of the vision is cut from the raw pile and many a passersby are able to passively participate in the creation hour by hour, inch by inch, until finally, the artist steps back and what was once just an idea is now a fully formed castle as elaborate as the Hotel del Coronado in the background. Spires reach high, turrets delicately hang off of the main castle screaming, "I'm made of sand, I might fall!" But they don't fall. Instead they are of sound foundation and draw out the depths of imagination where the sand creation is a mere gateway to the fire-breathing dragons swirling above as the castle guard prepares its arches along the narrow walls in defense from a great beast. Will the castle stand for another thousand years? The sand-mansion next door sparks excitement and fans the flames of hope of those who glance upon its intricate windows, gables, and life-like proportionality that says to viewers, "This could be my dream home if it were built to scale."

Each sand castle here is fleeting – they will retreat to oblivion as the Great Pacific tides reclaim them eventually. Yet, we build beautiful things anyways.

You too must build your own version of the sand castles of Coronado Island. What these artists have, and what you are working to develop in your own life, is the "un-system" that we've talked about so far. They, like you, want to create something more grand than the individual grains and each of us is tasked with finding a set of tools, actions, and thoughts that allow us to start ever so slowly towards the accomplishment of our respective visions for our lives. Like the sand castle artists, progress comes slowly at first as the raw materials are shaped, but like the debt-snowball rolling down a hill, acceleration and a quickened pace comes as we continue towards our end goals. No doubt there will be setbacks of all types, but when the light shines from the high points of the hotel and out onto the final sand castle creation to illuminate its brilliance, a satisfaction and sense of accomplishment takes over just as it will for you when you reach your financial goals. The only question then to ask is:

What will your sand castle be like?

Part 3-Financial Fitness

8. From Foundations to Financial Fitness

The Financial Foundations section is like going to a doctor, getting an annual checkup, and then starting a light regimen of walking exercise each day in the name of bettering your health. You are going to be much better off after this visit than if you haven't been to the doctor in a while and haven't really been exercising (but that couldn't possibly be you!). It's a start, but there's more you could do to improve your health, like drinking less pop (otherwise known as soda for all the non-Midwesterners) or cutting your Netflix watching down a bit from the 600 hours per year estimated average by cordcutting.com.[85] That 600 hours is hard to comprehend, so let's put it another way: that's 25 full days' worth of Netflix each year (I should take my own advice).

While the Financial Foundation section is the cornerstone to your financial health and wellness, just like regular visits to your doctor, it's time we take it up one level and talk about a broader level of financial fitness. This is really parallel to actually listening to the doctor, scoping out and following a more nutritious and healthier eating plan (I've been boycotting the word "diet" since circa 2007). For instance, instead of just walking, you are going to incorporate various forms of physically healthy practices such as jogging or running, swimming, weight training, or whatever exercise floats your boat and elevates your heart rate.

The financial equivalent here is not just to work on saving *some* amount, but a *specific target amount*. It's not just about paying off debt *sometime*; it's about setting an aggressive goal to get rid of, say, your credit card debt in 6 months and driving down other debt. We'll also dive into many secondary financial topics like intermediate savings goals for things such as a house, weddings, travel, prepping for kids, and more. We'll look deeper into various work benefits that can bolster your financial life as well as provide a quick overview of the evolving and expanding role of technology vis-a-vis your finances.

To position this section and the remaining portion of the book compared to the first section, it will be good to note that the Financial Foundation section is quite involved and explanatory. This Financial Fitness section and the one after, Advanced Fitness, are going to be much shorter per topic and targeted towards specific topics rather than defining and strategizing around general concepts. The meat of the book is truly the Financial Foundation section. You can always go back to it if you feel like a lost space cadet, but the remaining portion of the book is designed to start to push you towards more and more financially healthy practices and ideas. Neither can exist in isolation. Once you have a solid foundation, you must necessarily continue to learn and optimize your financial life, but if you ever find yourself needing to come back to center to get your bearings, skim back over the concepts in the Financial Foundations section.

Like all healthy practices in life, you have to learn about them first to truly understand how they fit into your specific situation. So without further verbosity: let's rock and roll.

9. Financial Parasites Exist! Be On Guard

As you continue on your financial journey, two important safeguards are going to help guide you for all time if you can remember to just look beyond the smooth-talking salesperson and a little deeper into the financial products and services you are using. The two things to watch out for are *bias* and *fees*.

Bias Blows

First, bias. The financial industry is set up in such a way that many many many people and companies are quite biased when it comes to working with you and offering you financial products and assistance. It doesn't matter how smooth-talking someone is, how sleek the website is, or how good or bad someone makes you feel about your finances, you should watch out for bias.

What exactly is bias and why is it dangerous financially? Bias itself is simply "prejudice in favor of or against one thing, person, or group compared with another, usually in a way considered to be unfair."

This financial bias lurks in the background of tons of products and services. It is particularly dangerous to you as a consumer because often times it isn't explained or shared with you in a way that is clear, transparent, or understandable. The bias really distills down to financial people trying to sell you things, even though it will be sugar-coated and not seem like it at first. It is also designed in a way that is parasitic so they can latch onto you for the long haul. A parasite's objective is to subtly latch onto you, hook into the system, and steal away just enough resources to a) keep itself alive and b) not kill you. If the parasite does its job right, you will barely (or never) notice its impact, but you'll still be worse off than if it hadn't latched onto you, sucking away your health and financial resources. As we saw already, these financial parasites can strip away thousands and thousands of dollars of your money, as was the case with the teacher retirement plans cited above. Oh, and the other thing about parasites: they're disgusting.

So, how can you guard against financial bias? Simple: ask how they make money. The baseline assumption you should drill into your brain is that everyone is out to make money, in one way or another, no matter how nice they are and no matter how many times they tell you that they won't make money by meeting or talking with you. If you don't believe this, start believing it. Most of these financial parasites will meet with you for free and then try to sell you something. That's the parasitic approach to watch out for, a sure-fire way to weed out and identify bias. Remember, you are David and most of these companies are Goliath. The companies have been doing that for decades or perhaps centuries. They have a tried and true mechanism that you should watch for. It goes something like this:

Goliath (them): Hey, want to meet to talk about some financial things?
David (you): I'm sort of busy, no thanks.
Goliath: It'll be quick, I promise, let's grab coffee on Tuesday. I'll see you there?
David: Umm...sure.

Tuesday rolls around

Goliath: Great meeting with you, check this out [*insert financial product of your choice –expensive mutual fund, strange retirement account, life insurance, disability insurance, new investing website,*

etc.]. Isn't it awesome? It doesn't cost anything to set up.* You need it, I need it. Your friends KaMar, Marisa, Katie, and your warrior friend Xena from space (#throwback) already have it and blah blah blah....
David: Looks interesting, let me think about it.
Goliath: Great, but you know it's really easy to start right now. Here, check it out.

Shows you tons of pretty graphs and charts. Says a bunch of numbers that may or may not actually make sense.

David: Nice, I'll have to think about it.
Goliath: Great, here why don't you just sign here and we can get started slowly. Then we can talk about it again soon.
David: Umm, I'd like to think..,.

Goliath turns up the sales heat

Goliath: Look, you really need this. I just want you to be in the best position possible.
David: Ok, I guess I'll do it.

Before you know it, you've bought their stuff. Goliath wins and is now officially a financial parasite in your life.

Furtive Fees

So what did Goliath just win besides eternal glory out on the fictional financial battlefield? Goliath just convinced you to buy something. No one sells (or does) anything for free (not even my company). So understanding just why Goliath is out there trying to conquer consumers like you and me is imperative to avoid his army of parasites waiting to nibble on your wealth.

---

* This is the magical line. It's technically true, you don't have to pay directly for these things or up front, but you will pay for it for sure. Nothing is free, even if someone says it doesn't cost anything immediately. Be optimistic, but not gullible when talking to financial types or when looking over financial websites and apps. Always press to see what the fee or commission structure is (i.e. how do they get paid?).

Most companies can genuinely say that their products (such as life insurance, mutual funds, web platforms, you name it) don't cost anything to *set up*. But you know better. It might be free to *set up*, sure, but going back to the question, "How do they make money?" it is essential for you to understand the answer.

Before signing up for anything or succumbing to their sales tactics, ask Goliath point blank how they make money. If they can't answer clearly and easily in one sentence, a red flag bigger than the one a Matador uses to lure in a bull should go up. Alarm bells should ring and treading very cautiously around Goliath should be your main concern. Essentially, Goliath makes money by charging very subtle fees, commissions, premiums, and a whole host of other words that essentially mean that you pay Goliath.

The goal here is to understand the impact of these parasitic fees on your life and to realize that most of them represent a high degree of bias. So let's look at some examples. First though, I will give you two examples of *unbiased* financial situations so you can compare them to the biased ones.

Unbiased

Case Study 1: Holberg Financial.

If you were to ask how we make money, we can give you a transparent and easy answer that is immediately clear and understandable:

We charge a "fee only" that is a fixed and flat $20/month for access to our website, information, and services.

One sentence. What you notice is that we don't sell financial products, nor do we sell your information to others (very common). Our underlying motivation is to teach you about your finances and to help you improve your financial health. Further, as an added bonus to you, we believe that if we're successful, you'll only use us for a couple of years and then not need us anymore (i.e., stop paying us $20/month). Sure, it might be "bad for business" but it's good for you. We care about getting results and about your success – that's it. There is also no stoppage or cancellation fee, which is another common trick of the trade that many companies bury in the fine print to make extra money off you. Fee-only companies are quite rare, most opt to be "commission" or "premium" based, which you'll see below in the biased case studies. Fee-only companies are able to adhere to the highest level of fiduciary standards as well since they aren't tainted by or tempted to sell you extra stuff that makes them more money.

Case Study 2: Mint.com and Creditkarma.com

These are for-profit companies. But they cost you, the consumer, nothing. They are free tools. Platforms and websites like Mint and Credit Karma come onto the scene every year and are helping to create more transparency and quality in an often murky and bleak financial world.

So how do they make money? They make companies pay for advertisements to show you, the consumer, various services. So long as you don't click on the ads, you can use the site for free.

That's pretty sweet and simple. You'll notice it didn't take a huge stack of paper or a tiny font to tell you about these two cases.

If you have to wade into the legal jargon and long documentation with all kinds of clauses and phrases that are hard to understand, you know you're heading into Goliath's trap. So watch out. It might be time to turn around and just say no.

Biased

Before highlighting some biased practices, let me point out a couple of things:

1. This is not just a problem that exists out there in some unrelated area of the universe – it impacts you directly. How much so? The Department of Labor is now *finally* passing rules that require a higher ethical "fiduciary standard" for people in the financial space that will "save middle class families **billions of dollars every year.**"[86] For the government to flat out say that companies are essentially ripping off Americans is unprecedented and calls out the true nature of exploitative companies and individuals.

2. Many companies are intentionally structured in a way to take "tiny" commissions, fees, and expenses that seem small at first, but add up to the collective billions and billions of dollars for them (and not you) every year. There are definitely some good products out there, but there are tons of garbage ones as well, so be on guard. These parasitic fees are often as small as "1% of your account value" or might be disguised as "premiums" on an insurance policy or even as "expense ratios" or "management fees." If any cost or fee is ever expressed as a percent, you should ask them to give you several hypothetical examples of how this translates to actual dollars in terms of cost to you. If they demure, give you a half answer (like when politicians "pivot" and answer a similar question with an incomplete answer), or can't give it to you straight, keep pushing them until they do. If they don't, it's probably best to walk away, *no matter how uncomfortable it may feel.* Further, ask for their fee charts or sections in the paperwork that expressly point out *all* of the fees.

3. The following case studies will focus on products and not on companies themselves. But as a proxy here, you should

be trying to identify what types of products each company you interact with is selling, whether it is a financial product like a mutual fund, retirement account, or other financial service. If you don't 100% fully understand a product, a service, or something someone is telling you about, it's time to walk away or learn more. Be a defensive consumer and as the apropos and well-worn phrase cautions: *caveat emptor* (in English: "buyer beware").

Before diving in, it should be noted that even if a financial product or person has some level of bias, it doesn't mean they are 100% bad 100% of the time. It just means that while the product or service *itself* might be good for you, the fees, the commission, the timing, or the appropriateness for you in particular might be ill-suited, too biased, or cost too much.

Case Study 3: Insurance

There are all kinds of insurance out there: life, short term disability, long term disability, term life insurance, whole life insurance, car insurance, insurance to insure against lack of insurance (as comical as this last one sounds, it exists), umbrella insurance (insurance for my umbrella? Not quite…but again, it's real insurance).

When it comes to insurance, most companies will charge you fees and/or premiums that are pretty costly if you add up the fees themselves. The opportunity cost may not be worth it if you are directing your money to them instead of putting it towards other goals that have a higher priority in your financial life, like paying down debt or saving for retirement or a house, for example. You might pay in the neighborhood of $15 – $100+ *per month* for the premium, which means if you're investing $150 a month towards a policy, then your account is only growing by $150 minus the premium, which might be substantially less than you think. This leaves you making slower progress than is ideal or possible elsewhere. These fees and commissions are the functional equivalent of running a race with weights strapped to your feet–not good.

Further, insurance is inherently designed to be more conservative than many other investments like the ETFs, some bonds, and stocks and committing money each month to insurance can severely erode your long term wealth. It's typical that an insurance policy makes somewhere in the neighborhood of 4% per year on your money, whereas we now know that the stock market returns 8% on average. Let's imagine you commit $150 per month to one of these two options for 10 years. What's the difference?*

After 10 years:

Insurance policy value: $22,706

Investment account value: $27,193

Bummer, not only did your insurance parasite take a steady $15 per month commission for a total of $1,800 over that time period, but you have $4,487 less than had you invested your money in some basic retirement account like an IRA or your work 401k. Ouch.

Additionally, what makes insurance sales notorious is the fact that the people offering it to you are *inherently biased* because they are working off commission and only earn money when you buy their policies. Again, no matter how they spin the story, they make money when the sale is finalized. The high-pressure sales tactics and slick ways to get you to say yes are scientifically studied at these companies. I've heard horror stories from people about being solicited to buy insurance via Twitter, Instagram, and even Snapchat. The insurance salespeople are generally trained to contact you anywhere from 6 to 15 times, and they know you are way more likely to say yes after repeated overtures than on the first interaction. I like to call it "legal harassment" and I've even heard several people say, "I finally said yes just so they would stop bugging me." Eww. Not only are they trying to hook into you as a parasite, but they are forcing themselves on you like a 7th grade boy who is

---

* Assumes annual compounding and doesn't account for tax implications for simplicity.

getting a little too handsy in the movie theater. No means no, even in the insurance world, so don't be afraid to be firm and tell them what's up.

When talking to people in the insurance industry, ask them what their credentials are. What you'll find is that many of them only have the license to sell insurance and nothing more. They may call themselves "Financial Advisors" or "Financial Planners," but the legal restraint on calling yourself one of these terms is actually pretty loose and doesn't necessarily mean that they can give advice beyond whether or not you should buy their insurance (which they'll almost always think you absolutely need as they paint some "end of the world" scenario).

Don't get me wrong, insurance is an integral and important feature of your financial life, but the way the industry is generally practiced, sales are predatory and laden with financial landmines. We'll cover what types of insurance are out there and when you should consider buying in a bit. But for now, don't get sucked into being *over insured,* which happens to a lot of young people just starting out in their careers when a fast-talking, suited up, insurance salesperson comes knocking at your door (or blowing up your email inbox or Twitter feed).

Case Study 4: High Cost Mutual Funds

65.5 million years ago, right at the Cretaceous-Tertiary Boundary (the "K-T Boundary") a giant meteor collided with Earth and wiped out dinosaurs. While there's lots of speculation still out there as to the precise chain of events that led to actually killing off the dinosaurs, one thing is for sure: T-Rex and Pterodactyls have been relegated to the fossil record and movies like *Jurassic Park.* The same type of monumental wiping out and extinction of high cost mutual funds is underway as of the last 15 to 20 years with the rise of different investment options. It breaks down like this: very few people, save the very wealthy, will find a compelling need to have high cost, *actively managed* mutual funds ever again. They will slowly fade into history, like the dinosaurs, and they will ultimately represent a past age. Why though?

Actively managed mutual funds are expensive and eat away at your wealth. If you're seeing expenses, expense ratios, or fees in the 0.5% – 1.5% range, you're dealing with high cost mutual funds. Additionally, many mutual funds will perform at or below a more passive investment like an ETF or index fund in the long run. For the most part, therefore, they cost more, and perform as well or worse. Now, anyone who works at a mutual fund will tell you otherwise, but they will struggle to back up their case scientifically. Just ask billionaire investor and Oracle of Omaha, Warren Buffett,[87] or one of the early pioneers and champions of ditching mutual funds, Burton Malkiel, who wrote *A Random Walk Down Wall Street* and introduced the first passive investment in 1975. (P.S. His bio is wickedly impressive in case you need any more reasons to believe that you should watch out for actively managed mutual funds.[88]) Their opinion is that low cost passive ETFs and index funds (0.05 – 0.4% expense ratios) are the way to go and that mutual funds should have a tiny place (if any at all) in their multibillion dollar investing strategy. Like them, you don't need high cost actively managed mutual funds either (As we'll talk about later, there are low cost, more passive mutual funds that are still legit.).

Mutual funds are biased because they have some highly paid person *actively managing* (buying and selling) the investments in the fund itself which incentivizes them to trade actively and more frequently than is arguably necessary. This bias ends up costing you, the investor, lots of money and it goes into their pockets (and the fund's employees and owners) all while delivering results, that are not always the best.

Moral of the story: avoid high cost, actively managed mutual funds and expensive life insurance policies.

Avoiding Financial Traps Pays Off

With your new knowledge of bias, fees, and various financial practices and products, you can now go out more confidently when assessing your financial options. The name of the game is for people to sell you stuff – that's the way America is built. And your new job is not necessarily to avoid buying anything ever again, but to make more informed and better choices. Your job is to avoid the financial traps like a cunning fox, keep your money rather than give it away via subtle and secretive fees and commissions, and feel comfortable saying no when the pressure and the salespeople turn up the heat. If you can do this, you'll avoid unnecessary costs, find things that actually add value to your life (and your net worth), and you'll avoid being preyed on by those little parasites looking to latch on at each step of the way. Remember, David *does* end up beating Goliath.

Joe Holberg

10. Budgeting 101

Are you the Scarecrow of budgeting? As Dorothy meets the new members of her curious caravan in the *Wizard of Oz*, they each sing a song about what they wish to gain from the Wizard. The Scarecrow sings, "if I only had a brain." The Scarecrow thinks that all of life's issues would be a lot easier if he could just get some of those bundled neurons inserted upstairs. Like the Scarecrow, millions of Americans are skipping down the yellow brick road singing their version, "if I only had a budget," thinking that it will magically solve their financial woes.

The word budget itself is probably the most abused and trampled upon word in all of finance. It means everything and yet it means nothing. People allude to their "budget" all of the time, but is it really something that is central to your finances? The budget may be helpful, but it can also be a topical solution like the time my soccer coach put a Band-Aid over my left eyebrow after I crashed into a goalpost while playing soccer. I really needed stitches – not a Band-Aid – since I had ripped open my flesh to the point where my teammates could see my skull (in retrospect, I really wish I could have seen my skull. Alas I was preoccupied with the pain at that point). The Band-Aid did help, a little, but it was a solution that was used in lieu of the more adequate one.

It turns out the Scarecrow, my eyebrow, and your budget all have something in common – they've been ripped apart. The Scarecrow gets attacked by those blue-faced winged monkeys (which are terrifying, btw), my eyebrow succumbed to the metal post, and your budget gets torn up every couple of months when income and expenses change unexpectedly and all of a sudden, you're back to square one.

Is the budget worth putting back together again like my face and the Scarecrow's straw legs? The answer is *yes*. The budget itself is only a tool, however. It isn't something that needs to be put on the pedestal of financial awesomeness. The budget is more like a rudimentary navigation instrument that Magellan would have used in circumnavigating the globe. The instruments themselves are important, but what is more important is the vision and the goal of completing a trip around the world. Knowing that you want to pay off debt or create longer term savings is the vision. The budget is the navigational tool to get there. Another way of phrasing it is the budget is the means, not the end itself.

So how do we use the budget as a means to our ends? We find a system that works for us. There are two primary ways to budget and many times it's advantageous to do both simultaneously in a constant cycle of analysis and reflection. First, you should *proactively* set budgets so that you can do some basic forecasting for the month ahead. You can use whatever time frequency works for you: weekly, biweekly, monthly, but I wouldn't do it less frequently than monthly.

Secondly, you can *retroactively* analyze your budget. With the forward-looking approach, you can see the road ahead: is it more or less a normal month or is there some obstacle ahead that we can see? Just as in the Mario Kart, there might be a financial speed booster ahead (good) or there might be a banana peel on the road (bad). Are summer months more or less expensive? How much do you want to carve out for birthday or holiday gifts for family and friends? By being proactive, you can start to anticipate what is about to happen, even if imperfectly, which allows you to better capture opportunities and avoid unnecessary costs. The name of the game isn't about having 100% unyielding fidelity to this proactive budget, but being cautious and realistic so that you can meet most, and hopefully all, of your financial goals. It's about weeding out outliers and aberrations that threaten your financial fitness.

Each month inevitably comes to a close: January happened. July ended. All of a sudden it's Halloween and October just slipped away. What now? From a retroactive budgetary perspective, look back at what just happened. Did you increase your new year expenses because you signed up for a gym membership for $30/month? If you're going to keep it, then build it into February's budget. The 4th of July cookout was awesome, but you dropped way more on hot dogs, chips, and American-themed accessories (and of course, fireworks*). Dropped $50 on Pumpkin Spiced Chai Lattes *and* $35 on bags of Halloween candy? What the heck October! Whatever it is, you are better off taking a hard (and sometimes painful) look at what happened the month before. The more you look, the more patterns you'll see and the more honest you can be with yourself about spending habits and behaviors going forward. The point of retroactively looking at your budget isn't to castigate yourself for your personal splurges on things like Chipotle lunch (because you know that burrito was divine), it's to help guide you in making more informed and educated decisions that (once again) help you move towards your larger vision and goals.

Everyone veers off course at times. As an example, let's say you're a coffee junkie (I'm essentially talking to myself at this point). You tell yourself that you only "treat yo self" on Fridays so you guess that you spend something like $20 a month on coffee. That's not bad, if you ask me. But then you look at your credit card statement and realize that you actually went twice that many times last month. You did consistently go on Fridays like you thought, but there was generally one other day of the week that you slid through Dunkin', Starbucks,† or your local, specialty coffee shop with an aroma and beans to die

---

* I always spend too much on fireworks. But I love them so...I build it into my budget towards the end of June so I can make some noise for my home sweet home, 'Merica! Public Service Announcement: only buy the fireworks that are legal in your state. Once I was pulled over by a police officer and happened to have a sizeable box of fireworks in a state that might not have been as big of a fan of fireworks as I was... but that story is for another time.

† To date, I still haven't purchased anything from Starbucks. Waiting to get my first cup with Howard Behar in Seattle at store #1 in Pike's Place Market.

for. That $20 turned into $50 because you either grabbed a little side snack or maybe bought your friend's coffee too. This has happened for the last 5 months to varying degrees...it might be time to adjust your mental framework around your coffee consumption (as I had to). Just recalibrate to the fact that you spend $50 and not $20. You can either make the mental adjustment and keep up the coffee habit or you can make the financial adjustment and go back to spending $20. The choice is yours, but having dissonance between the two is unacceptable as it will distort the true nature of your given budget category.

Whether or not your vice is coffee, Target, books, shoes, fluffy hats, or whatever else floats your boat, the retroactive budget analysis is crucial for taking a bird's eye view of yourself and your spending. Nine times out of ten, just being aware of your actual budget can provide the impetus needed to start making minor, reasonable changes. You don't need to go on a juice cleanse and commit to never drinking coffee again. Instead, maybe you buy yourself a $20 gift card each month to spend on coffee. Once it's gone, it's gone. Now you have to wait until the next month to get another one and you can only drink coffee at home where it is much cheaper per ounce consumed. (The same holds true for beer or wine or really obnoxiously expensive bottled water whose container simultaneously pollutes our environment.) This logic can be extended to pretty much any expense or budget category you have in a given month.

Fortunately, tracking this type of data is much easier now than ever before,. You don't have to whip out your pencil and paper to create and manage a massive budget these days. In fact, just one powerful tool that I love and cannot recommend enough can help you achieve the same goal of proactively and retroactively budgeting effectively: www.mint.com.

If you've never used Mint, now's the time to try. Mint is ultra-powerful (and free) and links to all of your bank accounts, credit card accounts, and other important financial accounts including student loans, personal loans, and retirement accounts. Essentially it is a one-stop-shop for an overview and assessment of your financial picture. You can see all kinds of pretty charts and data that will satisfy even the nerdiest data-lovers. This data-richness is also the very same thing that turns a lot of people off from Mint because it can be too powerful and too overwhelming. So if you've used Mint and it hasn't worked for you, give it another chance!

However, I think there are two main features that are most useful and important when it comes to using Mint for a better grasp on your budget. First, on the proactive side, you can set a very basic budget by categories. You should set some constraints in common spending areas and in aggregate so that you can see how your expectations match reality. For example, if you think you spend $10 per month on fast food, set your Mint fast food budget to $10. Mint will track your expenses by category and it will shoot you an email if you are approaching or have gone over your fast food budget (you can disable emails if you want). Replicate this for other areas of your budget to your heart's content.

Two mandatory budgets to set are for "food and groceries" and for "restaurants and bars" since most of us do a little self-denial in these categories (myself definitely included). These two can be "budget busters" for sure, so tracking them is ultra-important. Once you have your budgets set, you can go about your business and simply watch for an email from Mint if you're hitting any given budget. This will be a little alarm bell going off to warn you that you might be spending more than you think in a given category.

Secondly, from a retroactive standpoint, Mint amasses all of your spending and income data and puts it together in various ways so that you can look at it if you so choose. One of the most valuable ways to do this is by clicking "Trends" at the top of the page once you're logged in. The trends show you how much you've spent, where you've spent it, and how this spending changes over time. This is amazing, if you think about it. You can watch all of your historical data build up so that you have a more complete picture of what's going on. One of my favorite things to do with people is to help them look through various categories of spending over the last 3, 6, and 12 months. Once you start digging in, you will find that the numbers don't lie and it will be quite a surprise to see how your spending fluctuates over time. Uncovering places that are higher spending categories or categories with lots of fluctuations can be one of the best ways to use a budget to better serve your long term goals.

For instance, if the data says you bought $35 in art supplies on average for the last 6 months, then this is something you can count on doing in the future unless you change your behavior (you may or may not want to). If you notice you throw away lots of veggies and fruits that spoil (40% of all food bought ends up getting thrown away, as sacrilegious as this sounds) *and* you're still making weekly trips to the grocery store, then maybe it's time to think about going to the grocery store twice a month instead of four times. Maybe you'll decide that to cap your weekly grocery spending at a certain amount instead of just free-wheeling it through the store and grabbing whatever looks good. (I'm a sucker for those tasty olives and cheeses, but dang they are pricey!)

With the thousands of people I've worked with and talked to, "food and groceries" and "restaurants and bars" are the two most underestimated categories in people's budget. One of my favorite lines is, "Oh, I rarely go out to eat," or "We only go out twice a month or so." But upon inspection, they've eaten out during lunch multiple times per month, swung by for breakfast a couple of times, chilled for several rounds at the bar after dinner on the weekends, and still shop at Whole Foods too. There is absolutely nothing wrong with any of this, whatsoever. Truly. I will never criticize you or anyone else for eating food or for having any other expenditure for that matter. I will, however, be absolutely adamant about two rules in these categories that are the biggest sources of "money seepage," and you should observe them as well:

1. **Be Honest:** If you are honest with yourself about how much you spend, it's all good. You need to know where your

money is going, so look at the numbers, look at the data, and be honest with yourself about what you typically spend in each category.

2. **Make Progress:** If you are fully aware of the tradeoffs that you're making and how it impacts your entire financial picture and progress towards your goals, it's all good. If you want to save $200 in your IRA each month, but you're only saving $100 consistently, then there has to either be an increase in income of $100 to meet your savings goal or there has to be a $100 decrease in expenses (or obviously some combo of the two).

There are categories galore that can drive the "invisible budget leaks" like food and restaurants, which leave people thinking at the end of the month, "Where did my money go?" You know your rent/mortgage is a fixed cost, you know that gas for your car is relatively constant, etc., but where did the rest go? The leaks might be big or small, easily spotted, or a little harder to uncover, but just like the children's story of the little Dutch boy who plugs a dyke's leak on the way to school so the city doesn't flood, you too should start identifying and plugging leaks in your budget wherever possible. I'd wager you'll find leaks in your budget dyke, many related to food, groceries, restaurants, bars, and shopping, so pay particular attention to those categories.

In closing out our discussion about budgeting, it's important to remember a couple of key things that will help you be a better budgeter and ultimately drive you towards a greater degree of financial fitness and health so that you can meet your goals:

- Budgeting is a means, not an end. Your budget should help you learn about yourself, your income, expenses, and savings.
- Budget regularly and be willing to put in the time to budget. Spend an hour or so a month just looking over all your expenses. (This is a great fraud prevention mechanism, too, so you can spot any fishy charges in the event they occur.)

- Proactively budget to plan for the coming month. Plan rigorously, but allow room for flexibility.
- Retroactively analyze your budget. Use data to inform yourself about you! Be honest and make progress towards your goals. Make small, realistic changes instead of life altering massive tectonic shifts.
- Use tools like mint.com, Google spreadsheets or Microsoft Excel, pencil and paper, stone tablets, etc. to help make your budgeting life easier and more successful.

Go forth and budget!

Make Key Goals Automatic

One of the single best actions you can take in order to make your life a quadrillion times easier is to make your key goals automatic. We've touched on this lightly in previous sections, but it's worth accentuating. Far too often people manually contribute to various accounts like savings, retirement, and debt pay-down.

You know how this pans out: the direct deposit from work comes in and hits your checking account (woohoo), you have some expenses (boo), then at the end of the week or month you look and you think hmm...do I have enough to save? Maybe I'll save $25 and you send that money over to your savings account (woohoo). But then the next paycheck rolls around and you're out of town and you forget to save some. And the next paycheck you realized that you didn't have enough left over to save, so you skip saving again. In the long run, the intent to save is there, but the system isn't. So make it automatic. Now.

If you already have a savings account, login and set it up so that you are automatically and regularly committing some amount every time, not just sometimes. The best thing to do is to make the savings contribution come out on the same day (or a day or two after) as your direct deposit goes in. You should start with a small amount that won't throw your budget into a crazy tailspin. Ambitious savings goals are great, but work your way up to them so you can see how they affect your lifestyle and budget. Have it repeat at whatever frequency you are getting paid. So for example, if you are paid weekly and you want to save $100 per month, then save $25 per week. If you get paid biweekly, then set up a $50 savings contribution for twice a month. This "smoothing" of your savings will more accurately match your cash flow, which makes the "pain" of savings easier.

The same thing goes for your debt pay-down, retirement, and any other financial goal that you have. Whatever the goal is, it is almost certain that you can automate it these days since almost everyone has an online payment portal. Student loan debt is a great example. Why the heck would you want to have to log on to your student loan website every month to pay your bill? If you know you always owe $250 per month, what is the benefit of having to remember each month to log on and do the same thing? It not only wastes your valuable time, but it exposes you to the risk of forgetting (oh but I *never* forget!). As we'll see later, even forgetting once can have deleterious consequences on your credit and credit score, so why risk it? It's simply unnecessary. Automate. Bills also fit nicely into this category, whether it's utility bills such as electricity and gas, or the monthly cable/Internet bill. If you can automate, then automate.

Let's think of two simple scenarios to highlight this. First, you've got Taylor who set up an automatic biweekly savings contribution of $40 so she can save $80 per month. Taylor also has a credit card that she isn't using and has a 0% APR for 12 months. This card has a balance of $1,200 so she sets up an automatic monthly payment of $100 so that on the last month before her interest rate increases, she'll pay off the balance. Each month, $180 total is automatically transferred to these two accounts and quite honestly, she forgets about them because it comes right out of her checking account around the time of her direct deposit. At the end of the year, she has saved $960 and paid off her $1,200 credit card balance. She is $2,160 better off, with less (or no) credit card debt and a solid start to her savings. She can proceed from here with more confidence and stability. #winning

Anthony, on the other hand, really wants to save $2,400 in the next year. So he saves as much as he can at the end of each month after looking at his bank account. He is usually able to save in bigger, irregular chunks, but sometimes has to draw on his savings to pay for things like bills or travel. He too has $1,200 in credit card debt at 0% APR for the year, like Mary. He never forgets to make payments (fortunately), but he often makes big payments one month, followed by the minimum in the next. Over the course of the year, Anthony has his eye on his savings prize and for the first five months he makes solid gains and saves $1,000 ($200/month). He made the minimum payments on his credit card though so he could save more. He paid $40/month for 5 months on the credit card so his balance is down to $1,000. He's not doing badly, but then in month six he doesn't save anything because expenses were a little higher than he thought they were going to be. Consequently he just dumps $100 onto the credit card as a payment. Same $1,000 savings balance, $900 credit card balance. Months 7 through 12 are hit or miss and he ends the year with $1,500 in savings, but still has a $700 balance on the credit card so he decides to use some savings to pay off the credit card (strong move since he'll avoid interest). His savings balance declines to $800 and he's paid off his credit card. Anthony hasn't met his savings goal, nor was he able to save as much as Mary, who saved less in each automated transfer, but transferred funds to savings more regularly. #notwinning They both paid off their credit cards, but Mary's slow, automated system got better results.

This is obviously fictitious and simplistic, but it absolutely works. One thing I have heard repeatedly over the years is, "I don't have enough right now to save," and "I can't make extra payments quite yet." Yes, you can. If you have a checking and savings account and you're feeling the pinch, set up a $5 per month automatic savings contribution. You can save $5 now. It's not about the amount, it's about the habit. Period. So do it. Increase it later as you're able, but for now, start harnessing the power of automating your goals. Further, this applies to other areas like retirement. Most people are defaulted into contributions that are equal to 3% or so of their salary. This is better than 0% for sure, but why not go in and turn up your contribution to 4% or 5%? It might be the equivalent of $20 – 40 per paycheck, but the result in a 1% contribution difference is staggering over a long period of time.

How staggering? If you make $50,000 per year, your 3% contribution is $1,500 compared to 4% which would be $2,000 saved per year. You've already saved $500 more just by notching up by 1%, but that's just the start of the story since it is invested and compounded. Let's assume your growth rate is 8% and you do it for your working life (22 to 67 years old). By saving $500 extra each year (that's only ~$19 per paycheck!) for 45 years, you have increased your savings by $22,500, but it turns out that puny 1% difference *with interest* yields a "measly" $208,713 extra once you retire! Awww, cute, you now have almost a *quarter of a million dollars* extra. Just because you decided to automate and push your savings up just a little bit in the short run, but over a long period of time it creates a massive windfall. #reallyfreakingwinning #themoreyouknow

At the end of the day, leaving it to your brain to remember and then act each time on your goals exposes you to the "tyranny of the urgent." If you do it manually, you'll not only end up forgetting to revisit the goal itself, but in case you do, you'll often rationalize or make up some reason about why this month or week isn't a good time to actually act on your goal or you'll end up only contributing a fractional amount towards said goal. Life is crazy and busy and there is always something "else" to focus on. So don't do it manually. Instead:

Automate. Automate. Automate.

Below is a quick list of things to automate. If you aren't doing it already, seriously consider starting. If you are already doing it, then push yourself to "up it" just a little bit to get better results:

- Debt payments, especially high interest accounts such as credit cards.

- Savings goals, especially if they are larger, like saving for a trip or for a home down payment.
- Retirement goals, especially if you are getting a match or have a lot of working years ahead of you.
- Bill payment goals, especially if they are the same amount each month. Why spend more time than you need to on paying bills?

A quick closing note; this automating is for the actual *act* itself related to your goal. You are automating the *mechanism* of your goal (the transfer or the payment of your money). This is intended to bolster the achievement and success rate of meeting your goal. But it is absolutely 100% not removing you from the higher level cognitive process of actually paying attention to the flow of your money, your budget, or your actual allocation of funds. You are still in charge of your budget and financial life. Automation should never be used as a replacement for the proactive and retroactive budgetary analysis that you should be conducting regularly. In fact, automating certain areas should actually directly increase your ability to spend more time on the review of your budget. This is great news because lots of people don't budget because they "don't have time." If you just freed up 30 minutes a month because you've automated many of your goals, you now have 30 minutes to spend on budgeting and other financial best practices.

Budget Priorities vs. Luxuries

Budgets can be broken down into all types of categories and frameworks such as "essential vs. discretionary" and "pre-tax expenses, post-tax expenses, and savings goals." There are "gurus" out there who say their system is the best system or the only system, blah blah blah. The budget is really important and there are lots of good systems out there, but I don't think this is an area where a prescriptive formula or framework works for everyone. People's lives are highly customized and individualized, so having a way to allow people to adjust for their circumstances is important.

While there are tons of templates and ideas out there, a simple T-chart that you can construct on a piece of scrap paper should get your budget ball rolling. You can supplement with whatever other budget system you like along the way. On the left side list all of your priorities. This includes essential things like housing costs, food, and utilities, but it also includes things that you really, really don't want to give up or that you know are super important to you. This includes things like your savings goal, your retirement contributions and, in my life, for example, coffee, my magazine subscription to *The Economist,* and getting my laundry picked up and done for me (it's a game changer). On the luxury side, list the things you spend money on, but could do without. Truly if push came to shove, you could bail on them entirely or at least reduce them considerably.

Priorities	Luxuries
Rent ($750)	Netflix ($10)
Utilities ($120)	Eating out-nights and
Gas for car ($40)	weekends ($120)
Car insurance ($35)	Eating out-breakfast on the
Health insurance ($140)	go and lunch at work ($60)
Food ($150)	Clothes ($50)
Unlimited coffee card ($20)	Sports League ($60)
The Economist ($15)	Gym Membership ($50)
Laundry service ($25)	Tickets to shows ($40)
Monthly savings ($100)	Red wine ($25)
Retirement savings ($120)	White wine ($10)
Student loan payment ($175)	Beer ($25)
etc...	Gifts for friends/self ($20)
	More coffee ($35)
	Books ($15)
	Uber/Lyft ($13)
	Music streaming app ($7)
	etc. etc. etc.....

Using this simple framework, you can quickly scan your own list and find areas that might be weak areas that you need to address. For example, if you're finding that you use the gym 1-2 times per week because you're always playing in a sports league or choosing to run outside, then you might be able to drop the gym membership. Boom, fifty extra bucks. You might also realize that you are buying a lot of regular food for home ($150), but you're still going out to eat quite a bit. Not only are you likely to toss out food at home, but you're paying a premium to eat out. The two-sided solution here is to either eat out less and eat more at home (reducing luxury spending) or to actually stop buying so much food when you go to the grocery store to load up for the week ahead (reduce priority spending, keep luxury spending the same).

As you separate the list into these two distinct categories, don't judge yourself too harshly. It's ok if you put your haircut and clothes in the priority category and put vegetables in the luxury category. The worst thing you can do is trick yourself into putting items into the wrong category because of various messages out there about what is and isn't important or unimportant. Everyone is in a different place and you might think the world is going to end if you can't see a blockbuster movie, but you'd be perfectly fine with boxes of mac and cheese instead of fresh veggies. Further, the items in the list may change sides over time. For instance, maybe Netflix is absolutely crucial and a priority this month, but it might not be utilized much during the summer months and you could decide to do without it for a while. There are tradeoffs that we all have to make and when you're working on your budget and an exercise like this, you have to be honest with yourself in order to get the best results.

The takeaway from this exercise is to make you cognizant of how you prioritize your spending so you can determine whether you want your world to remain as it is, or if you need to make changes. Once you see that you've got a ton of luxury expenses, you might decide it's time to trim your spending down in a healthy and realistic way without completely robbing yourself of life's joys. Alternatively, you might look at it and realize that there are items in your priority list that you aren't quite happy with. For example, maybe you need to bolster your savings or perhaps your retirement progress has become stagnant in the last year or two.

Whatever the case may be, you are looking for increased opportunities to rebalance towards the things you prioritize, while clipping or trimming things from the luxury category that might be out of balance. You don't have to be a weekend hermit and never go out with friends. But if you're going out 3 times during a weekend and the bill is always higher than you thought it would be, then maybe it's time to stay in one of those nights and trim ever so slightly. Again, there is no judgment assigned by you, me, or anyone else; there is just the cold, hard reality that each of us has only a given amount each month and we have to make a set of constrained choices to move towards what we want and need in our lives, whether priorities or luxuries.

Joe Holberg

11. Intermediate Life Goals

It's tempting to think that the world is carved up into a nice short-term vs. long-term structure. There is the immediacy of today and then there is the metaphorical light at the end of the tunnel barely visible, but definitely there. As a society, we talk so much about things like budgeting and saving, then we turn around and talk about this distant idea of retirement. But looking out across the time horizon, you can quickly see there is a huge stretch of time that is neither far away nor pressing against the present. If the short term is defined as anything within the next year and the long run is defined as retirement and beyond, then what is in between all that time? Let's call it the "intermediate" time frame. Lots of goals will fit into this intermediate time horizon and we should be developing ideas and strategies to tackle these goals just as intentionally as we tackle short-and long-term goals. In fact, in this category are some of life's most challenging goals. Without a concrete action plan and roadmap to figure out the best way to accomplish them can lead to forced decisions, less than optimal decisions, or perhaps even foregoing the goal entirely.

Some intermediate goals that people have include traveling, buying a house, donating to causes or charities, planning for marriage, and getting life insurance. Each one of these has a long "ramp up" time. This means that the goal generally costs quite a bit and the time in which it happens is usually foreseeable in some sense since it will happen in the one-year-plus time frame. The most practical way to approach each of these goals is to figure out what needs to be done each month leading up to the goal itself and what the best route to get to said goal is. This "backwards planning" or "reverse engineering" approach is powerful since it shifts the ambiguous future event into the realm of confidence and control. It puts you in the driver's seat and it allows you to course-adjust as needed. These intermediate goals come on the heels of the automation section since you can (and should) use some form of automation for intermediate goals as they are gnarly large beasts to tackle manually.

Finally, as we dive into these intermediate goals, you may or may not think these intermediate goals are relevant to you specifically, and that's just fine. Home ownership for example, is becoming an intermediate goal that lots of people are reevaluating. If you aren't sure whether or not you're going to buy a house, the best default position is to assume that you are, and work towards it. Then if you decide you aren't going to buy a house, you have at least created a reserve of cash savings that can be allocated towards new and emerging goals, whether they themselves be short, intermediate, or long term. The rationale here is that you'd rather over-plan than under-plan. If you are planning on traveling and you save up $2,000 for a trip to Greece and then decide not to go, well now you've got a head start on your house down payment!

Let's cover some of the major intermediate goals in turn. Just because you aren't totally sure that you are going to pursue something doesn't mean that you shouldn't plan and create a strategy for it. The military is a great example of how to plan for the unknown future – they do disaster and catastrophe planning and execute huge military exercises across the globe with other countries so regularly even though the likelihood of needing to respond to these hypothetical events is miniscule. If they plan for things rigorously that are extremely unlikely to happen, shouldn't you plan for things that are much more likely to happen like traveling, getting married, or buying a house?

Time to Travel the World!

There are two major ways people pay for travel. One way is by throwing it all on a credit card and worrying about how to pay it off once the travel concludes. Eek. Don't do this. Before you burn me in effigy for suggesting you give up your travel points and rewards, just hear me out. This style of "go now, pay later" is widely used and subscribed to and plays to the "worst angels" of how we make decisions. As seen already, simply by using a credit card, people spend more (12 – 18% more) and traveling is no exception. It allows us to be more freewheeling and impulsive. We end up after said travel looking at the bill or credit card statement with eyeballs the size of saucers. This way will leave you feeling more burned than the airplane coffee...not good.

The other way to travel isn't that much of an adjustment from the first, believe it or not, and ultimately it is just setting up a simple savings goal in order to pay for the trip along the way. This "go now, pay now" strategy doesn't reduce travel ability. It just puts you in the position to avoid the travel hangover for months afterwards whereby you are left with great memories *and* a big credit card bill.

You should care about this for two main reasons:

1. "Go now, pay now" will allow you to travel more regularly, within budget, *and* to the places that you've put off that are higher cost. Lots of people dream of going to France or Bali, but few go.

2. It will allow you to avoid the pains of loading up a credit card. As you've seen already, carrying a balance adds up and can greatly increase the cost of your travel in the long run by using the "go now, pay later" method.

So how do you proactively save for travel? Believe it or not, it's ultra-simple. As you might have guessed, it's about setting up the system to achieve the goal more so than it is about anything else. In order to set this up, the first thing you will need is a separate, dedicated savings account for travel. I *strongly* suggest not using either of your two savings accounts that you learned about in Section One (general savings and emergency savings. P.S. If you don't have those yet, go get them now!). The reason here is the same: you are creating a distinct account so that you can create a more concrete psychological and actual barrier between your funds.

Once you have the savings account established, figure out how much you need to put into it in order to achieve your goal. If you're trying to go to Puerto Rico for a week, you'll need a much different amount compared to visiting family in California for a 3-day weekend. Estimate (loosely, it doesn't have to be perfect) the amount you'll need including airfare, lodging, food, travel, souvenirs, and anything else. Then divide that total amount by the number of months left before your trip. Say you're going to Puerto Rico 8 months from now and you'll need $1,300. Then you'll need to save $162.50 per month until the plane takes off. This will also give you enough runway to buy your tickets in a timely fashion prior to the trip. By the time you leave, you'll have funds for your "on the ground" expenses. By the time you get back home, you'll have postcards, a tan, some good memories of beautiful beaches and a great culture, but you won't have the nasty balance on your credit card.

Likewise, if you're headed home for the holidays to see family and you know you've got 12 months to save, then just sock away a small amount each month. It might only cost you the airfare since lodging is theoretically free (even if your childhood bedroom still has cute wallpaper and a twin bed with your stuffed animals waiting for your return) and food costs might be lower. Say, $500/12 = $42 per month. Not too shabby.

This simple system is easily extended to more complex travel situations. If you travel several times per year and you mix international and domestic travel destinations, it's not really that much of a stretch to extend this "go now, pay now" mentality. I work with a lot of people to help them understand their travel patterns so they can budget a realistic amount towards travel savings each month. Let's say you travel domestically every other month and you travel once internationally per year (if this seems like a stretch, just wait till you see the numbers). Then how much will you need to save per month? Let's assume that your type of travel domestically relies on crashing with friends (i.e., avoiding hotels) or finding cheap Airbnb lodgings. You'll still buy good food and do fun things, but given this cheaper, value style travel, you are spending money on the plane ticket plus a couple of hundred dollars once on the ground. (One thing I like to do is estimate that domestic travel costs essentially 2x the cost of the airfare, so if you spend $250 on a round trip ticket, you'll most likely spend at least another $250 on the ground for a total of $500). So, you travel six times per year and each time you need $500 door to door. Your annual domestic travel costs $3,000 which means you need to save $250 per month. You might bump it up or down on a given year, but at least now you are building the funds to actually pay for the trips you take.

Now, adding in the international trip to Peru (spin a globe and pick the place where your finger lands? I dare you). Peru is going to set you back $1,000 (expensive airfare, but once there, relatively cheap) so you throw an additional $83 per month into your savings account. Now you're saving $333 per month for travel and each time you go, it's already paid for. Turns out, the world is your oyster with this straightforward, automated savings system. It's just up to you to implement.

Remember when I said "hold your horses" regarding your precious travel points/miles/rewards? Well, it turns out you should definitely utilize your rewards credit cards to *pay* for the trip and the expenses itself. Swipe away when paying for your flights, hotels, and costs. There is no reason not to accumulate your rewards and points, but recognize that you are now *immediately* able to pay off the expense with your savings rather than having to pay for it under the "go now, pay later" model. The credit card is just a channel and thoroughfare for your expenses. It is not a funding mechanism since there are no funds that actually come from using the credit card. Those funds have to come from somewhere and they either come from this new, proactive savings model or they come in the form of the travel hangover where you're paying off your Daytona Beach excursion for

Joe Holberg

way too many months afterwards. This proactive savings for travel is a good method that clearly spans across travel styles whether you like 5-star hotels or 0-star hostels. It works for frequent travelers as well as once a year traveling and it works for road trips to the state next door as well as Southeast Asian adventures to the other side of planet earth. Whatever it is for you, "go now, pay now" and definitely have fun.

Quick steps to proactively saving for travel:

1. Save each month for an upcoming trip by calculating your travel budget: $ Cost of Trip / # Months to save.
2. Pay for your trip either with cash, debit, or credit (yes, you can still get those points!) *beforehand and during* the trip.
3. Go on your trip/travel/vacation/grand world tour and have fun.
4. If you used a credit card to pay for expenses, pay them off entirely upon return.
5. Return home with pictures, memories, and good stories, but no credit card debt.
6. Repeat to your heart's content.

Down Payments, Buying a House, and the Cornerstone of the American Dream

This one's a doozy. Talking about buying and owning homes (and by extension, condos, townhomes, flats, bungalows, dwellings, etc.) has the peculiar effect of both exciting people and nauseating them. Flip the TV on and HGTV has the *Extreme Home Makeover* or flip through any number of magazines like *Architectural Digest* and our little hearts and minds flutter with aspirations of buying a piece of the American Dream in the form of our own place to live. This excitement is further bolstered by the knowledge that the alternative to buying is renting – a dreary long term prospect as you know your money is going straight into the pockets of the landlord or whoever actually owns the place.

The cute 3-bedroom row home in D.C., 1,800 square foot ranch with a big backyard in the Midwest, or the condo on the 22nd floor with a panoramic city-line view keeps us all thinking about home ownership on the regular. But it's also becoming more difficult to figure out a way to actually lock down said dream home these days as millions simultaneously have large amounts of debt earlier in life coupled with rising real estate prices. Unfortunately, this has been the general trend for decades (save a couple of blips like the Great Recession).

With home prices in the hundreds of thousands of dollars it can seem an almost impossible scenario to envision buying a home when you look at your bank account and see your savings account balance at a couple hundred or a couple thousand dollars. So what can you do to avoid paying rent for the rest of your life?

The answer to this is surprisingly similar to the proactive savings scenarios that you just read. It does get a little more nuanced and specific, so we'll take the analysis item by item. There are several core components to thinking about how to get your hands on that elusive property and future home, but the main ones to consider are:

- Determine the ideal mortgage for you (go back and reread the mortgage section if you need to)
- Identify your expected home purchase price
- Identify your expected home purchase timeline
- Calculate what you need to save each month for a down payment
- Select your optimal account for savings

Taking each one of these in turn, as we've seen already, the 15 and 30 year fixed mortgages are going to be your best bet in almost all scenarios even though the variable mortgages will be alluring. It's worth reminding you that the variable mortgage is inherently risky since you don't know when your rates will change nor by how much, so steer clear if possible.

In thinking about the home itself, most people will have a target value in mind and this purchase price will vary significantly depending on more factors than we can realistically cover. Either way, the purchase price is where people can get into a lot of trouble. The first thing to think about is how much house you actually need versus what you want. As Americans, we are trained to believe that bigger is better and we totally have the "keeping up with the Joneses" syndrome when to comes to buying a house. The purchase price is going to dictate your monthly payment, so if you are feeling the pinch in your current budget or just don't want to end up with a house with tons of empty rooms, then think "less is more." As a corollary to that, you'll need a smaller down payment to go along with it which could help you get into your home faster in the first place. Next, think of the timeline. Are you trying to buy in the next year, 5 years, or some point in the distant future? You're going to need some cash for the down-payment, so you'll want to get that savings put into the right account along the way. Finally, we'll do some quick "back of the envelope" calculations to figure out how much you need to save each month and where you should ideally save it.

We start by looking at the expected home purchase price in more detail (go back to the mortgage section if you still are wondering about types of mortgages or need a quick review). In terms of the purchase price, there is going to be the value of the home which will most likely be close to the sale price. If the home is on the market for $200,000 it might be worth more or less than that, so make sure you get the paperwork with the most recent assessed value or get your own assessment of the value before making any decisions. The best question you can ask yourself when looking to buy a home is "Can I afford this?" There is definitely going to be a sweet spot in the range of what you can afford. The tip here is that homes end up costing more per month than you expect. So there is absolutely nothing wrong with sticking towards the low end of what you can afford because taxes, insurance, repairs, fees, closing costs, etc., are all going to pop up along the way and pinch your wallet and your ability to make monthly payments.

Next, even before deciding how much you need to save for the down-payment, realistically determine when you would like to buy your home. This can be a tough question, so try to narrow it down to a range if you're not completely sure. The ranges to pick from are:

- Less than 1 year.
- 1-3 years
- 3-5 years
- 5 years or more.

The first three are relatively "soon" and especially if you are in the 3 and under crowd, you need to get cracking. We'll cover this momentarily, but there is a special trick if you are in the 5 year or more timeline. This approach can help you strategically (and legally) avoid paying taxes and penalties on a portion of your down payment, which is pretty cool and valuable. If you are in the 5 and under crowd, it is going to be a mix of paying attention to debt pay-down so you don't have too high a debt-to-income ratio (see mortgage section), and of saving up funds. Then, if you have a longer time horizon, you can start building a larger base of funds for your down payment.

Now, in terms of saving up for a down payment, the "golden rule" is to put 20% down and yes, this is great, but it's also a lot of cash. The three main advantages of putting 20% down are: 1) lenders love to see larger down payments and you will be more likely to get approved (and approved for a larger mortgage too – even though you might not need one), 2) you won't need as large a mortgage since more will be paid in cash, thus reducing your overall interest, and 3) you will be able to avoid Private Mortgage Insurance (PMI), which is valueless to you, since it is insurance to insure your mortgage.

If you put less than 20% down, Private Mortgage Insurance can range from roughly $50 to $100 per month on top of your mortgage which can really add up in the long run, so putting 20% or more down will help you avoid it. However alluring and advantageous putting 20% down is though, it is often not realistic for many

Americans. In fact, according to an NPR segment, the median down payment amount is 3.5%.[89] Whaaaa?! I thought you had to do at least 10% or something, right?! No. Not. At. All.

This lower down payment amount cuts both ways. It's good for consumers like you and me because it makes buying a house easier since you don't have to walk in with gobs of cash. But this also means that consumers are incentivized and allowed to take out larger mortgages than they might otherwise utilize and thus have a higher monthly mortgage that can strain their budget. On top of this, folks end up getting behind the metaphorical 8-ball because the ratio of the home value to the mortgage balance is often very close to 1, meaning they are close to being "underwater" on day 1 of their mortgage. This makes it especially difficult to sell your house and move because you might end up selling and not being able to make enough to pay off your mortgage.

Knowing this, even if you do end up having a smaller down payment, such as 3.5%, the best thing you can do for yourself is buy a house that is reasonably priced and not going to tax your budget too hard – so be thoughtful on the purchase price. All this being said, we still need to cultivate an actual down payment strategy. So let's go back to the drawing board with our example home with the $200,000 purchase price. The chart below shows the monthly savings amounts given various time frames for purchasing the home. If you have a short time horizon, you're more likely to end up putting less down compared to when you're able to save for a little bit longer.

Monthly amount to save

Home Purchase Price of $200,000	Length of time until purchase			
% Down payment		1 year	3 years	5 years
	3.5%	$584*	$195	$117
	10%	$1,667	$556	$334
	20%	$3,334	$1,112	$667

As you can see by the table, if you have an inkling in your brain about a future home in the next five years whatsoever, the bare minimum you should be saving per month is $117. The biggest assumption in the table above is that the house purchase price is $200,000. You can play with the numbers proportionally if you'd like to get an idea of what you'd need to save given your own home purchase price.

One thing that complicates most people's current housing situation is going from renting to owning. This first time home purchase is especially important and comes with two additional questions, all of which have links associated with them:

- Should I continue to rent or does buying make sense? Absolutely check out the interactive Rent vs. Buying tool provided on the N.Y. Times website.[90]
- How do you learn about the actual process? I consider it mandatory that you do your own research <u>and</u> attend a home buying class. Banks, cities, and lenders are just a couple of the places that you can find information and classes (all should be free). Two of my favorite resources are the Consumer Financial Protection Bureau (CFPB) and

---

* For each of these values, I assumed that they are in non-interest bearing accounts since the savings rate for shorter term accounts is virtually zero in today's market and two, they are in fact shorter term goals that while you could invest the money, it would be reasonably risky given the ultimate goal of having the certainty of having the cash at the necessary time to buy the house.

real estate website Redfin.[91] Both have great free resources that are spot on.

The Coolest IRS Rule Ever: Rule 72t

If you haven't heard of this rule, I wouldn't be surprised. It's buried deep within the tax code.[92] Very few people have. But it's pretty cool and useful when you're buying a home for the first time, so check it out. While you'll get smoked for early withdrawals on most retirement accounts, the rules for a distribution on IRAs are bent slightly by good ole Uncle Sam when you're looking to buy your first place. Normally, you would face a 10% early withdrawal penalty if you took your funds out early from either a Traditional or Roth IRA, but this is waived if you use the funds towards acquiring a home (the actual house, financing, or closing costs). This 10% penalty is waived up to $10,000 for *each* person, so couples buying a home together can withdraw up to $20,000. Woot! This is great news since you might have built up quite a bit of savings in your IRA, but maybe you don't have cash elsewhere. However, one consideration against doing this is that presumably you have contributed to your IRAs because you'd like them for the long run in retirement. So if you can use other funds, this will be a better option so you don't eat into your retirement funds.

If you are taking funds from your Traditional IRA, remember that you'll still pay normal taxes on the amount withdrawn since it hasn't been taxed yet. But given your specific tax situation, this still might not be a bad idea.

The Roth IRA is a little different though. Since you have already paid taxes, you won't have a tax liability since the earnings are tax-free (double woot!). However, you do need to have your Roth account for at least 5 years before being able to use Rule 72t to your advantage. If it has been open for less than 5 years, you don't qualify for the 10% early withdraw penalty waiver. Sad, I know. But there is a silver lining with the Roth. The 5 year "timer" retroactively starts ticking at the beginning of the year in which you open your

Roth IRA and ends on the first day of the year in which you would complete the 5 year period; therefore, the actual time period needed to fulfill the "5 year" requirement would range from, at a minimum, 3 years and 2 days (you open the account on December 31, Year 1 and the "5 year" period is met as of Jan 1, Year 5) to, at most, 4 years and 1 day (you open the account on Jan 1, Year 1 and the "5 year" period is met as of Jan 1, Year 5).

That's a little confusing, so as an example, if you open your Roth IRA on October 18th of 2016, then for the purposes of the 72t rule, your Roth has been open since January 1st of 2016. This means that your Roth IRA will meet the "5-year" requirement on January 1st of 2020 (an actual period of 3 years, 2 months and 15 days). You do not have to wait until October 18th of 2021 (a full 5-year period), as 2016 and 2020 both count as full years for the requirement even though the account was only active for 2.5 months in 2016 and 1 day in 2020. Hence, in this example, you could use the funds from your Roth IRA for Rule 72t as of January 1st of 2020.

Pretty cool right? The great thing about leveraging your IRA funds towards your first time home purchase is that the investments within the IRA generally earn more (fingers crossed) than by simply leaving the funds in your bank account. This is a good example of an "optimal" allocation of funds since the return helps your money grow quicker. The obvious risk here is that investments like ETFs and anything related to bonds and stocks have inherent risk, so choose carefully whether or not you want to use your IRA and Rule 72t. If you're afraid your funds might lose value around the time you are about to take them out for your home purchase, it might be better just to keep the money in a savings account, a money market account (not guaranteed, but very low risk), or a Certificate of Deposit (CD) – all of which allow your money to grow in the interim period.

There are some other fine nuances that are worth understanding and bankrate.com has a great article[93] pointing out these intricacies if you are thinking that leveraging Rule 72t is a viable pathway for you as you gear up towards your first time home purchase.

This is one of Uncle Sam's truly kind rules out there, so strongly consider leveraging it, as these rules are few and far between.

Giving Back: Charity and Tithing

If you ask me, humans have evolved to have the innate desire to give back to community and to others. Giving back can be found across countries, regions, nationalities, clans, tribes, and virtually all other social constructs. Individuals who aren't regularly giving often express the wish to give more than they currently do. Even individuals who are currently able to give express the desire to give more. Knowing this, there are two angles to talk about: the practical and the taxes. Both of which are pretty straightforward.

First, practically speaking, I am a fan of finding small, recurring opportunities to give to charity or via tithing (tithing is generally associated with giving in the religious context). This repeating smaller amount is nice because it makes it a little more amenable to the monthly budget. A lot of websites and charities are now setting up the ability for you to opt into recurring donations. They might bill these as memberships or subscriptions, so if you care about a particular cause, see if they have this option.

The other nice thing here, too, is you'll most likely get an automated receipt or giving summary for tax purposes. One thing to pay attention to is whether or not the donation processing platform charges either you or the organization you are donating to an administrative or similar fee. If the fee is small and reasonable, it might be a non-issue, but I've seen sites attempt to charge several dollars to process a donation and on smaller amounts like $5, $10, or $25 it might be a high enough fraction to be a deterrent. If you find yourself wanting to give "more" but things always seem a little too tight, then I'd suggest keeping your admirable goal of giving more. In the meantime, just start small with your giving goals and grow it over time as you're able. Alternatively, focus on giving more of your time and talents to your favorite organizations and incorporate monetary donations when you have more room in your budget. You'll feel better giving a little bit now compared to continually saying you'll give a larger donation later!

From a tax perspective, keep your receipts, as these can be used to lower your overall tax liability and thus save you money. There's nothing wrong with doing good *and* getting a break on taxes. However, be aware that if you aren't currently itemizing your deductions, you'll most likely take a standard deduction ($6,300 for individuals and $12,600 for married filing jointly in 2016) and logging your tax deductions from your charitable giving will be a moot point. This point is nice if you know you aren't going to itemize your deductions since it gets rid of the hassle of tracking, logging, and then filing your donations.

Either way, carve out a small line item that fits your budget and your lifestyle if you want to give more regularly. Even if you don't have the option to give automatically in a recurring fashion, you can still carve out a small portion from your general savings account. If you're saving $50 per month, why not save $60 a month and just contribute $10 per month towards your chosen cause or simply save up for a couple of months and mail a quarterly or semiannual check of $25 to $50? Whatever the frequency and amount, start small and work up from there.

Don't Let Love Break the Bank: Weddings, etc.

Engagements, bachelor/bachelorette parties, wedding showers, weddings, and honeymoons galore. The love and the excitement couldn't be more palpable during these special times and while everyone certainly wants to focus on the people and the events themselves, there is still an onus to focus on the financial aspect. Failing to do so can leave you spending way more in the heat of the moment than you either planned on or thought was reasonable. Personally, this section still hits my bank account hard every year. To give you an example, I had three out of town weddings within the same year. There's no chance I would miss them, but I needed to approach with caution as it relates to making preparations financially as you need to do for your wedding or for your friend's and family's weddings.

Texas wedding (flight + lodging + suit): $600
California wedding (flight + lodging): $550
Park City, Utah wedding (flight + lodging): $450
Total (at bare minimum): $1,600

Ouch. And I'm still single? Even if I started saving 6 months in advance, that means I would be tasked with socking away $267 per month! And there are more weddings to come...including my own at some point (fingers crossed).

This type of situation is perhaps extreme in the amount of geography that we're covering (3 trips in less than 8 months) and not all bachelor/bachelorette parties end up in cities outside of the groom or bride's local area, but it can happen. Being prepared is obviously more advantageous than not. Regardless of wedding destinations, pre-celebrations, and travel costs, weddings add up for the couple getting married, the various paranymphs,* as well as the guests.

The throngs of young love and the associated wedding costs generally hit us harder and more regularly when we are in our 20's and 30's since that's when the majority of Americans get married. By extension, this is usually the height of our wedding attendance and involvement. This wedding season of life is something we gladly partake in to celebrate with friends and family alike and it can last for several years in a row and even extend beyond a decade. Knowing it's a significant part of our young adulthood lives actually helps us respond more proactively and a lot of the central ideas here are going to parallel the traveling section – even more so if you actually have to travel a far distance to partake in the festivities.

At this point, if you have a savings account, an emergency savings account, and other savings accounts, you're probably pretty

---

* archaic word for the groomsmen and bridesmaids, I had to use it at least once in the book!

comfortable with the idea of separating savings accounts to help psychologically distinguish them according to their various purposes. However, if you think it's overkill to have this many savings accounts, I'd challenge you to see if you have 3 months' worth of income saved in an emergency account (remember, I'm here to be brutally honest). If you do, you get a free pass on creating another savings account, but chances are you don't. Perhaps it's time to set up just one more for weddings specifically. Plus, what is the drawback? Savings accounts are not only easy to open (virtually all can be done online), but they are almost always (and should be) free to open and maintain. So do it. For realz.

We'll look at weddings from two angles. You should, of course, adjust according to your own situation. The first angle is the wedding attendee angle. In this scenario, the process is easy. Look to the next year or two and ask yourself, "How many weddings am I either going to attend or be in?" If you aren't sure, but the past couple of years you've been to anywhere between 1 and 3 weddings, then perhaps settle on guessing that you'll be invited to two weddings. The next step is to simply figure out what your potential cost is going to be for each. Obviously it will be higher if you're in the wedding than if not, but additional costs such as travel, flights, lodging, and length of trip all should be added to the estimated total of the wedding.

Once this exercise is done, add it up and divide by the number of months remaining until the wedding (this is essentially the same process as the proactive traveling section so you've already got the knowledge and the skills to do this). Let's pretend you know you've got a wedding out of town and it's going to set you back $300. Another friend is getting married in the town next to where you live and all you need for that is a hotel for one night at $80. You've got $380 to save. The cheaper one is in 5 months and the other is in 8 months. If you want to have all your money saved up by the time the first one comes around (way to be proactive!), you need to save $76 per month. If you're looking to stretch it out over the full 8 months, then you only need to save about $48 per month. Pick one that works for you and roll with it, but don't get caught spinning your wheels trying to figure out how to pay for the intensities of wedding season with credit – that isn't good for you or your wallet.

Now, if you are about to enter the wedding pathway of your own or are currently in the middle of planning for your wedding, you've got a whole other set of questions and concerns to deal with. The first and biggest one is to manage expectations. In the heat of the moment, things can get pretty expensive. When you're about to buy a wedding ring, planning the wedding, or spinning the globe to decide where your ideal honeymoon should be, the last thing you want to do is start off a lifetime of partnership closer to the impoverished end of "for richer or for poorer." By no means whatsoever am I about to espouse a doctrine of frugality and bare bones wedding planning – it's your moment and your life. But I do think that having frank and honest discussions with yourself and with your partner can make a world of difference. It doesn't even have to be an awkward or uncomfortable conversation (if it is awkward, then perhaps some more intense conversations around money should be had first so you can get on the same page).

Looking at the major components that lead to "happily ever after" we've got the engagement, the wedding (and related events), and the honeymoon. I'd suggest throwing out maximum costs that you'd be willing to spend on each one of these to get the ball rolling. Is the ring $200, $2,000, or $20,000? Are you willing to drop $3,000, $10,000, or $50,000 on the wedding? Where is it at? How big will it be? Are you taking the honeymoon right after or in 6 months? These are the types of questions that should be asked in order to form expectations around individual costs as well as the overall costs of the wedding process, from engagement to honeymoon.

There is obviously an initial challenge around the engagement because our culture and tradition set it up as a "one-sided" decision whereby the ring purchaser usually buys it discretely and secretly without the other's knowledge. This is a momentous act and of course everyone wants it to be a lasting memory when coupled with the engagement. But when you're in that store about to buy a ring, just remember: there is almost certainly a ring that is bigger and better (no offense). There will be rings that are outrageously gorgeous in each of the 4 C's (cut, clarity, carat, and color) that certainly come with a higher price tag. If you go in with a preloaded maximum purchase price in mind, you'll be more likely able to resist the upsell and the "ring next door" that is just a wee bit more expensive. The way the shops are set up, they are specifically designed to get you to slowly, but surely "ladder up" whereby you look at a stunning $500 ring and then the ring next door that is $750. The jeweler proceeds to show you the $1,200 ring and then finally suggests the $1,500 rarity that is part of some special collection. Boom, you just tripled the price of the rings you're considering and even if you "pull back" from the $1,500 ring and decide on the $1,200 ring, you just bought a ring that was 240% more compared to the first ring all the way back at $500.

Now, in fairness, McDonald's does the same "upselling" that jewelry shops do, as does almost every other retailer out there – they are trying to make more money, of course. The point isn't to criticize the jewelers or the ring buying process. It's to help you be mindful and aware of the pitfalls – especially when the stakes are that much higher than supersizing your French fries.* The big temptation here is to buy into the message that the bigger the ring, the better. While bigger can bedazzle, it shouldn't make you go bankrupt.

Further, the overarching point isn't to dissect each and every one of these aspects in detail – that part is up to you. But what is important is looking at the larger arch and scope of the process. Just doing a quick calculation can leave even the most strong-willed Romeo and Juliet crumbling with anxiety over the total expected cost: $1,000 for the ring. $15,000 for the wedding, $3,000 for the honeymoon, and $2,000 in flex costs that you don't anticipate – $21,000 in total. Prices are going to vary significantly depending on more factors than are worth going into detail over, but weddings generally on the cheap end cost $5,000 and on the upper end can balloon to $100,000 or more.

---

* My Achilles heel.

If your heart and mind just crumbled a little bit at the thought of spending six figures on a wedding, then grab a sticky note and a pencil and jot down what you think each of the major areas will cost. Weddings are further unique in that both families usually chip in to help out the soon-to-be-couple with all types of costs, so estimating how much support you can count on is definitely challenging to ask about, but helpful in the planning stages. At the end of the day, estimate the total cost, then assign relative proportions of the responsibility to figure out how much you and your partner will be responsible for covering. Check out the example scenario below and feel free to sketch out your own scenario when the time is right:

Mickey Mouse & Minnie Mouse Wedding Estimates & Expected Costs

Item	Low Cost	Expected Cost	High Cost
Ring	$1,000	$1,250	$1,500
Bachelor/ Bachelorette Party	$800 ($400 each)	$1,000 ($500 each)	$1,200 ($600 each)
Wedding	$8,000	$12,000	$14,000
Honeymoon	$1,000	$2,000	$3,000
Subtotal	*$10,800*	*$16,250*	*$19,700*
Extra & Unexpected (make this 5-10% of the other items)	$1,080	$1,625	$1,970
Total	*$11,880*	*$17,875*	*$21,670*

Who's Chipping in?

Using the total of the expected costs above, for simplicity ($17,875)

Who?	Rough Percent (or dollar amount) chipping in
Parents	35% (~$6,256)
Family Friends/Other Relatives	10% (~$1,786)
Left Over For Couple to Cover	55% (~$9,831)

After this exercise, the soon-to-be-newlyweds know that they should expect to cover just shy of $10,000, so this can be their target amount when laying out a plan and a strategy for making it work. The crucial thing to realize as you're planning this with your significant other is that it might not be feasible to have 100% of this saved before the events themselves start taking place. It's a huge cost and it generally happens pretty quickly. If you meet someone and decide to get engaged one year later, you realistically have one year (plus or minus) from the engagement date until the wedding to save. This creates an unrealistic and burdensome savings goal of roughly $1,000 per month. For almost everyone, this isn't going to be possible.

So, given the enormity of the financial commitment that couples the couple in their lifelong commitment, what's the strategy? It's going to vary, certainly, but if you've got decent credit and a healthy amount to utilize, you might be able to pay for some of it on credit or you might be able to borrow from family or relatives. Another consideration, even though you might have to trim the guest list or the ultra-fresh, over-the-top flower arrangement down a little bit, is to simply reduce costs in various areas, as tough as this might seem at first – it's a sure-fire way to control the headache of starting off married life with residual wedding-related debt.

Another trick-o-the-trade is to open a new credit card and load it up with expenses so you can earn travel or bonus miles that you can use towards honeymoon costs to offset that expense. This isn't necessarily an ideal plan since you could lower your credit score by having too high a balance and/or your points might take too long to become available if you have the honeymoon soon after the wedding. This would then be defeatist, so only pursue this trick if your honeymoon is a ways out and you have very, very little or no credit card debt already.

In the example above, "The Mouses" still have to figure out how to pay for their dream celebration. They decide that they are going to do a mixture of paying for it up front and utilizing borrowing. They decide that they can cut costs by 25%, then pay for the remaining by saving 50% and using credit cards for 50% (obviously not highly recommended). They figure out with cost-cutting they'll only need $7,500, which leaves $3,750 to save and $3,750 to put on cards.

"I do" want to save with you!

The wedding is 10 months out (2 months have gone by since the engagement – they lost track of time since there were so many people to call and share the good news with!). The Mouses set up a joint wedding savings account and decide that they should each put in an equal amount each month. Since they need to save $375 per month, they'll each put in $187.50 and since they both get paid biweekly, they obviously set up an *automatic recurring* savings contribution of $94 that gets moved into their wedding savings account every other week. All of the sudden, that original $10,000 amount seems a little more manageable and conquerable. The soon-to-be-Mouses feel pretty good about the plan. While it's not perfect, it's going to get them moving in the right direction and working in tandem towards a mutual goal. This is especially empowering since they have really had separate finances up until this point and they experience the added benefit of being able to have more direct and open conversations about finances.

As they approach the wedding, they still have $3,750 in expenses that they don't have savings for, so they open a credit card, and pay for the remaining expenses with that card. They have the wedding (the cake was delicious, by the way) and take their honeymoon. Once back, they then switch from saving each month to an automatic payment on their credit card of $375 per month so it's paid off in 10 months. (The 0% APR is for 12 months, but they're used to allocating $375/month to savings, so they figure, why not keep going at this rate with the debt pay down?)

Winning Weddings

Attending and having weddings can cost an arm and a leg, but it doesn't have to destroy your progress financially, nor does it have to come at the expense of your other goals. It's realistic that you can tackle the finance portion with more intentionality rather than just freewheeling it whenever the wedding bells start clanging. These are high-priced items regardless of role and frequency so lock down a strategy that works for you. The wedding savings often overlap with travel savings, so think carefully about which expenses go in which bucket. Maybe wedding-related flights still get saved for in your wedding savings account. Or maybe no matter what, you want flight and travel costs to come out of your traveling savings account – it's totally up to you. But have consistency and think about it along the way. It's all about finding that un-average, rogue system that works for you so that you don't have to feel unprepared and stressed out when you should be enjoying and celebrating the precious wedding moments with your friends and family instead.

The Black Abyss of Life Insurance

Let's get something out in the open: talking about insurance is not fun. Insurances of all types have the feel of a dark, black abyss where your hard earned money disappears, but never returns. It is "important" but it's not always clear why. And to top it off, the language and the terminology is as opaque and confusing as trying to read Herodotus' *Histories* in the original Greek. Fortunately for you, I'm going to lay out some simple, clear rules to help guide you out of the black abyss and back into a place of clarity around insurance. Specifically, we are going to be talking about life insurance. At this juncture, we are not going to address health, car, renters, home, or any other type of insurance – we'll touch on those later. With the simple guidelines I am going to lay out, we will aim to primarily achieve a singular objective: have the appropriate level of life insurance. There is also a substantially important secondary goal that was touched on earlier: avoiding financial parasites that sell high cost insurance policies.

Even before considering what types of insurance are out there, let's ask a more primitive question about insurance: why do we need it in the first place? Additionally, do we need it at all? The answer to the latter question is clear cut: yes, you do need insurance. The former question about why we need it is quite simple to understand, even if a little morbid. You need life insurance so that if you die, those you care about (i.e., the beneficiaries) will receive the value of your life insurance policy which can help pay off any outstanding debts, funeral costs, and be used for their continued financial security. They will most likely use some of the proceeds to pay for funeral and burial expenses and the remaining amount will be used to offset the financial pain of losing you as a person. While it's unlikely that people die early, it does happen, and that is one of the primary reasons that life insurance exists. It helps to offset (or "hedge") against this unlikely and burdensome event. Knowing this, you'll want to play *Goldilocks and the Three Bears* with life insurance. Like Goldilocks trying out the porridge, you don't want it too hot (being over-insured, a.k.a. more life insurance than you need) nor do you want it too cold (being underinsured, a.k.a. having too little insurance). You want your insurance porridge "just right." For many people, that means getting a term life insurance policy.

As you stroll around looking for the perfect life insurance porridge, you'll need to know what's out there being sold by the "Life Insurance Bears." Let's look at a couple of basic types of life insurance. There are lots of options out there, but we'll focus on the ones that are most common.

Term Life Insurance ("just right," the best option for many people): insurance for a specified time range. It might be 5, 10, or 20 years. If you die during this period, your beneficiary(ies) will receive the policy value which might be $25,000, $100,000, or even $1,000,000. Term life insurance is relatively cheap and provides significant coverage.

Whole Life Insurance ("too hot," only good for a select few): insurance for your whole life, so long as premiums (monthly payments) are made. This is doubly touted as an investment, since your principal earns interest (albeit a low amount) and your funds will build a "cash value" meaning you can use them along the way for various reasons. It also grows tax free. The good thing here is that whole life insurance policy premiums generally remain constant over time. But there are two drawbacks, 1) very large administrative fees that you'll pay each month, *and* 2) the investment grows slowly compared to many other investing opportunities you have such as paying down debt or investing in things like your 401k, IRAs, etc.

Universal Life Insurance ("too hot," only good for a select few): insurance for your whole life, like whole life insurance. The main difference here is that universal life insurance premiums will fluctuate over time, as will the returns earned on your investment. Universal life insurance still has tax advantages and a cash value.

Variable Insurance ("too hot," only good for a select few): Anything with "variable" in it means that your premiums are generally going to be both invested in a low-earning insurance investment as well as a more aggressive investment component such as bonds or stocks. This is good for people who want higher yields, but still want insurance. They can't guarantee high rates of returns, but many will have a "floor" where you will make at least some percentage return. You'll see all kinds of names like variable whole life, variable universal life, etc.

Work Only Insurance ("too cold" or "just right," good start, but might not be enough): Insurance through your work isn't a distinct type of insurance; it's generally just term life insurance that happens to be provided by your work. Lots of times, this is a great start, but it can be quite minimal insurance. So research it and see if the policy is at a value that you feel comfortable with. Many will cover 1 to 2 times your salary level, meaning your policy value is tied to your salary. You might find it's good, but not quite enough to meet your insurance needs.

If you'd like to know more, Investopedia has a wealth of information on insurance policies, types, and definitions and the link is included in the endnotes.[94] In terms of having appropriate life insurance, follow this quick guide to see what type of life insurance is best for you:

Step 1: Are you single with no dependents (most likely children)? If no, proceed to step 2. If yes, then it is highly probable that the best insurance option for you is **term life insurance**. Many employers have basic term life insurance bundled into your benefits so check to see if your employer has insurance that is either paid for by them, or is paid for by you. You can check your paystub to see if you are paying for life insurance already, look for a line item for insurance that is a couple of dollars per month. This is pretty common and if you have it, you are probably covered in the "too cold" to "just right" amount, depending on your situation.

If you don't have insurance at work, then consider a very low cost term life insurance policy. They typically range from $15 – $80 and will change based on your age, gender, health, whether you smoke, and other factors. Nerdwallet has a great guide and tool on term life insurance (they call term life insurance "the most affordable way to buy life insurance" and I agree[95]).

Step 2: Are you are married and/or have kids? If you are not married or you do not have kids, go back to step 1 and strongly consider **term life insurance**. There are very few cases in which you need something other than term life insurance if you aren't married and don't have kids even though the insurance companies will try to show you why you need whole or universal life insurance.

Step 2a: If you are married (with or without kids), then ask yourself the following question: do I have debt? If you do, focus on paying off debt before getting a whole or universal life insurance policy. However, you should still consider **term life insurance** in the meantime to protect against an unlikely and untimely death (again, check to see if your employer is offering it first).

Step 2b: If you are married (with or without kids), then ask yourself the following question: am I maxing out my other investment options (such as a 401k, IRA, etc.) that might get better results than a life insurance policy? If you aren't maxing them out, then it almost certainly makes sense to first work towards maxing them out before getting into an expensive, low yield insurance policy. It still makes sense to get a low cost **term life insurance** policy if your employer doesn't already provide one.

Only two steps to consider? That wasn't as painful as you thought, was it? In summarizing life insurance, the easiest way to think about it is twofold. First, you need some type of life insurance and secondly, you most likely only need to get the basic term life insurance policy to be covered adequately. The people and companies out there are going to try to sell you the more lucrative policies (for them anyways!) such as whole, universal, and variable life insurance, but realistically, you should only be considering those once you are married (or have kids) *and* have paid off all of your debt *and* have maxed out other more advantageous investment options. I don't have a statistic, but my guess is that the percentage of people who should be considering a life insurance policy other than the basic term life insurance is quite low and that term life insurance will be adequate until you have a much stronger and complete financial picture. We'll leave it at that, eh?

Joe Holberg

12. Get Healthy with Health Care and Health Insurance

In discussing health care and health insurance, I've asked Matt Bauer, a budding force in the medical field, to write a guest chapter. Below is a wealth of information on the surprisingly interesting origins of insurance, a quick breakdown of health insurance (in a lucid and understandable manner!), and some ideas around health care more generally speaking so you can pair your increasing financial health with your physical health. Enjoy!

I'm afraid that if I begin with a historical overview of insurance, I'll bore you, but it's challenging to describe health insurance without a quick summary on the origins of the business of insurance as an institution. So I promise to be brief.

Several years ago, a man named Peter Bernstein wrote a book about taking risk. Honestly, I bought the book because I thought it might explain why the French and Swiss don flying wing suits to graze the surfaces of the Alps at speeds unimaginable to me. I was wrong; most of the book was about the origin of probability, the advent of insurance, gambling, and the economic quirk that is the stock market. No explanation of Darwin Award winners for me. Despite my initial disillusionment, I read on, and I'm glad I did.

Insurance companies are the natural extension of the early work on theories of probability. While the fundamental notion of insurance dates to pre-modern times, the concept of aggregated risk assumption seems to have formally started in London in the late 1680's with the *underwriting* of ships' passages to distant reaches of the globe. Captains seeking assurances that the cost of any damages accrued during their voyage would be covered sought out an individual insurer. This insurer would then distribute the policy to a larger crowd of similarly like-minded risk takers who were willing to accept a small premium in exchange for a promise to cover any potential damages, thereby spreading the risk among multiple people or parties. They sanctified their agreement with a written contract and their signatures at the bottom (underwriting).

Ships that fared well by avoiding pirates, voracious Sperm Whales, and Neptune's fury generated money for the insurers because there were no damages to cover. Ships that were aggressive towards lighthouses and rocky shoals rapidly discovered that "rock-beats-wood," and had a deleterious effect on the pocketbooks of their insurers.

From this humble beginning arose the creation of the insurance behemoths. No longer was risk assumed by a single individual, or even by a group of individuals. The arena of risk was given over almost entirely to corporations with substantial capital and the power to appropriately forecast, in order to insure an ever-growing population seeking protection against the unknown. And that's really what insurance is about – protecting yourself against the unknown.

During the time of the American Revolution, a few insurance companies began to make their debut in America. In 1752, Benjamin Franklin helped form a mutual insurance company called the Philadelphia Contributionship, primarily to help insure buildings against fires. It's still around today and offers many more types of insurance, but the underlying structure of insurance across the world remains virtually the same as it was in the early days of ship voyages.

Now, modern advances in insurance are mostly predicated upon basic tenets of capitalism and the free market, federal and state policies, the use of complex algorithms, and obtaining larger data sets. Every time someone wrecks their car, the person's age, sex, car model, income level, and location becomes data. When aggregated and analyzed, all of this data allows insurance companies to calculate the risk disparity between insuring an 18-year-old novice driver who is paying more attention to their friends in the passenger seat than the road ahead of them and the 40-year-old parent with kids to get to and from school. Can you guess which represents less risk?* Based on the risk, they come up with a price you have to pay to get insured. For example, the younger you are, the more accidents you've been in, or the more expensive your car, the more you'll pay every month for car insurance.

This all makes intuitive sense, so why is insurance so complicated? The answer is that it usually isn't if you're talking about car, home, or life insurance, but there is one exception – health insurance. This topic is no doubt confusing and opaque so let's dive in.

First, we have to understand who's who in health care. The main players in the health insurance market are:

1. You and/or your family, known as the "patient(s)"
2. The insurance company, often known as the "payor"
3. The hospitals, private practices, and groups of doctors who practice together. Each of these are known as the "provider."

Next, we have to look more closely at the *providers* themselves since there are many types of "Managed Care Organizations" (MCOs) that actually provide health services. Three of the most well-known are Health Management Organizations (HMOs), Preferred Provider Organizations (PPOs), and Exclusive Provider Organizations (EPOs). Each one is different, so look at the definitions below to get a sense of what each entails:

---

* Answer: The parents. Even though kids in the back seat can be pretty distracting too!

Health Management Organizations (HMOs)

You pick one primary care physician (PCP), such as a family doctor, with an HMO. Your health care first goes through that doctor and if you need to see another health care professional, you would need to get a referral. Access to providers outside of your network aren't normally covered by your insurance. While your premiums could be a little higher, total coverage is often more complete. Every time you visit your doctor, you will pay a small copay, but the insurance will pick up the rest of the tab.

Preferred Provider Organizations (PPOs)

PPOs have become very popular, and you'll likely recognize some of the associated phrases quite easily. It's simple: the insurer makes deals with a list of providers. The way the payment structure works is that if you go to a doctor in the PPO network, the insurer will usually pay 80% of the bill and you'll pay 20%. If you go out of network, your percentage typically increases to something close to 40% of the bill. One of the aspects of PPOs that some people like is that your ability to see a specialist is not typically limited by having to go through your PCP. While this is a great feature, you should still consider seeing your PCP first so they can help you coordinate your care, follow up on test results, and follow your progress and health over a long period of time.

Exclusive Provider Organizations (EPOs)

Exclusive Provider Organization plans (EPO) are similar to PPOs in that you don't need a PCP to coordinate your care, but you're typically not allowed to see anyone outside of the network.

These types of MCOs are only a sample of the options out there and there are others to choose from including Point of Service (POS) and Private Fee-For-Service (PFFS). They can get quite specific quickly so make sure you are reading up on the fine print and details before selecting a plan.

Before we get down to business, we need to define a few more terms so you'll know how to interpret all of your pedantically-written insurance documents that often feel like they are designed to be more confusing than enlightening and reassuring. These terms are simplified so that they are easily understood and you can quickly come back and reference these at any time, especially if you're working your way through reading over your health care options.

Subscriber: you, the person buying insurance, also known as the patient.

Dependents: your spouse and/or children.

Premium: the amount of money that you pay *every month* just to even *own* the insurance plan.

Co-pay: the amount you pay each time you go to see a doctor. It will differ depending on where you go. It may be $15 if you go to your primary care doctor appointment and it may be $50 if you go to the Emergency Room. Most insurance plans have copays, although some don't.

Deductible: the amount of money that *you* have to pay before your insurance even starts to kick in. For example, if you have a high deductible such as $5,000 and your total bill for visiting the doctor for the year was $3,000, you would still have $2,000 to go before your insurance pays for anything. If your deductible is low, say $1,000, once you pay for $1,000 worth of medical services, your insurance will pay for the rest.

Coinsurance: Instead of a fixed cost for seeing your primary doc or going to the emergency doctor (ED), you pay a fixed percentage of the overall fee. If the bill is $2,000 and the coinsurance you have to pay is 20%, you will pay $400 while your insurance company will pay $1,600.

Maximum out-of-pocket expense (MOOP): This is the maximum amount of money you would have to pay in one year before your insurance covers *all* of the cost of your care. It includes your deductible and the amount you have paid in co-pays and coinsurance during the year, but does not include your monthly premium. For health plans purchased through the Affordable Care Act (ACA) marketplace in 2017, the out-of-pocket limit is $7,150 for an individual and $14,300 for a family.

Here's what this means. Let's say your deductible is $1,500, your co-pay is $20 for every primary care visit, and your coinsurance is 20%. You've been to the doctor twice with a co-pay of $20 each time, totaling $40. Now your belly starts to hurt and you go to the Emergency Department. You find out that you need your appendix out, which of course you have done, and the total bill is $15,000. Okay, so you will pay *all* of your $1,500 deductible, which leaves $13,500 left. Your coinsurance is 20%, so you will pay $2,700 (20% of $13,500) on top of the deductible, while the insurance pays the rest. They will pay $10,800, which should come as a relief since you won't have to pay the full cost. When we add your copays ($40) + deductible ($1,500) + co-insurance ($2,700) we get $4,240 that you'll be responsible for covering. Since your MOOP is $7,150 (if you're single), then there is still $2,910 left before you reach the MOOP limit. That means that if you need a second surgery that costs $8,000, you'll pay $2,910, at which point insurance will cover the rest. If you need more care after that throughout the year, then insurance will cover you because you've reached your maximum out-of-pocket expense. Just remember that this total doesn't include your monthly premium. If your premium is $200/month *and* you spend enough to reach your MOOP, the most you will ever pay in one year is $9,550 ($2,400 in premiums + $7,150 MOOP). That's really quite a bit of money, but at least there is a max so at some point you will get the rest covered. Unfortunately, the amount you've paid towards your MOOP will reset to $0 every year as well.

Lifetime and yearly maximums: These used to exist in the old system. Be thankful they no longer do. In the old days, these limits were the maximum amount that your insurance would pay in a year and over your lifetime. Once you went beyond that, you paid *everything*. Ouch. There are no lifetime or yearly maximums anymore, fortunately.

While these definitions can be muddled and confusing, health care is broken down in a pretty clear way if you're dealing with Obamacare and state plans.

Check out the table below. This is taken directly from the ACA website – healthcare.gov, which categorizes plans according to "metal" type:[96]

Metal Type	Premium	Cost of Care	Deductible	Good Choice if:
Bronze	Lowest	Highest	Can be thousands of dollars per year	You want a low-cost way to protect yourself from worst-case medical scenarios, like serious sickness or injury. Your monthly premium will be low, but you'll have to pay for most routine care yourself.
Silver	Moderate	Moderate	Usually lower than those of Bronze plans	You're willing to pay a slightly higher monthly premium than Bronze to have more of your routine care covered or if you qualify for "extra savings."*

---

* For those within the income ranges, you may qualify for extra savings, but you must pick a Silver plan. To see if you qualify, check here: https://www.healthcare.gov/lower-costs/save-on-out-of-pocket-costs/

Gold	High	Low	Usually low	You're willing to pay more each month to have more costs covered when you get medical treatment. If you use a lot of care, a Gold plan could be a good value.
Platinum	Highest	Lowest	Very low	You usually use a lot of care and are willing to pay a high monthly premium, knowing nearly all other costs will be covered.
Catastrophic †	Very low	Very high	Very high	You want an affordable way to protect yourself from worst-case scenarios, like getting seriously sick or injured. You pay most routine medical expenses yourself.

5 Simple Steps to Picking a Health Care Plan

Phew, finally after all that information, we're ready to get down to the business of actually selecting a health insurance plan. Here are some helpful tips on how to choose the right insurance. Remember, these are just tips and you will have to account for your individual circumstances in order to pick the one that is right for you:

1. If you're younger than 26 years old, you should consider staying on your parent's plan, provided that they have "good" coverage and can afford it. If their insurance doesn't

---

† You must qualify for Catastrophic plans and they are generally only available to those under 30 and with a hardship exemption. You can learn more here: https://www.healthcare.gov/choose-a-plan/plans-categories/#catastrophic

cover the medications you need, or if you aren't covered as fully because you live away from home, then you will need to consider another option.

2. If you're too old to stay on your parent's plan and/or that plan won't work for you, the next question to ask is whether or not you are employed. If you are employed by a company, firm, school system, etc., or you are a graduate or professional student, you need to get a list of all the insurance options that they offer so that you can compare them. If you are self-employed or don't have health care at work, then you will need to buy insurance through either the Obamacare health exchange marketplace during the enrollment period, or you'll need to buy insurance on the open/private market (this latter option is typically not a great idea as it's typically quite expensive).

3. If it's between November 1st and January 31st, then you are in the open enrollment period during which you can sign up for "Obamacare." What this means is that you can go to www.healthcare.gov and buy insurance. You will have to input quite a bit of information, including your social security number, mailing address, income level, whether you're married or single, and information about your current insurance if you have it, among other data points. When this is complete, you will get a list of plans that are rated on the following scale: Platinum, Gold, Silver, Bronze, and Catastrophic. If you just want to check out the exchange without divulging your darkest secrets, go to https://www.healthcare.gov/see-plans/.

4. If you are not in the enrollment period, you may still be able to enroll in a private health care through the Marketplace if you qualify for a "Special Enrollment Period." You could qualify if you recently lost your job, had a baby, or got married.[97]

5. Next in terms of picking a plan itself (employer's, Obamacare, or other) you might see various options. They'll have different combinations of deductibles, premiums, etc. The next step is to determine how much healthcare you really need. If you are healthy and don't visit the doctor very often, consider choosing a high deductible, lower premium plan as exemplified in the table above. This plan will still include things like birth control and your yearly physical. If you have one or more medical conditions, see specialists, and/or take several medications, then your level of health care usage is generally higher. You will most likely be better off choosing a higher premium and lower deductible plan if you suspect you'll hit your deductible relatively quickly from all the doctor visits and prescription medications. If you have a chronic condition requiring lots of care, it makes much more sense for you to choose a high premium, low deductible plan. If your company has plans that include Health Savings Accounts and Flexible Savings Accounts, then you can utilize an HSA or FSA paired with a high deductible plan and start saving tons of money for health-related expenses (HSAs and FSAs are covered in the Work Benefits Work chapter, in more detail).

One additional life event to pay attention to is what happens to your health coverage when you change jobs, which many young people do frequently early in their careers. Insurance provided by your previous employer will only cover you for a certain amount of time after you leave if they participate in COBRA (usually up to 18 months after departure). Even COBRA will eventually no longer cover you once you leave, so you have to be careful when switching jobs and make sure to fully evaluate how you'll maintain your health coverage. With COBRA, all of a sudden you now have to pay not only your part, but also the part that was contributed by your previous employer. Sound expensive? Yep, it is.[98]

When looking for a plan that works for you, you should find a plan that offers a wide array of preventive care so that you can reduce your risk of getting diabetes or heart disease in the future. Fortunately, Obamacare has helped us out here by mandating that all insurance companies pay for a basic set of preventive care services. Once you sign up for your healthcare, you should take advantage of these preventative services to boost your health, which can ultimately keep your medical expenses lower. Some of these preventative services that are relevant to millennials and young people (that are easy to forget about or skip entirely!):

- HIV, Hepatitis, and Sexually Transmitted Disease screening
- Blood pressure screening
- Immunizations (Including the HPV vaccine* and Flu shot!)
- General check-ups

Additionally, there are those that are specific to women:

- Anemia screening
- Contraception (Birth control pills and implantable devices such as IUDs)
- Prenatal care screening and vitamins
- PAP smears (cervical cancer screening – see HPV vaccine above and below)
- Well-woman visits (general checkup by your doctor)
- Breast cancer screening (for women over age 40 or for younger women with a family history of early breast cancers – this includes BRCA testing and mammograms)

Special Circumstances Related to Health Care

* HPV stands for human papilloma virus. In men it can cause genital warts. In women it can cause warts and cervical cancer. This is one of the few vaccines ever created (the other one being Hepatitis B) that can PREVENT cancer. It is made for men and women aged 26 years or younger. If you're 26 or younger, you should seriously consider getting it. Learn more here: https://www.cdc.gov/std/hpv/stdfact-hpv.htm

There are several circumstances where you may qualify for alternative types of insurance coverage. Many are state or federal plans. These include Medicare, Medicaid, CHIP, the VA, and TRICARE. Medicare is for the elderly and permanently disabled people. Medicaid is like Medicare for very low-income individuals with payment coming from both state and federal funds. The Veterans Health Administration (VA) has plans for veterans while TRICARE is for active duty military. We're not going to go into details about these programs – not because they're unimportant, but because if you think you qualify for any of these, you should seek out the programs themselves as they have many more details that are great resources to tap into now that you're aware of them.

Health Care Closing

The healthcare marketplace can be a fire-breathing and outlandishly complex beast with numerous heads swirling about, but you can protect your own health and interests by knowing something about how the system works. Just remember, the point of health insurance is to protect you from physical and fiscal ruin if something truly horrendous happens to you or a family member. From there, it's about assessing the devil in the details. In general, if you don't see the doctor often, try to get a high deductible, low premium plan paired with a HSA. If you're on the other end of this health spectrum, spring for a more comprehensive plan with a higher premium and lower deductible. You can't predict what will happen with your health so it is essential to have some type of health insurance in your life. Consider health insurance your emergency savings plan for your life. Beyond this, try to stay proactive and healthy – eat well, exercise, sleep, go on vacation, try to reduce your stress, surround yourself with loving family and friends, get your teeth cleaned every six months, and sit up straight while at your desk or while using the computer!*

---

* No seriously, ergonomics research has estimated that there were 16 million health care visits for neck, hand, and wrist pain in just one year. https://www.nap.edu/download/10032

13. Other Essential Insurances To Protect Yourself

It was a Friday afternoon and I was coming home from work. My phone rang and one of my roommates sounded shaken. "Are you almost home?" I said, "Yeah, five minutes." He hung up. Other than by the tone of his voice, this was a pretty typical phone call. I showed up five minutes later to a busted open door. Once inside it was clear that my roommate was upset because we had been burglarized. There were four of us living together and we were all teaching at the time. We had all kinds of laptops, cameras, watches, iPads, and money laying around. Well, we *used to have* all that stuff laying around. We watched the security footage from the building with the cops once they arrived: within 12 minutes, the two burglars were in and out with what I estimated to be $10,000 worth of stuff.

We didn't have renters' insurance.

That meant that we had to replace our stuff with our own funds. I had just gotten back from a trip and had beautiful photos from halfway around the world on my computer that I was so excited about sharing with my friends and family – gone. While there was definitely an emotional loss from losing the photos and sense of security, there was a very real financial loss too. I had to go out the next day and buy a computer since it was also the one I worked on. My roommates had to replace all kinds of stuff, and boy did we take a big hit financially that summer.

Renters insurance generally costs $10 – $15 per month.

In retrospect, I have to laugh at myself for neglecting to do something as easy as getting renters insurance.

So how do you learn from my mistake and make sure that you have the essential insurances to protect yourself and your stuff? You see if you're properly covered by looking at the short list of *mandatory* insurances for your life:

1. Health Insurance – Don't go without it. Even if you think you don't need it. You do. And now you'll pay a penalty for not having it, so you might as well get it. It's covered in the preceding chapter.

2. Life Insurance – Most people have this provided through work. If you don't, consider a *term life insurance policy* before any other types as this is the least expensive and still can have a policy value that is large enough. Make sure you read up on the chapter about watching out for bias and being over-insured so you don't end up with a costly plan that isn't the best option.

3. Disability Insurance – Again, most people have this provided through work. It comes in short term and long term flavors. Short term is usually sufficient for low risk jobs and those that aren't physically demanding. Long term disability insurance is more appropriate for those whose livelihood is closely tied to their physical ability to do their jobs, such as dentists, medical professionals, and construction workers.

4. Automobile Insurance – It's legally mandated so that's a good enough reason to have it. I believe we are on the precipice of an insurance revolution (generally speaking) with larger and more insightful data sets. One way this will first show up (specifically speaking) is in the auto insurance industry. Pricing is going to become customized and highly individualized which will be a great boon for consumers in that your risk-adjusted premiums could go down

significantly if you have a good driving history. Look for companies that will start to spring up in the next five years that offer individualized pricing. Right now, Metromile. com is leading the charge (although only offered in certain markets, they will continue to grow). I pay substantially less than I used to for auto insurance, in part because I don't drive a ton. Regardless, get auto insurance and realize that your premiums will go down if your car is older, you are older, and you don't drive a lot. If your car insurance company has an option to get a data transmitter so they can track your driving, I'd encourage you to get it since they will usually offer you a discounted rate in exchange. Just make sure you are on your best driving behavior if you have one of these since poor driving can increase your rates!

5. Renters/Homeowners Insurance – You are mandated to have home-owner's insurance in most cases and it's a good thing to have anyways. As you saw from my example above, whether you rent or own you need insurance to protect against natural disasters, fire, burglars, etc.

Pro Tip: Many companies will bundle or combine your various insurance policies and give you discounts for doing so. Ask about these options and see if they can combine several together for you. Also ask them for discounts associated with things you might be a part of like AAA, your university, professional organization, or anything else. I'll often just ask them what all of their discount options are to get the full list before telling them what I am a part of to make sure that I'm catching all the discount opportunities.

Insurances are essential even if you don't think they are. They protect you against "long-tail" and "black swan" events. These events are statistically very unlikely to happen, but they are extremely costly when they do happen, heaven forbid. Fires, burglaries, car accidents, Dean Winters (a.k.a. the Allstate "Mayhem" guy[99]) pretending to be a deer or giant pile of snow on your roof... Whatever it is or when it happens, you'll be glad you had coverage so go get it and be protected adequately.

Joe Holberg

14. Credit Cryptology 101

If you haven't ever seen *Last Week Tonight* with John Oliver, I think it's fair to say you're missing out on living life to the fullest. He's uproariously hilarious with cantankerous monologues on stymying topics that range from the criminal justice system and the Olympics to Canadian elections and credit reports. One episode in particular lambasted the credit score and reporting industry for being unfair, opaque, and riddled with erroneousness that makes a kindergartener's spelling look picture perfect (up to 25% of reports have errors, by some estimates[100]). In particular he said that "credit scores are the basis for the most important three-digit number in your entire life"* and that might in fact be understating how truly important both your credit reports and credit scores are.

Alas, the credit scoring and reporting system can feel more like a cryptographic nightmare of your financial life than the asset it can truly be if understood, monitored, and nurtured. In order to move credit and its inner workings from being a scary sealed secret to intelligible information, we will explore several key facets surrounding credit including why you should protect it like a pearl, what it is, how it is calculated, and where you can get access to it so that you aren't perplexed by credit. After the next section, you'll have the credit cipher which will allow you to start to own your credit score, rather than having it own you.

---

* Well worth the 20 minutes: https://www.youtube.com/watch?v=aRrDsbUdY_k

Protecting your Credit Pearl

Your credit score is worth a whopping $250,000 over the course of your lifetime, according to the Annie E. Casey Foundation.[101] A quarter of a million dollars. 25,000 ten dollar bills – enough to fill a couple of briefcases for sure. This dough stays in your (obscenely gigantic) pocket *if* you have a good credit score compared to a poor score. If you have a bad score, that cash goes into someone else's pocket. So yeah, your credit score is important and valuable like a rare pearl and it's still only three digits long since scores typically range from 300 to 850. The $250,000 number comes from the average amount of interest and fees saved by consumers with good scores over the course of their lifetime. Essentially, when companies are about to lend you money (such as banks, auto lenders, credit card companies), they will first look at your "creditworthiness." and one of the major factors determining this creditworthiness is your credit score. If you have a good (700-749) or great (750+) score, you'll get better deals which ultimately means lower interest rates. If you have a mediocre (650-699) or poor (< 650) score, you'll get worse deals which ultimately means the converse: higher interest rates, higher fees, stricter terms, less leniency, etc. This all means that it costs you more over your lifetime, and sometimes hundreds of thousands of dollars more. Turns out your credit pearl is something worth knowing more about!

Credit Scores and Reports

Your credit score is just a number that is computed based on the underlying information that makes up the credit report itself. All of the data in your credit report is hard to analyze and synthesize just by glancing over it, so the Fair Isaac Corporation (FICO) created a highly guarded and prized algorithm that computes your credit score so it is easier for lenders to understand what type of borrower you are. (Whether or not it's actually accurate is certainly arguable, but this is one of the areas where it's worth playing by the rules). You can (and should) check your credit report multiple times each year and you are legally allowed to do so via the only federally sponsored website out there: annualcreditreport.com. Just note that you are entitled to one credit report from each of the three major credit bureaus (Transunion, Equifax, and Experian) per year so use them wisely. You are not entitled to your score for free via annualcreditreport.com, but fortunately you can now find it via www.creditkarma.com which is the only credit score related website that I will recommend even though there are others out there. Credit Karma is awesome because they get you up to date scores and tons of educational information. Using it won't affect your score, and they will never ask you for your credit card or billing information like other scammy websites. (Credit Karma makes money by servicing ads on the site just like Google and Facebook, so just be aware when clicking on ads on the site). Once you get your score, you should know which category you fall into and its associated implication.

Credit Scores and Their Categories

Category	Score	Implication
Excellent	750+	At or near 100% approval, best offers, lowest rates
Good	700-749	High approval rate, top offers, low to lowest rates
Mediocre	650-699	Approval or denial likely, excluded from best offers, face higher rates
Poor	< 650	Denied frequently, few offers with highest interest rates possible

While your score isn't static, it can be hard to control and to move in the positive upward direction. In order to start building your score, you have to know what factors influence your score so you can start to consciously control each one of them to the degree that you are able.

Looking at your credit report itself can be quite daunting, but your score is more comprehensible as it is distilled and computed based on five factors, each with a different weight. Knowing exactly how the score is computed is impossible for everyone but FICO,[102] but you can still start to figure out what's most important to pay attention to and how each component may impact your score for better or for worse. Once you get a sense of the factors, you can pay closer attention to ensure your actions are in line with building and protecting your credit report and score itself so that you can move up over time to the most favorable position of having a score of 750+.

Payment History (35% of your score's weight): making all of your payments on time is crucial and is the single largest factor contributing to your score. Missing just one payment can drop your score significantly (as much as 50 – 100 points!) and it can take many months to rebuild your score. Don't miss payments and always make at least minimum payments. If you can set up automatic payments, do it! Anything less than 100% repayment history can be a red flag to lenders.

Amounts Owed (30%): Just because you have debt, doesn't mean you're going to have a low score. To have this component work favorably towards your score, aim to have each of your revolving account (such as credit cards and retail cards) balances at or below a 30% "utilization rate." Your utilization rate is the amount owed divided by your credit limit on debts. For example, if you have a $5,000 credit limit, you should aim to have your balance at or below 30% of $5,000, which is $1,500 (preferably $0. Am I right or am I right?!). Even though you have the ability to spend up to the credit limit of your $5,000 "credit pie," try not to fall into this trap as it will lower your overall credit score. Further, you might have a mortgage, car loan, student loans, or other debt. Use a small slice of your credit pie.

Other non-revolving debts will count towards your score, but you will be scored on the amount and not on the utilization rate since non-revolving accounts don't technically have a utilization rate in the first place. Just because you owe "a lot" on your mortgage, for example, doesn't imply that your score will go down, per se. In fact, per this dimension, it's really hard to say with any level of certainty how it will impact your score. The key here is to consistently work on paying debt down overall at a pace that works for you.

Length of Credit History (15%): The older each one of your lines of credit is, the better. Having a long credit history is tough at the outset, but you'll get there. This simply takes time and there is a tradeoff between opening new accounts (which will build your overall available credit, which is good) and lowering your average age of credit history (which can be bad). However, it can be argued that having a larger "credit pie" is more advantageous than the length of credit history since the Amounts Owed component is worth 30%.

Either way, in the long run if you keep old accounts open and sparingly apply for new lines of credit and debt, this will become a minor issue. I get the question all the time, "Should I close my account?" and the answer is emphatically "NO!" You should keep accounts open so long as there's nothing fraudulent happening and you aren't misusing them. Pay off a balance and toss the card in a sock drawer, but don't close it. Ironically, closing it can hurt your score since your "credit pie" length of credit history will go down by closing more mature cards. Every once in a while, credit cards companies will close your account because of inactivity, so if you want to ensure that they don't close them because they've been in the sock drawer for too long, take it out and make a small purchase. Then pay it off right away to keep the account active. It's hard to tell what each company's policy is around this so you can call and ask if you're inclined. I have heard of cards being closed after a year without activity and I still have cards that are open that haven't been used in five or more years...

Credit Mix (10%): By having different "types" of credit, you are demonstrating that you have the ability to manage an array of credit. Just having credit cards, for example, doesn't allow lenders as much insight into you as a borrower compared to having a diverse set of debt. Now, you shouldn't go get a mix of debt just for the sake of building your score, but it does help to have various types such as retail cards, credit cards, auto or installment loans, student loans, and mortgages. If you are looking to diversify your mix a little bit, one of the easiest ways to do so is by getting a retail card from somewhere you shop at (such as Target, Best Buy, etc.). However, I would strongly encourage you to get a retail card from somewhere you actually do *not* shop at often so that you can self-mitigate by virtue of not being a frequent customer at said retail location. If you get a retail card from somewhere you shop at regularly, you are more apt to spend even more which is not going to help you out in the long run. (Recall bonus: how much more do people spend with credit cards compared to cash?*)

New Credit (10%): New credit can be good, but too much new credit is bad. When you apply for credit, the lender will conduct what is called a "hard inquiry" which will show up in your report. Having three or more hard inquiries can damage your score so be careful when applying for credit. Fortunately, hard inquiries will be removed from your credit report two years after it first showed up so you will be able to continue to open new lines of credit if you so choose without being too severely penalized. Often utility companies, cell phone companies, and cable companies will ask to check your credit before starting service with you, so if you're ever unclear whether or not it is a hard or soft inquiry (soft inquiries don't show up on your credit report), just ask. They can only check your credit with your permission so you can always decline. You should be aware of how many hard inquiries are on your credit report, but with a relatively low weight, this factor is not likely to cause a major dip in your score and it will rebound quickly if your other categories are tended to.

These categories are the proportional weights that determine your score and minding them is a first step towards actively controlling your credit score. With the average credit score in the United States

---

*   Research shows that people spend 12-18% more when using plastic compared to traditional paper tender.

being 692, it is an uphill battle for many to improve their score, but it can be done. This will ensure that you are in the best position possible financially . Gaining access to the best and lowest cost options out there will ultimately make up that $250,000 difference over the course of your life. The way I like to think of your credit report and score is that it is essentially a financial resume that you have to give to lenders when attempting to borrow. And just like applying for a job, you want to put your best foot forward and have a clean, crisp, and strong resume to show. Like a resume, it takes time and work to craft one that gives lenders a good sense of who you are and it can make all the difference when applying for and using debt and credit.

Counterintuitive Credit

If you're confused by the complexity of the credit score and the amount of ambiguity surrounding it, you're not the only one. However difficult this beast is to understand, there are some tips and tricks that will make taming your credit score a little easier and more manageable. With all of the information and misinformation out there regarding credit, these tips may actually come off as counterintuitive, but they can help you adapt and play the credit score game with dexterity that ultimately gets positive results.

- Actively and frequently monitor both your credit reports and scores. As mentioned, my top recommendations are to use creditkarma.com and annualcreditreport.com.
- At minimum, roughly 25% of credit reports have errors so be on the lookout and use Credit Karma's automatic dispute feature to resolve any errors on Transunion and Equifax reports via Credit Karma,[103] but be aware that you will need to check your Experian via annualcreditreport. com to make sure it is accurate. At any time, you can use the FTC's guide to disputing errors on any report.[104]
- If you miss a payment, call your lender and kindly ask if they can remove the derogatory mark from their files, which in turn may show up on your credit report as paid

instead of late. Many companies, like Discover, are starting to offer this.

- If you only have one line of credit, consider opening another line so that you have less of a "thin file" which can bolster your score. The common misconception is that more lines of credit will hurt you, when in fact having a more robust amount and mix can actually help your score. Just don't apply for them all at once and mind your hard inquiry level.

- Call your credit card companies and ask for a credit line increase. I do this once every 6 months and they usually consent. This helps build your available credit "pie" which helps to keep your credit utilization lower. Just remember that having more "pie" doesn't mean you should use more of it. Continue to work towards paying off all your revolving lines of credit each month even while your credit "pie" is growing.

- Be aware of the fact that just because you pay off your credit cards in full each month doesn't always mean your score won't be negatively impacted. If you use a high proportion (30%+) of your available credit on any given card, you still might be dinged because FICO can recalculate your score at any time. As such, always try to keep your current balance below 30% so your utilization rate looks the best.

- Conduct "rate shopping" cautiously. When applying for larger ticket loans like car loans and mortgages, you'll want to find the best rate out there by "rate shopping" (a.k.a. getting quotes from various lenders), but you'll have to cautiously consider the potential negative side effects of too many hard inquiries. Many of the credit scoring models will take into account "rate shopping" to encourage people to find the best offers out there, but stick to applying for the same type of loan (such as a looking for a mortgage now and waiting to apply for a car loan until later). When you do, bunch your quotes and applications into a narrow window of time, generally within 14 days, since many of the credit scores won't ding you as hard for shopping around. It's not perfect, but it's better than sporadically applying over a longer period of time or not "rate shopping" at all.

With these tips and tricks up your sleeve, you can play the credit game with more cunning ability that will hopefully help edge your score up over time. No matter how many of these tips and tricks you utilize, the best and surefire way to build and maintain the best credit score is to make sure you keep your debt levels low, especially on revolving lines of credit, and that you consistently make 100% of your payments 100% of the time. In reality, it can take years to build a solid credit score so if yours doesn't jump overnight, keep at it. The scoring models are more or less designed to be "sticky" so that it is tougher to make large swings in either direction. In building your score, we have to heed Yoda's sage advice, "Patience you must have, my young Padawan."

In closing, we have to acknowledge that having so much ride on a single score sort of sucks, but it's part of a gigantic system and it's not likely to change anytime soon. So the best we can do in this scenario is to suck it up and play the game. Knowing that it is a bigger "machine" should make you that much more proactive in safeguarding your score, not less so. Don't be one of the nearly 60% of Americans who don't know their credit score.[105] Dealing with your credit is one of the easier financial topics to act on and monitor. Your score might not be where you want it to be, but at least you only need 5 – 10 minutes to actually *do* something about it to take control immediately.

Seriously though, put this book down and go get your credit score and report right now if you haven't already. I'm watching you…

Joe Holberg

15. Work Benefits Work

The work benefits world is changing as highlighted in movies, TV shows, and pop culture. What counts as a "benefit?" Coffee machines, kitchens filled with snacks and Le Croix flavored water, flexible work locations and hours, day care for kids, gym memberships, health care, retirement matches, and pretty much anything that your employer offers you on top of your normal monetary compensation. Benefits are popping up as additional workplace perks all across the country and the globe as employers seek to attract the best talent, keep employees motivated, happy, and feeling like they are adequately compensated for their long hours and work product. If you've seen *The Internship, Silicon Valley,* or *The Social Network* you've seen these benefits (a.k.a. perks) portrayed as companies try out a completely new way of compensating employees for their labor. This monumental shift might not have resulted in a massage chair in your office quite yet, but the role of benefits as an additional component of compensating you has been taking an increasingly prominent role in the 21st Century.

Ultimately, work benefits work to your benefit (tongue twister!), but only if you work to take advantage of them. They can be quite valuable and sadly enough, tons of employees either don't know about all the work benefits available or they don't completely understand them or take advantage of them properly. Nationally, employers spend billions upon billions of dollars on benefits for employees and other than your monetary compensation at work, these represent one of the largest opportunities to significantly extract more overall value as well as decrease costs in your life, especially if you have a more generous employer that has many perks available. In this chapter, we'll cover some of the most common work benefits out there so you can head into work ready to capitalize on all that's offered to you as an employee.

Ironically, you actually have to work harder initially to get the most out of your work benefits. Ugh, I know, no one wants to work harder. But at least in the short run you are going to have to do more research, reading, learning, and perhaps even inquiring to an HR person in order to take advantage of your work benefits. In the long run though, most people find that this upfront work is well worth it. If you have to spend 5 hours reading up on the educational benefits your company offers, for example, but learn from your investigation that they'll cover 75% of the cost of grad school and you end up leveraging that for a $30,000 degree, you will walk away immensely better off – $22,500 better off to be precise. Or if you read up on a cell phone reimbursement program that compensates you each month for work-related phone use, you might net several hundred dollars each year in reimbursements and thus drive down your personal monthly expenses #savvy #winning. The whole research part is definitely annoying and tedious, but the silver lining is that you only have to spend a lot of time upfront learning about your benefits once. From then on, it's just a matter of utilizing them at the appropriate time.

The Dangerous Default (Reprise)

I mentioned earlier in the book that simply accepting the default retirement set up at work is a plan for disaster. This is doubly true for the rest of your benefits. Most people just get overwhelmed during the hiring and orientation process and this is almost always when your benefits and perks are discussed. It's easy to miss them in the heat of the moment. But don't just simply sign up for stuff you don't understand and don't ignore it entirely – be proactive and on guard. With the paperwork and presentation panoply, I don't blame you for letting things move to the back burner, but the benefits are worth inspecting in closer detail. Ultimately they are designed for you anyway so why throw away a great opportunity that could amount to thousands of dollars each year?

As you read about each of the benefits below, keep in mind that you may not have access to said benefit. If you don't, there's no need to mope around in sadness. Instead, become an advocate. Tell your boss, HR peeps, or CEO that you're interested in a certain type of benefit. It might seem awkward at first, but the worst that can happen is they say "no." However, just think how cool it would be to ask for something like public transportation reimbursement and have it become a real thing that saves you and everyone at work $50 – $100 per month. Be gentle and inquisitive when asking for additional benefits and not demanding. As they say: you catch more flies with honey than with vinegar.

Retirement Accounts

Even though this was covered in detail earlier, it is well worth repeating: if you get any type of match for putting funds into your retirement account, then do it. There is virtually no equivalent out there in life that is this beneficial. It's as close to free money as almost anyone will ever come, so do it! However, if you don't get a match, be a little more cautious and consider an IRA instead, especially if you don't have a lot of retirement investment choices or the fund managers charge a lot for administration or for the investments themselves. Don't underestimate the value of this over the long run.

Want a mind-blowing example? Imagine your company offers you a 100% match (for every dollar you put in, they put in a dollar) up to 6% of your salary and you make $50,000 a year. Well if you just accept the 3% retirement default (quite a common default amount) you'll wind up with a cool $1.2 million by the time you retire. Not bad, right?! Now imagine you proactively upped your contribution to 6% so you could get the maximum match from your company. You just set yourself up to retire with ~$1.3 million more, for a grand spanking gigantic total of $2.5 million.* Now who's feeling sweet sipping Mai Tias on the beach? Get the match. See ya.

---

* Assumes you saved from age 22 to 67 and that your rate of return was 8% and compounded annually. For simplicity, it does not take into account taxes.

Health Care and Health Savings Accounts

Our healthcare system is jacked up. It's undeniably opaque, confusing, and disadvantageous to consumers. Navigating all things related to health care and health insurance is akin to needing to cross the Amazon River whilst knowing that there are famished piranhas lurking just below the surface, a 15-foot anaconda slithering on the opposing shore, and a jaguar running up on you from behind. There's nowhere to go, but you've got to wade in anyways. Good luck. This is one of the more treacherous areas financially. According to a Harvard University study conducted by Elizabeth Warren, medical expenses were at the heart of 62% of all bankruptcy cases.[106] While bankruptcy might not be a current concern, the simpler and more routine medical expenditures like getting a checkup, paying for basic medical care, health care insurance, and prescriptions can still add up to significant amounts of dollars and elevated headaches and stress (ironic as the latter two effects may be).

The panacea for this? Focus on the solutions, not the problems. The first thing to note is that, as of publishing this book, every American is technically mandated to have health coverage in some form. Regardless of your views on health care writ large, you still need health insurance for yourself and for the sake of your own health (even if you're perfectly healthy, immune to everything, and invincible, like I am) as well as for any spouses or dependents. It's non-negotiable that you have health care for your own self-preservation. We'll leave the policy and political discussion for another time. Further, as this is in the context of the benefits section, we'll look at what's available to you at work specifically.

Most employers will offer several health insurance options and to keep it mostly topical, suffice it to note that plans are either a high deductible health plan (HDHP) or not. HDHPs have lower monthly premiums, but high deductibles. Thus, these are generally favored by healthier people with the expectation that they will have relatively low costs as they relate to medical expenses throughout a given year. They are also easier to justify for single folks or younger married couples without kids since children's health care costs can vary widely.

Deciding on an HDHP versus a non-HDHP can be quite difficult and the decision also inherently relies on you making assumptions about future variables that are unknown. While not perfect, a quick way to help decide what's best for you is to simply look back at the previous year's medical expenses to see how much health care you actually used. If you spent way more than you realized, it might be time to go with the high premium, low deductible account. On the other hand, if you opted for the high premium care and only got an annual checkup, it might be time to switch to the HDHP. Amidst the plan choices, terminology, and the general sucky-ness of dealing with health insurance providers, one thing is clear and easy: if you have a Flexible Spending Account (FSA) or Health Savings Account (HSA) offered at work, you should be using them.

HSAs and FSAs All the Way

Health Savings Accounts (HSAs) and Flexible Spending Accounts (FSAs) are fantastic ways to save money for medical care while simultaneously taking advantage of the fact that they have special tax advantages so Uncle Sam takes less from you each year. In order to utilize them well after you've set up and enrolled in the FSA or HSA account itself, you'll need to pick a regular amount to contribute from your paycheck into the account. The best way to select this amount is to look back at medical expenses for the last year or two, and/or forecast your upcoming year's likely expenses. For example, if you look back to last year and realize you spent $900 on various medical expenses, then you'd want to save $75/month. If you had a pretty normal year last year and paid $200/month for premiums and had $300 in medical expenses for a total of $2,700 in expenses, then you'd want to save $225/month in either your HSA or FSA. (In most cases, you can pay for your premiums with your HSA or FSA.)

While the FSA is simply an account for your medical funds, the major caveat here is that FSAs in particular can really make you shed tears because almost all of them will *wipe out* your remaining balance at the end of the calendar year. That means if you diligently saved $50 a month and didn't have any medical expenses over the year then your $600 end of year balance would vanish faster than Houdini in a magic show. Houdini = cool. FSA funds disappearing = not cool. Why do they do this? Legislation, duh. Does legislation always make sense? No. But we still have to deal with it.

Unfortunately, you can only change your contribution during open enrollment, if your family size changes, or if you change employment, so this adds another level of risk and complexity in terms of trying to get the amount you put into the account right. If you're thinking well hey, this sounds like too big a hassle, think again. Because it is tax exempt, you are essentially saving whatever tax bracket you're in. So if you're in the 25th percent tax bracket and you save (and hopefully use) $1,000 in your FSA, you'll end up avoiding $250 in taxes which is well worth it since your adjusted gross income would drop by $1,000. It might be a pain to manage (pun intended), but you'll be surprised how flexible the FSA really is. The IRS has a full list of expenses that you can use your FSA (and HSA) funds to pay for.[107] A short list includes doctor visits, dental care, eye exams, glasses, medicine, pregnancy testing kits, and even lactation expenses for families with newborns and babies! With the annual FSA contribution limit at $2,250, it's time to get your FSA on.

HSAs are more or less functionally equivalent to FSAs except for one big con and one huge pro. The con first. HSAs are only available to people who choose HDHPs. The IRS defines a high deductible health plan as any plan with a deductible of at least $1,300 for an individual or $2,600 for a family. So if your insurance deductible is lower than that, you aren't eligible for an HSA. However, the huge pro here is that the funds do not expire like FSAs. Not only do they roll over from year to year, but they are transportable, meaning that if you change jobs, you can take your HSA funds with you. Case in point, I loaded up my HSA when I worked at Google and I haven't really used it even years later and I still have over $3,000 chilling there for when I do something dumb and hurt myself (which is likely sooner rather than later). On top of this big plus, the contribution limits are quite a bit higher for individuals at $3,350 and for couples it's a whopping $6,650 annual contribution limit.

In closing, using a health savings account is a no brainer so double check what your employer offers and keep pace with the ongoing changes to contribution limits on a site like Forbes.com[108] so you can use them most effectively. Simple guidelines for reference:

- If you have an HSA or FSA, use it.
- If you are eligible and have an HSA available, use it!
- Otherwise, use the FSA!

Public Transit and Transportation Benefits

Many companies are now helping to offset the cost of travel to and from work, especially in urban areas with more public transit options. These benefits come in three flavors:

1. Prepaid benefits such as preloaded gas cards or transit passes.
2. Reimbursements for transportation costs.
3. Tax-advantaged transportation accounts.

Companies will generally opt for one main type, but may have several additional options available given various circumstances surrounding how you and your company commute to, from, and during work. This is "low hanging fruit" like several other benefits in that, if it is available, it should be utilized. There are essentially no drawbacks or cons to consider other than the infinitesimal annoyance of setting up the benefit itself.

Case in point, when I was teaching, we had a tax-advantaged public transit account available to us meaning we were able to create an account (literally took 5 minutes online) and direct money to it each paycheck so that we could pay for public transit with our funds from this account. Since it was tax-advantaged, it lowered my taxable income by the amount put in. Since my monthly transit pass in Chicago was $90, I just put in $90 per paycheck, then used my account to pay for transit instead of using my bank account or credit card. Pretty simple. I was in the 25th percent tax bracket so I was able to avoid being taxed on $1,080 worth of income, meaning that I had about $270 less in taxes that I had to pay. Once again, the amount is sizeable enough in its own right to justify utilizing, but once you start to look at it from the 10,000-foot level view, you can see just how quickly each of these smaller chunks add up to and quickly surpass the thousand or thousands of dollars mark per year.

Use it or lose it.

Education Reimbursements

Most benefits distill to a more or less financial case for utilizing them since they are geared towards offsetting your costs, giving you access to tax breaks, or providing something you would otherwise not have. However, education and tuition reimbursement programs at work definitely go much further than this in that they offer employees access to increasing skills and knowledge which in turn drive your own career advancement and ability to be an innovative, creative, and productive person. Education itself is a societal, economic, and personal backbone of society. Taking the opportunity to continually learn and advance self-knowledge is a hallmark trait of successful individuals across time. It represents a core pillar and an individual and continuing education when possible can be one of the best and most rewarding opportunities out there. I was recently reading a biography of John Adams, who thought that education was so central to the individual and to the prosperity of his home state and the country that he forever spelled it out directly in Chapter 5, Section 2 of the Constitution of the Commonwealth of Massachusetts, entitled *The Encouragement of Literature*, etc.:

Wisdom, and knowledge, as well as virtue, diffused generally among the body of the people, being necessary for the preservation of their rights and liberties; and as these depend on spreading the opportunities and advantages of education in the various parts of the country, and among the different orders of the people, it shall be the duty of legislatures and magistrates, in all future periods of this commonwealth, to cherish the interests of literature and the sciences, and all seminaries of them; especially the university at Cambridge, public schools and grammar schools in the towns; to encourage private societies and public institutions, rewards and immunities, for the promotion of agriculture, arts, sciences, commerce, trades, manufactures, and a natural history of the country; to countenance and inculcate the principles of humanity and general benevolence, public and private charity, industry and frugality, honesty and punctuality in their dealings; sincerity, good humor, and all social affections, and generous sentiments among the people.

It's stunning to realize that this was the first and only time a special carve-out regarding the imperative of government to attend to the educational and intellectual pursuits of its constituents was directly and explicitly penned. Weighty in its nature, it reinforces the value of education. Looking across the history of our country, we should note the particular inextricable linkage between the private sector and education insofar as companies and institutions are greatly invested in affording their employees the opportunity to continue their own education under the financial auspices of the company. How much so? According to a 2013 research report by the Society for Human Resource Management (SHRM), a full 61% of companies surveyed offered tuition reimbursement for graduate educational assistance.[109] And get this, the average reimbursement across companies was quite high at $4,980.

Larger companies tend to have more education reimbursement programs than mid to small sized companies since they are pretty expensive to have as a benefit. If you're at one of these companies, take advantage of it while you're there so that if you end up switching jobs to a company that doesn't offer this benefit, you will have made the most of it. Further, you don't necessarily always have to enroll in intense, demanding, or long-duration degree programs that span years right up front. Some employers will allow you to take a single class at a time without committing to a rigid degree program, and this can be a great opportunity to get your feet wet.

When I was at Google, I took advantage of their education reimbursement program to take a class at Harvard so that I could learn a little more about the mathematics of computer science. I felt I needed more background knowledge as it related to the fellowship I had where our team built a pretty sweet (and free!) computer science educational platform for 4th – 8th grade students to learn how to code. The program was called CS First (www.cs-first.com), in case you want to share it with your teacher friends or friends with kids.

Like at most companies, I had to ask for manager approval, but they consented because I had a good reason for wanting to take the course. I paid for the course up front and the only contingency was that I get a B or higher in order to get the reimbursement. The hard part wasn't related to the process at Google, it was the course itself, which I found thoroughly enjoyable albeit quite demanding. I would get up to study from 6-8 a.m. before work Monday through Thursday, get quasi "office hours" from my generous math-loving friend Sarah during lunch times and after work a couple of times a week, and attend classes and do homework at night, all while prepping for the exams, which were scheduled on the weekends. It was a ton of work, but I felt like I was more capable in my job. The knowledge, in part, has even helped to inform various components of Holberg Financial as well, so thanks Uncle Larry!* Once I finished the course, I submitted my grade and got a reimbursement check for the course.

---

* Co-founder Larry Page is affectionately referred to as "Uncle Larry" by many at Google.

As you look at your educational reimbursement programs, it's important to think through the following:

- What percent of your expenses will be reimbursed? Employers may cover anywhere from a small fraction, such as 25%, for example, all the way up to 100% of your costs.
- Are there contingencies like finishing within a certain amount of time or getting a certain grade or GPA?
- Do you have to commit to staying at your company for a certain amount of time if they pay for your continued education?
- What kind of course load can you handle given your schedule, work demands, and life priorities? This was the most revealing aspect for me. It was quite demanding and I'd personally have a difficult time taking more than one class at a time while having a full time job.
- Is your employer willing to allow you a reduced workload or grant you a temporary hiatus on working in order to pursue education? This isn't as common, but it's often found in engineering and business fields, especially for those interested in pursuing an MBA.
- If you are pursuing a degree, would it make sense to leave your job and enroll full time instead? This often means giving up the education reimbursement opportunity, but arguably increases the likelihood of completing the degree and could significantly shorten the amount of time to get said degree or certification.
- What are the tax implications? Your reimbursement may count as income which could raise your tax burden, but you might be able to claim a tax credit or deduction for some of your expenses.[110]

What If Your Company Paid Your Student Loans?! It's True...

The newest and hottest benefit that employers are offering employees is student loan repayment assistance programs to help ease the increasingly large student loan burden that millions are facing. Employers are taking note that the millennial workforce has an increasingly large burden of student loan debt and that there is over $1.2 trillion in student loan debt outstanding making life more difficult,[111] especially at the beginning of people's careers when debt is high and income is relatively low.

As such, imagine a world in which your employer actually pays some (or all) of your student loans each month!

It's real. Mind blown.

It's awesome and it's happening now as companies are setting up programs to pitch in towards their employees' student loan balances. A company called Peanut Butter* helps other companies set up these student loan repayment assistance programs to help employees out and provide them with a great benefit. Employers might opt to match employees' payments or they might offer a fixed amount so that they can, together with you, make a dent in what is a sizeable student loan burden. This benefit can quickly add up to several thousands of dollars per year if your employer is generously contributing to or matching your student loan payments. So it's well worth inquiring about. There are several companies out there like Peanut Butter that help bring this benefit to you, the employee, but since it's such a hot new benefit, you are most likely going to have to advocate for it at your workplace. This is a great opportunity to make gains financially so I'd highly encourage you to muster up the gumption to suggest it to your employer, especially if you think others at your workplace would also benefit.

---

*   www.getpeanutbutter.com

A note for transparency: my company, Holberg Financial, is partnering with Peanut Butter to provide additional financial health benefits to employees. We're honored to be part of this exciting new environment that is helping to address the student loan issue facing millions of people across the country as it's an issue that both of our companies care deeply about.

This is a super valuable benefit for those with student loans. You'll want to catch the wave by actively advocating for yourself and others at your own company. Peanut Butter even has a quick and easy page available to you so that you can get in touch and learn more about their services: www.getpeanutbutter.com/get-started.

Holberg Financial As a Financial Health Benefit

One big way we help millennials and young professionals improve their financial health and wellness is by offering our platform and services to companies as a benefit that they can give to their employees. This ultimately allows employees like you to have access to our service, tools, materials, and information provided by their employers – much like a gym membership or some other benefit like the ones we've just discussed.

There is lots of research that supports a tandem problem that we are trying to address: first, employees want to become more financially successful and secure while simultaneously reducing stress and worry about money. Secondly, this stress and worry translates to your job and impacts all kinds of work-related metrics including reduced work productivity, increased distractibility, lower engagement, and reduced job satisfaction.[112] Essentially, we believe (and the research shows) that by helping you achieve financial health, we will make you better off, which in turn helps you perform better at work, which in turn helps your employer create a better workplace for everyone while reducing their costs and increasing their overall productivity.

Since this section is obviously a little self-promotional, I'll keep it short. Essentially, like all other benefits, you can advocate for yourself and tell your employer about us if you'd like. We have a quick and easy page available to you so that you can get in touch and learn more: www.holbergfinancial.com/forbusiness

Cell Phone & Internet Reimbursements

Companies are ditching office phones and relying on employees to use their cell phones and their home internet for work-related purposes. Lots of work places are now offering to compensate employees for the use of their cell phones and home internet either in full or in part. If you're using either for work, then see if your employer offers this reimbursement. Many of these reimbursement policies will cover the "work related portion of the cost." This means that if you use 50% of your cell phone minutes, messages, or data for work and you've got a $120 monthly bill, your employer might cover $60 of the bill or they might offer a fixed plan or reimbursement for your usage. Internet reimbursement will most likely function the same way even though both of these are admittedly difficult to monitor for accurate usage proportions. Many policies rely on good faith estimates of usage so try to be faithfully accurate when submitting your reimbursements. These alone could be worth roughly $900 in reimbursements per year if you get a 50% reimbursement on both, assuming your bills are $100 and $50 for your cell and internet, respectively. A big note here is that while you might not have a formal company reimbursement policy for phone and internet, many managers and departments will reimburse you on a case-by-case basis if you use either regularly for work purposes. Definitely ask for some type of reimbursement if you find your bills increasing due to work-related usage. Otherwise consider drawing more clear cut lines between work and personal accounts so you don't have an unnecessary personal expense increase.

Advocating for Benefits: 3 Easy Steps

It's almost a guarantee that your employer doesn't offer *all* the benefits out there and as such, you might not have a benefit that is valuable and appealing to you. You have two choices regarding your employer's benefits offering. First, you can do nothing, remain silent, and leave getting the benefit you desire in the hands of Fate. Or, you can be proactive and advocate for yourself. Guess which one I think you should do?

Yup, go advocate. As in any relationship, you can't expect someone to know what you need or want through ESP or mind reading alone. You wouldn't expect your significant other or spouse to know exactly what you're thinking all of the time. Likewise, you have to communicate with your parents and family that daily phone calls and texts are too much (or too little!); they won't know it just because they are related to you. Right? Communication and advocating for your needs and desires is crucial to navigating relationships.

This is virtually identical in your relationship with your employer, as strange and as it may seem. Admittedly, advocating for yourself is not something that is widely discussed, so it's important to realize that this is relatively new and uncharted territory. But just think – if you have tons of student loans and would love love love to have a student loan repayment benefit, you have to let them know. How would they know otherwise? If you like hitting the gym after work, but don't like the $50/month membership fee, maybe your employer would think it is a good investment to pay for it (plus working out increases health and reduces stress!). But they won't know if you don't say anything.

This logic is fairly straightforward if you buy into the fact that your employer is interested in getting you benefits that you want. Now before you roll your eyes and say, "No way they'd go for this," just remember that the worst that can happen if you discuss it with them professionally and appropriately is that they say "no." At least if you hear a no, then you can say you tried. But the prospect of getting a "yes" should make the idea of advocating for yourself inherently attractive. So how do you "advocate" for various benefits?

1. Gather the facts. Using data and reasoning about how these benefits will be an advantage for you, your fellow employees,

and the company are key to advocating for your position. Consider seeing if other employees are also interested so you can demonstrate more interest.

2. Determine who is the best point of contact in your company. It may be prudent to ask those that are closest to you organizationally, such as your manager, so you can lightly bring up the topic. A casual inquiry at first might be more appropriate than a long-winded explanation and research paper.

3. Once you've found the right person to communicate with, ask for a quick meeting to share your thoughts and data. During the conversation, don't demand an answer. Instead, leave the door open for a continued conversation since many benefits decisions take time to consider, analyze, and adopt. Be persistent, but do not overburden in your follow up communications as you continue to advocate for yourself and others.

This should get the ball rolling and many times a hard yes or no won't actually happen right away. Be open to working with your employer and encourage them to continue to think about it while offering to help them understand why the benefit is valuable to you and others. By being open and communicative you allow your employer to gather additional reasons to say yes. In my opinion, it's important to view your employer as an asset, a partner, and a resource rather than an obstacle or blocker to overcome and convince. With this advocating mindset you will be able to more genuinely and positively align yourself with them to get better results. After all, if you can figure out a way to describe it as both beneficial to you *and* to them, they are more likely to say yes. Try it out and see where it goes!

Part 4-Advanced Financial Fitness (Yes, You're Ready!)

16. What Does It Mean To Be "Advanced" Financially?

Being financially advanced simply means that you are exploring and pursuing concepts that exist on the outermost areas of your financial life. Everyone can do this and yes, you are ready! Even if this means that you are in a learning phase and just reading through this section without quite needing to act on these topics. Whereas concepts covered in the preceding sections like earning and income, budgeting, paying down debt, and saving for retirement are core foundations to your financial life, there is a whole realm of "advanced" areas that round out and optimize your finances like education savings accounts for kids, diversifying your investment portfolio, and thinking through ways to buy property so that you can generate additional income through real estate. The concepts in this section are designed to cover various financial concepts and ideas that are the outer layers of your financial life much like the outer layers of a tree that include the bark and the skinny branches and leaves high up in the canopy. These outer layers are essential to the tree, but they develop *after* the foundations have already taken root. The innermost rings and trunk will always be the heart, the foundation, and the strength upon which the rest of the tree continues to grow and thrive.

As you read through the financially advanced section, your task is to learn about the various elements of the outer layer of your financial tree and as things become more stable with your foundations (like paying all your credit card debt off #coughcough), you can start to act on the information here so that your tree starts to bear fruit and become the most mature and complete version of itself.

17. The HF Unsexy Investing Strategy

If you thought that I was going to teach you some secret and clairvoyant investing strategy that will help you get rich overnight, I'm sorry, but I'm about to burst your audacious and aspiring investing bubble. Before I do, I want to give you some definitions that will be helpful in this section. Each is a shortened variation from Investopedia:

Index Fund: An index fund is a type of mutual fund with a portfolio constructed to track a market index, such as the Standard & Poor's 500 Index (S&P 500). An index mutual fund is said to provide broad market exposure, low operating expenses and low portfolio turnover. These funds adhere to specific rules or standards that stay in place no matter the state of the markets.[113]

Exchange Traded Fund (ETF): An ETF, is an investment that tracks an index, a commodity, bonds, or a basket of assets like an index fund. Unlike mutual funds, an ETF trades like a common stock. ETFs typically have lower fees than mutual fund shares, making them an attractive alternative for individual investors.[114]

Target Date Fund: A target-date fund is a mutual fund in the hybrid category that automatically resets the asset mix of stocks, bonds and cash equivalents in its portfolio according to a selected time frame that is appropriate for a particular investor. A target-date fund is structured to address some date in the future, such as retirement.[115]

Expense Ratio: The expense ratio is a measure of the total costs associated with managing and operating an investment fund such as an index fund, ETF, or mutual fund. These costs consist primarily of management fees and additional expenses, such as trading fees, legal fees, auditor fees and other operational expenses.[116] Most will be between 0.05% and 1.5%.

Now that we have some definitions, it's time to break it to you: the tried and true way to invest is also the most unsexy way that you could ever imagine. There's no *Wolf of Wall Street* or *the Big Short* glory to be had in the HF Unsexy Investing Strategy. But this plan will help you hone your inner tortoise and slowly, but surely, work on making steady progress over time so that you can reach your goals and that illustrious, envisioned finish line. Maybe by the time you reach retirement they will make a sequel called *The Tortoise of Main Street* about you or me. I don't know, but what I do know is that the Holberg Financial Unsexy Investing Strategy turns out to be a pretty easy one to enact and doesn't require you to read up on dense investment theories, complex strategies, or get a computer science and financial engineering degree to build your own robo advisor or high frequency trading platform.

Ready for it? The HF Unsexy Investing Strategy is to:

Use tax-advantaged accounts when possible, invest your money in low-cost, diversified investments, and contribute regularly and over a long period of time.

Don't be fooled because of its short length. Sir Isaac Newton wasn't: he only needed two short sentences and a single, simple equation (*Force = mass x acceleration)* to fully write out the Laws of Motion. Let's break down each one of the HF Unsexy Investing Strategy portions so you can start your own tortoise journey towards retirement.

Use tax-advantaged accounts when possible

First things first., you probably are past the starting line already even if you haven't caught up to the napping Hare way up the road. If you are at a job with a retirement plan that you are contributing to, you're well on your way. In either case, the first part of the HF Unsexy Investing Strategy dictates that you should be using some type of tax-advantaged account when possible. That just means that if you are at a job that has a retirement plan, you should be using your 401k, 403b, or whatever else is available *especially* if you have a match. Get as much of your match as humanly possible. Don't leave free money on the table.

If you don't have a plan at work, then set up an IRA (Roth or Traditional) and contribute to that account. With an IRA you can save up to $5,500 per year. Further. you can contribute up to $18,000 per year towards your retirement plan at work, meaning you could potentially save $23,500* before needing any other types of non-tax-advantaged account. It's quite a feat if you are hitting this amount per year. Even if you don't have a work account, it's still great to be able to save $5,500 each year – this will add up quickly over time and grow in a compounded fashion, as described earlier. So get cracking.

It's worth noting that there are several other miscellaneous rules surrounding IRAs. A couple of things to research and pay attention to when contributing to an IRA are your income (for high income earners, this impacts your contribution limit for Roth IRAs only), your tax filing status (single, married, etc.), tax deductibility (this phases out as you earn more and is based on whether or not you have a retirement account at work), and age ("catch up" contributions allowed if you're 50 or older). At the end of the day, most of the rules surround Roth IRAs and even if there are caveats, most people can still contribute at least something to them. The IRS has some pretty understandable information that's useful to double check especially since the contribution limit changes often to adjust upwards to account for inflation. Be sure to check out their rules before determining what you'll contribute each year.[117]

---

* These limits change periodically and the ones here are based on 2016 limits. Further, there are special "catch up" contributions for those age 50 and older. In 2016: $1,000 and $6,000 for IRAs and work retirement plans, respectively.

For those who are self-employed or work at smaller companies without work-based retirement plans, there are both SIMPLE and SEP IRAs available that have even higher contribution limits and are intentionally designed to be easy to set up. For 2016, the SIMPLE IRA has a contribution limit of $12,500 and the SEP plan has a huge limit of up to $53,000 per year. If you don't have a work retirement account, consider asking your employer about these options.

At a bare minimum, you should have access to either the Traditional or Roth IRA and the vast majority of people should have a $5,500 contribution limit. This implies that you can save up to $458 per month, which for many is a stretch goal in and of itself. So start small (tortoise style) and work your way up to higher contribution amounts as you're able. The biggest thing here, on the way to becoming un-average, is to actually set up the proper accounts and to start utilizing them. There is no advantage to waiting so go out and do it. How much you put in is up to you, but try to save something rather than nothing. The gulf and distinction between saving and not saving is as wide as the Mariana Trench and you want to be on the saving side, not the side of inaction.

Invest Your Money in Low-Cost, Diversified Investments

Just having the proper retirement accounts isn't enough. You actually have to select and moderate what investments you have. For many people, this happens automatically when you enroll in your account at work. The big risk here, as previously discussed, is allowing yourself to select the default investment options. This can be ruinous and strip out tens of thousands and potentially hundreds of thousands of dollars of your wealth over the long run.

How do you avoid this risk and sadness?

Know what investments you have and what is available to you. You want to make sure that you have a solid mix of low-cost, diversified investments such as low-cost index funds, ETFs, and target date funds. These investments are what millions of people are flocking to in order to avoid expensive *actively managed* investments (expense ratios roughly at or above 0.5%). The reason many of the top investments out there are low-cost is because they are *passively managed* investments (expense ratios roughly at or below 0.5%). These passively managed funds have continued to gain market share and as of December 2014, there were over 1,800 ETFs available worth over $2 trillion dollars.[118]

All the hubbub and definitions aside, the practical implication is to look at what you are invested in, and verify that you aren't paying too much. This means logging into your retirement account and looking at the expense ratios to see if your investment costs are above or below 0.5%. If it's higher and you have other lower-cost options available, consider changing your allocation. If there is a lower-cost investment is in line with your risk and reward objectives you can switch to this. This is one of the more difficult areas to figure out independently, so you can reach out to your company's retirement plan administrator-or Holberg Financial-for help with this to make sure you get all the proper information.

In terms of figuring out the ambiguous concepts of cost, risk, and return objectives, there are lots of ways to understand this, but the basics to remember are that 1) the higher potential return, the higher potential risk, and 2) always try to keep your money in low-cost investments. This is one domain in which a financial Goliath is actually working on your side rather than thwarting you. A great baseline to figure out the approximate trifecta of cost-risk-return is to look at the financial behemoth, Vanguard, to better understand what's going on. Vanguard has a rock-bottom average expense ratio that is 82% less than the industry average for their mutual funds at 0.19% compared to the industry average of 1.03%. Further in terms of risk and return, 93% of their mutual funds performed better than their peer-group averages over the past 10 years.[119] What this means is that if you are looking at an investment, you can check out a similar investment that Vanguard offers and compare their cost and performance. Chances are that Vanguard will be cheaper and get solid returns that rival or outperform other companies that sell ETFs and mutual funds. They are considered by many to be the industry leader and gold standard. Therefore, you can use them to learn about your actual investment choices to make sure you aren't paying too much in fees.

The point of calling out Vanguard is to compare the market in terms of cost, risk, and return. There are tons of other companies that make investments, including Fidelity, Blackrock, and Invesco. While these companies have some good options, it would be wise to check Vanguard's options to see if there is an equivalent so you have an informed baseline.

Let's now look at and compare two major investment types to explore in more detail the two notions of diversification and underlying assets: ETFs and target date funds.

First, diversification is the breakdown and spread of what is inside the investment itself. Target date funds and ETFs are composed of hundreds or even thousands of stocks and bonds (a.k.a. underlying assets) which represent a huge amount of diversification. Comparatively, buying individual bonds or stocks (like Apple, Whole Foods, or Pfizer, for example) represents a low amount of diversification. More diversification helps to balance out the various ups and downs of individual stocks and bonds and is something most investors strive to build into their investments to lower their overall risk levels while gaining exposure to lots of different assets that could potentially grow in value. In diversifying, people use the logic put forth by the idiom, "Don't put all your eggs in one basket." By spreading things out, you're lowering the chance that you lose your entire basket or that something bad happens to it like a wily fox nabbing your eggs for dinner.

Let's look at the diversification of one of Vanguard's most popular ETF's: the S&P 500 ETF (its shorthand name, or ticker, is "VOO").[120] VOO itself invests in stocks in the S&P 500 Index which represents 500 of the largest U.S. companies. The goal of VOO is to track the S&P 500, which is one of the most closely followed indices used to track the overall U.S. stock returns. (If you've ever heard people talking about the stock market on the news, they are often talking about either the S&P or the Dow Jones Industrial Average, the "Dow"). As of December 6, 2016, a share of VOO costs $203.61,[121] which means if you bought one share of VOO, you would technically own a wide array of underlying stocks including Apple, Alphabet (formerly Google), Microsoft, Amazon, General Electric, and over 500 other companies (VOO itself has 507 stocks).

Whereas many ETFs are either all stocks (like VOO) *or* all bonds, target date funds will be composed of stocks *and* bonds. Target date funds are built so that the percentage mix between stocks and bonds changes over time, so that they can function as target retirement funds. The point of the target retirement funds is to gradually change your fund's risk and return level to more accurately reflect your tolerance and age. For example, Vanguard's Target Retirement 2010 fund is almost 69% bonds and roughly 31% stocks.[122] The 2010 date indicates that it is designed for people who were planning on retiring within a couple of years on either side of 2010. Vanguard makes Target Retirement funds in 5-year increments, as do many other companies. For people who are 25, retirement might be 40 years away, which equates most closely to Vanguard's 2055 Target Retirement fund. This fund is more heavily weighted towards stocks at just under 90% and has far less of a percent dedicated to bonds at roughly 10%.[123]

In general, younger people have a higher degree of risk tolerance so they are more able to invest in riskier ETFs like VOO and target funds that have a higher percentage of stocks compared to bonds. Over the course of time, as you age, have kids, and get closer to retirement, most people don't want to take on that same level of risk. Since you will be closer to using your retirement funds, you will be more concerned with stable, lower growth that is afforded through less risky investments such as bond-based ETFs or sticking with target retirement funds (this is referred to as capital preservation). It's important to recognize that most large ETFs themselves won't change what they are composed of. VOO for example, will always be composed of the U.S.'s largest stocks. The largest stocks do change over time, but not very frequently since large companies tend to stay large for years and even decades at a time. Therefore, unlike ETFs, the benefit of the target date fund is that you don't have to change and adapt your retirement portfolio as life continues – the fund itself will do that. This is both good and bad. It's good because it is automatic and handled "behind the scenes" so even if you get caught up with kid's soccer practices, music lessons, and advancing your career, your retirement portfolio will adjust along the way. However, this is also the drawback because you might find that by shifting your investments automatically at a given age, you might actually be in a position that is too conservative or too aggressive.

As you scope out both ETFs and target date funds, keep in mind that while it might be automated and relatively straightforward to participate in these investments themselves, they still require a conscious and active check-in from you at regular intervals. While retirement is way down the road like a Disneyland family road trip across country, it is still imperative to make sure you are getting on and off the right highways along the way or else you might end up in a far flung corner of the U.S. and not at your intended destination chilling in the sunshine with Mickey and Minnie Mouse. Try checking in at least once a year and perhaps even semiannually, and do a mental spot check with yourself by considering a couple of questions to see how things are going in your life as it relates to your investments:

- Have my expense ratios or costs changed? If they're higher, should I move my money into lower-cost options?
- Am I achieving a level of return that is satisfactory based on my retirement goals? As a reminder, the stock market has returned on average roughly 8% for decades on end, with various ups and downs.
- Do I have a comfortable level of risk? If you're trying to aggressively grow the value of your funds, then you'll have to take on more risk. If you are more concerned with slowly and steadily growing your funds, then you'll want to have

lower amounts of risk. Look at the overall proportion of stocks versus bonds to help guide you in this area. Remember, there isn't a "right" or "perfect" answer.

In closing, you are certainly acting in a rogue fashion if you are willing to suck up the "pain" that it takes to check in on your retirement account. Millions of people just set it and forget it or only think about it a couple of times a decade (if that). They're in for a rude awakening if they do this! I have to ask which scenario is better – checking hardly ever and being whacked with unpleasant surprises, or checking in regularly to make sure you're on track to meet your goals? Often times, checking can take 15 minutes or less, so it's a minor pain like getting a flu shot – annoying to do, but very good for your long term health.

Contribute Regularly Over a Long Period of Time

The final clause in the Holberg Financial Unsexy Investing Strategy is to simply become the tortoise you were meant to be, which means that you contribute regularly over a long period of time to your investment and retirement accounts. We're talking a healthy amount, each month, over decades of time. This is probably the least sexy part of the strategy since it's predictable, methodical, and spans a long period of time. We've already covered this notion at the beginning of Chapter 6: Retire Like a Boss, but it bears repeating since it is so central to your long term wealth accumulation prospects. While lots of the discussion in this chapter has focused on the types of accounts and the investments therein, everything is essentially rendered a moot point unless you are actually investing real, regular money into said accounts and investments.

Don't be fooled by the banality of this point. The implicit action item is that you can (and should) start now and implement this over time. There are 4 different buckets that you can fall into in terms of your investment contributions. Take a look at the list below and ask yourself, "Which category do I currently fall into?

Which one would I like to get to?"

1. Not currently saving.
2. Currently saving some each month, but below your target amount.
3. Currently saving target amount each month.
4. Currently saving above target amount each month.

If you need a refresher on how to find a monthly target contribution amount, head back to Chapter 6: Retire Like A Boss. You can count yourself as advanced and definitely un-average if you put yourself in group 3 or 4. If not, work to get there. Going from 1 to 2 takes action to set up the accounts (which are most likely free to set up and take less than 30 minutes), especially if you're logging in to your work retirement for the first time or using a platform like ETRADE. Going from 2 to 3 is a little tougher, but you could log in each month for 12 months and adjust your contribution up by $10, $50, or whatever amount is comfortable so that you can slowly and surely move into group 3. And who knows, eventually you might even find that you're able to squeeze into group 4.

That's it! The Holberg Financial Unsexy Investing Strategy is complete and is yours to implement: get the right accounts make solid investments and put in a healthy amount. Not too shabby, right? Now that you have this in your brain, it's time for some ultra-short addendums that will truly set you apart and optimize your financial life as it relates to your investing strategy. These are the granular tweaks that, while small and almost unnoticeable, have consequences and are valuable to get right.

Tweaking Your Strategy To Optimize Your Investments

Check the "DRIP" Box

DRIP stands for Dividend Re-Investment Plan. Many stocks, bonds, and funds will issue dividends, which are usually in the form of cash. If you do not enroll in DRIP, that cash will end up in your retirement account or your bank account as cash which will earn you either nothing or a paltry amount. By enrolling in DRIP, you are automatically taking your dividends and reinvesting them into the investment that gave you the dividend in the first place. There are two awesome reasons to do this. First, you can get additional small fractional shares. You can't generally buy fractional shares outside of DRIP plans. This drives the second point, which is that your new fractional shares will now be invested and earning the same rate of return as your other full shares. You are now getting the most exposure to compounding interest opportunities which can help your account grow faster. Moral of story: enroll in DRIP if you can. Not all investments disburse dividends and not all accounts allow you to enroll in DRIP. Furthermore, sometimes enrollment in DRIP is automatic and sometimes it's manual so make sure you're eligible and that you intentionally note whether or not you're enrolled for funds with the DRIP option.

Avoid "Professional" Money Managers

As detailed several times in this book, *active and professionally managed* funds and accounts not only cost more, on average, but they have not been able to consistently outperform more passive funds and accounts in the long run. Watch out for people claiming that they can "beat the market." If words like passive, broad-based, index, and low-cost aren't coming out of their mouths, it's time to walk away. Further, even if they are willing to invest your money in passive funds such as ETFs, index funds, or target date funds, make sure you ask whether the account itself has fees, charges, or any type of cost and whether or not they themselves make any money from investing for you. There are fees all over the place, so check, check, and recheck (and re-ask) to make sure they aren't lurking in the background like Slenderman.* As a company, one of our goals is trying to make sure people aren't getting taken advantage of by "professional" money managers who charge a lot and hide fees all over the place, so if you ever want us to look over your stuff just hit us up and we'll take a look with you. You can get ahold of us at holbergfinancial.com.

---

* Just Google it.

The Efficient Market Hypothesis (EMH) Explained

This might constitute the closest thing to an economics lesson in this book, but it will help clarify the HF Unsexy Investing Strategy as well as show you why stock markets and investments act the way they do and why "professional" money managers keep coming up on the losing end of the argument. In short, the EMH states that because of market efficiency, all factual and relevant existing information about companies and investments is reflected in the price of each investment.

This essentially means that no one is able to know anything about stocks and investments that isn't already folded into the price. This implies that no one can "beat the market." Further, no one can consistently in the long run continue to get above average rates of returns. Remember, numbers can be tailored to show you a compelling case, but what most companies will do to convince you of their prowess is show you the most favorable time frame that highlights their best performance. For example, in the last two years, they might have earned 4.5% on a given investment, but in the last three years, they might have earned 8.9%. No doubt they'd prefer to show you the better return, and many will do just that.

While the EMH is a hypothesis as opposed to a theory, it is widely accepted. For anyone who tries to convince you that they can outperform or beat the market, ask them for their proof which should include your ability to access and compare *all* the various time frames. *And* you should be able to compare it to a near or approximate competitor or index to see if it is actually a solid investment. Just remember, numbers can be coaxed to tell compelling stories, but as you become more financially rogue, you'll be able to spot a financial tall tale faster than Paul Bunyan can chop down a tree.

Day Trading Is For Losers

If you think you've got some special investing sauce and you hop online to trade frequently, good luck. Day trading is for losers and virtually the only people who should day trade are people who are trading *other people's money* in the millions and sometimes billions of dollar range. Day trading is almost a sure way to slowly lose your money if you're playing with less than a million bucks (which consists of almost certainly 99.9% of people). Why? Because of commission and trading fees. Trading isn't free and even super inexpensive platforms like ETRADE still cost money. If you trade regularly, let's say once a week and you make two trades (one to sell and one to buy), and each trade costs $10, you would spend $20/ week which would add up to $1,040 each year.

It's desirable to minimize your trading fees and keep them right around 1% of your account value (which, remember, is still pretty high-cost). Therefore, you'd need to be actively trading on $104,000 so you weren't eating too much into your potential return. Most Americans, including myself, would quiver in their boots at the idea of actively trading on $104,000 each week. Not only do the trading fees and commissions make this highly unfavorable, but you too are essentially buying into the idea that you can beat the market, which as we just saw, violates the Efficient Market Hypothesis. If you decide to actively trade your own money, be my guest, but all I have to say is good luck. Just know that you are at a massive statistical disadvantage and even companies controlling trillions of dollars of wealth are working to avoid this type of investing strategy. There are very, very, very few compelling reasons why you should be trading at the daily, weekly, or monthly level, so stick to simple and don't get caught chasing a fantasy down Alice's rabbit hole.

Rollover Previous Retirement Accounts

When you change jobs, you'll stop contributing to your previous work retirement account (or other accounts like FSA or HSA accounts, for example) and you might open up a new retirement account at your new job. If this is the case, rolling your old funds over is simultaneously an awful process and an important one. The reason it is awful is because it is tedious and difficult and they don't make it easy to do. Among other distasteful aspects, there can be paperwork, confusing instructions, and not-so-helpful support. The reason it's important is that by rolling over and consolidating into one, or a select few accounts, is that it's easier to manage and track. Further, you may be subject to account maintenance fees once you leave your employer. Some can be upwards of $50/month, which can substantially eat away at your investment balance.

Believe it or not, I've had people actually tell me that they don't remember how much money they have in previous accounts and when I ask them where it is, they literally don't know where thousands of dollars of their money is! At large, according to CNN Money, there is over $58 billion out there in unclaimed money.[124] Rolling over your retirement accounts can help your money stay in your control rather than have it float around in obscurity. You can either roll over your accounts to be housed within your new retirement account (they will most likely set up a distinct sub-account such as an IRA for your rollover funds) or you can roll it into an account anywhere you'd like such as ETRADE, Scottrade, or Wealthfront. When rolling over your funds, make sure that you understand the tax consequences and your old versus new costs and investment options. In terms of taxes, you can roll over funds from like account to like account without incurring a tax liability. This means that pretax money can go to other pretax accounts (most commonly 401k or 403b to a Traditional IRA) and post-tax money can go to post tax accounts (most commonly Roth 401k or Roth 403b to a Roth IRA). You can take a cash distribution or roll over your funds into "unlike" accounts, but you may have a taxable event (as well as additional penalties for early withdrawals) so read the fine print before submitting any paperwork or clicking any buttons.

If you do plan to roll over your funds, make sure that you have the ability to still find low-cost, diversified funds per the HF Unsexy Investing Strategy above. There's no point in rolling over your money if you have to pick inferior investments. But make sure you are keeping track of it until you find a good option! Not all accounts need to be rolled over, especially if your previous account was a good option for you. Just be aware of the increased need to keep track of it for the long haul and to double check whether or not you now pay any maintenance fees.

Rolling over previous accounts and playing things close to the chest is something you just have to suck up and do. By keeping your retirement accounts streamlined and consolidated, you're setting yourself up for long term success and you can therefore check off one more of your financial bucket list items.

Joe Holberg

18. Additional Advanced Fitness Items

As you read through these ultra-short advanced fitness topics, I want to fully acknowledge that each one is deserving of a much more detailed and expansive commentary and analysis than is included here. There are two reasons for keeping them short and sweet. First, these are the optimizing tweaks in your financial life that you can make as you build your financial foundation and become more financially fit. But the major focus of this book has been on creating and building the core components of your financial life and not on the numerous other topics that could have been covered. Secondly, each one of these topics has been written about by many other experts and there are great resources on each that already exist. As such, each one will have several follow-up resources for you to extend your learning if you so choose. Some of my favorite thought leaders, writers, and books are subsequently listed and I hope that if you do dive into exploring them, you enjoy them as much as I have.

Housing, Real Estate, and Becoming a Landlord

Housing and property ownership have always been central to America's societal and economic organization even before the founding of the country. It has vast consequences and has been used as a means to control wealth, power, and the political system. Many times, property and housing have been used in an extremely unfair way – most notably when owning property was a prerequisite to voting and participating in the political system. It's also been a key component and backbone of the U.S. economy that has driven growth and GDP for well over two centuries. Housing and property ownership have a multifaceted history and yet, it continues to be at the heart of the American Dream. No doubt an entire book could be dedicated to this topic alone.

Keeping on track though, we've already considered mortgages that are invariably linked to home ownership, but now we'll consider what options are out there for people who already own a house and are considering buying additional real estate as a means to invest.

First, research and learning must form the cornerstone of your real estate pursuits. Far too many people dive in without understanding the true cost, not only of the financial aspects of dealing with real estate, but the enormous amount of time it takes to own and deal in real estate. Whatever you do, read, read, and read more about real estate before diving in. If you don't have the time to read at least 10 books on real estate, I'd hazard a guess that you don't have enough time to actually go out and start to invest in various real estate options. #truth.

Secondly, since there is so much emotion and enthusiasm around extending your real estate footprint beyond your primary home, there are plenty of people and companies out there willing to exploit you. Now, many do actually offer tons of value and insight, but there are scams and shady dealings galore such as weekend seminars, online courses, house flipping schemes, online websites that promise access to all kinds of short sales, reduced price houses, HUD homes, and too many more to name. Being alert, defensive, and skeptical is essential if you are getting into real estate, which reinforces the previous assertion that researching and reading before going out and getting roped into something is absolutely crucial.

There are lots of different ways to get into real estate. Below is a list of common ways you might consider investing as you build your wealth:

- Buying land and building housing on it to either rent or sell.
- Buying land and holding it in the hopes that the value appreciates (a form of property speculation).
- Buying a home that needs fixing up in the hopes that you can sell it (or rent it out) for more than the sum of your purchase price + fix up costs (a.k.a. rehabilitation costs, or rehab for short).
- Buying a home or multi-unit property and renting it out.
- Etc…

There are several variations and certainly others that aren't on the list above, but this should get the wheels turning. In thinking about whether or not this is right for you, keep in mind that:

- It will almost always *cost more* than you expected to undertake and execute your endeavors.
- It will almost always *earn you less* than you expected.
- It will almost always *take way more time and energy* than you expected.

These dimensions can't be understated. I've seen folks buy a "quick fixer upper" thinking they were going to spend a few months fixing it up on the weekends with a couple thousand dollars then turn around and make a handsome profit. Instead, they watch their time and money slip down the drain while not even being able to recoup their cost once the property is sold. Properly estimating your willingness and capacity to deal with the unexpected events and setbacks is a fundamental trait of those that are successful in real estate.

By no means whatsoever am I discouraging you from pursuing this avenue – it can and certainly has been very lucrative for hordes of people who are savvy enough to get out there and roll up their sleeves. But one thing everyone can agree on in real estate is that it is *not* easy. I like to ask people whether or not they would be willing to have a part time job on top of their full time job. Many aren't too keen on investing in real estate when it's phrased like this, but that's exactly what it is. When there's water in the basement, a light goes out, or some appliance needs a fixin', it's on your shoulders. Maintenance and upkeep alone can be a large enough burden to dissuade people from undertaking the real estate adventures, and rightly so, as it's not for the faint of heart.

If you're ever considering investing in real estate or land or becoming a landlord for the properties that you rent out, start by reading some of these books and resources first:

- *The ABC's of Real Estate Investing* by Ken McElroy
- *What Every Real Estate Investor Needs to Know About Cash Flow...And 36 Other Key Financial Measures* by Frank Gallinelli
- *Real Estate Investing For Dummies* by Eric Tyson
- The *BiggerPockets Podcast* (www.biggerpockets.com)

Starting a Business and Becoming an Entrepreneur

According to a Bentley University survey, a whopping 66% of millennials say they want to start their own business.[125] It's an exciting prospect and it is arguably an outcropping and perfect example of our generation's ethos of finding more purpose and meaning in our work and career opportunities. But what does it actually entail? How do you do it? Should you do it? Is it worth it? What if you fail? Who? What? When? Where? Why? How? Gahhh....the questions are endless, but the seed of entrepreneurship is clearly lodged in the millennial mind and even more so, in the American spirit...

Compared to the preceding housing section, I will remain silent save to share resources, because this area is covered prolifically by those who have been around the block and can speak on it way more intelligently than I can. Admittedly, I am in the process of running and building my first company, but I am still looking to learn in this domain rather than speak on it myself. I have however, for years, read fantastic books that I absolutely know have been critical to my ability to run a company. I couldn't have done it without them. Below is a short list of resources (alphabetically arranged):

Books

- *Built to Last* by Jim Collins
- *Get Backed* by Evan Baehr and Evan Loomis
- *Good to Great* by Jim Collins
- *Influence* by Robert Cialdini
- *Just Listen* by Mark Goulston
- *Lean In* by Sheryl Sandberg
- *Mindset* by Carol Dweck
- *More Than Good Intentions* by Dean Karlan
- *Rework* by Jason Fried and David Hansson
- *Start Something That Matters* by Blake Mycoskie
- *The $100 Startup* by Chris Guillebeau
- *The Five Dysfunctions of A Team* by Patrick Lencioni
- *The Lean Startup* by Eric Ries
- *The New Digital Age* by Eric Schmidt
- *The Power of Habit* by Charles Duhigg
- *Thinking, Fast and Slow* by Daniel Kahneman
- *Work Rules!* by Laszlo Bock
- *Wikinomics* by Don Tapscott and Anthony Williams

Podcasts

- *Planet Money* by NPR
- *Startup* by Gimlet Media
- *Startup Grind* by Startup Grind
- *The Tim Ferriss Show* by Tim Ferriss

The rest, I'll leave to the above inspirational sources and will, for once, remain silent!

Savings Accounts for Education

The two most common types of savings accounts that can be strategically used for education are 529 Plans and Coverdell Education Savings Accounts (referred to as ESAs). These come loaded with both excellent advantages *and* tons of rules.

529 Plans

529 plans are also known as "qualified tuition plans" and are tax-advantaged savings plans designed to encourage saving for future college costs. There are two types of 529 plans: prepaid tuition plans and college savings plans. All fifty states and D.C. have at least one type of 529 plan and many have several options.

Prepaid tuition plans generally allow you to purchase units or credits at participating colleges and universities for future tuition and, in some cases, room and board. These units and credits lock in the price, which can be extremely advantageous given the rapid rise in tuition at colleges and universities. Most prepaid tuition plans are sponsored by state governments and have residency requirements so consider whether or not your child (or the beneficiary you're saving on behalf of) is going to attend college in your state or somewhere else as this can affect where you open your account. Further, many state governments guarantee investments in prepaid tuition plans that they sponsor. Prepaid tuition plans will allow you to buy the credits or units in bulk or over an extended amount of time, usually in regular installment intervals.

College savings plans help people save for their beneficiary's eligible college expenses (usually their kids). You will generally have several investment options, which the college savings plan invests on your behalf. Investment options often include stock mutual funds, bond mutual funds, and money market funds, as well as age-based portfolios that automatically become more conservative investments as the beneficiary gets closer to college age. Money in the account can generally be used at any college or university. One thing to note is that investments in college savings plans that invest in mutual funds are not guaranteed nor are they insured, so there is generally a higher degree of risk.

Both the prepaid tuition plans and the college savings plans have a considerable maximum contribution limit and the college savings plan max contributions will often exceed $200,000. Enrollment for college savings plans are open all year while prepaid plans have limited enrollment periods.

One primary reason that people will opt for 529 plans is because of the tax benefits. Earnings in the plans are not subject to federal tax. In the majority of cases you won't have to pay state tax either assuming you use the withdrawals for eligible college expenses. Premature or unqualified withdrawals will most likely be subject to income tax as well as an additional 10% federal tax on earnings. This makes them illiquid so one of the best things to double check on before setting up a 529 plan is whether or not you are really financially sound and healthy before investing in education-related accounts.

A *massive* warning about 529 plans is that you need to understand the fees that you pay, if any, as many can be extremely expensive to have. They come in two flavors; you can either buy them *direct* or via *advisor-sold* plans. As you're already financially un-average in understanding how small fees and differences in expense ratios can really add up over the long run, you should make a mental note that the direct plans (often managed directly by the state administrators themselves) will almost always have lower expenses and fees compared to advisor-sold plans. Advisor-sold companies can definitely help you pick a good plan, but it'll cost you and sometimes it will cost quite a bit, which can severely erode your earning potential. Just like a good ETF or target-date fund in your retirement account, so too should you be looking for more passive, low-cost funds in your college savings plans. There are many that will track benchmark indexes like the S&P 500. There are many other caveats, features, and dimensions to consider, so check out information about the account rules themselves on the web via the SEC[126] or via the IRS[127] and do a lot of research into your state's direct versus advisor-sold options before selecting a 529 plan.

Coverdell Education Savings Account (ESA)

Coverdell Education Savings Accounts, or ESAs for short, are similar to the 529 plans above, but with three main differences. First, the beneficiary themselves cannot have more than $2,000 in total contributed on their behalf in a given year. This is a much lower contribution amount than 529 plans. Secondly, your income can't be more than $110,000 as an individual or $220,000 when married filing jointly if you plan to contribute.[128] Third, and perhaps one of the main reasons why you'd use an ESA instead of a 529 plan, is that you can use the funds for elementary or secondary schooling (as well as postsecondary schooling) at public, private, or religious schools. ESA's can cover expenses like tuition, fees, books, supplies, tutoring, and special needs services. Again, there are lots of additional considerations and stipulations, so read up on the IRS website[129] before opening an ESA.

Talking Taxes

This one is ironically easy to address and I hope you find it alleviating since taxes are a gargantuanly ungainly and ginormous pain in the neck (like this sentence). The US Tax Code is several thousand pages long and exceedingly complex and confusing, but it doesn't have to be so when you file your taxes each year.

Taxes are becoming easier and easier, with technology and software tools that are quite cheap or even free. There are two gold standard ways to get your taxes done in the 21st Century.

First, you can get your taxes done for free through an awesome IRS program called the Volunteer Income Tax Assistance (VITA) program if you make around $54,000 or less. Over 3.4 million people filed their taxes via VITA sites spread out all over the country in 2013.[130] While that may seem like a lot (it is), millions more are eligible to utilize VITA services but don't. I've personally been involved with the VITA program in various ways since 2010 and can't extol its virtues enough. I set up and ran a VITA site in Providence, Rhode Island that went on to help thousands of people file their taxes over the next several years. I've also been on the Associate Board of an amazing organization called the Center For Economic Progress since 2011 and we are able to help roughly 15,000-20,000 hard-working individuals and families file their taxes for free each year. In both of these scenarios, it made a huge difference in helping people get hundreds of millions of dollars' worth of credits, deductions, and refunds.

The VITA software programs are designed, and the volunteers are trained, to help you get all the credits and deductions that can help you get a sizeable return while making sure you don't get extorted or charged through the roof from tax preparation companies. These companies will often charge people hundreds or even thousands of dollars while trying to get you to sign up for Refund Anticipation Loans (RALs), which can be loaded with fees and charge usurious interest rates anywhere from 35% to 400%+. These RALs are so dangerous to consumers, that the City of Chicago itself (among many others across the country) directly warns consumers about them on their website:[131]

"RAL's may sound like quicker refunds but what they are in fact are very expensive loans. Consumers should not be fooled – RAL's are expensive loans that come along with fees, finance charges, and high interest rates that are often not worth the price."

You'll find similar warnings regarding RALs, which begs the question as to why they're allowed to exist in the first place. But even if they suck as options, at least you now know to avoid them. If you qualify to use a VITA program based on your income, you can look up locations countrywide via their "Find a Location tool."[132]

If you do not qualify for VITA, but you make less than roughly $62,000 you can still file your federal return for free (and many state returns for free) using the IRS freefile[133] online software which is powerful and easy to use.

Regardless of whether or not you qualify for free tax prep from the IRS VITA program or freefile, a surefire way to get your taxes done efficiently is by using TurboTax (turbotax.intuit.com). You can still get your federal taxes done for free in a lot of scenarios, but you'll almost always have to pay for state filing. This usually costs only around $25 – $40 plus the fee for using TurboTax which ranges from $0 to $90, making it still one of the cheapest options out there.* For the raw power and ease of using TurboTax, I think it's well worth it. TurboTax scans for thousands of credits and deductions and optimizes your potential refund automatically. The advances in the industry that TurboTax has spurred have revolutionized tax preparation and made it as close to painless as possible, which is saying something for a notoriously agonizing season that thankfully at least ends on April 15th each year.

A final tax-related comment: the tax season is a perfect season for financial parasites and wolves in sheep's clothes to lurk around the periphery waiting for you to let your guard down so they can lunge at you with salivating fangs. There are all kinds of deals, offers, add-ons, and upsells that can be presented to you if you are filing your returns via private companies. The IRS VITA sites are one of the few remaining domains where you can be certain you won't be exposed to these vulnerabilities since the organizations that run VITA sites are heavily monitored by the IRS and trained extensively in ethics, compliance and quality assurance.

Other companies and individuals (legal and illegal), as we saw on the City of Chicago's website, shamefully attempt to lure you into

---

* The state filing fee is *per state*. There have been years where I've had to file in multiple states and I've even heard of people having to file in 6 or more states in one given year. Ouch. While a little more costly, it can still be really advantageous to use a program like TurboTax to help organize and make sense of what can be a convoluted situation.

voluntarily handing over large swaths of your return and milk billions of dollars from people's returns each year in the form of RALs, huge preparation and filing fees (anything over $200 is probably too much to pay), and other add-ons. In 2013 alone, the Government Accountability Office reported that the IRS was able to prevent or recover $24.2 billion in fraudulent refunds[134]-and that's just the *illegal portion* of the tax season bonanza! There are still billions of dollars that people are making legally off unsuspecting tax filers.

Be on guard as you get ready to prepare your return. Consider using one of the government's services or make sure you use a high-quality, reputable, and respectable company like TurboTax or H&R Block. The latter two will still charge you money and try to sell you add ons, but they will usually be much less expensive, much more useful, and not extortionary. TurboTax has been on the leading edge of online tax filing year in and year out and their software is arguably the strongest out there. I have filed my taxes with them repeatedly with great success and you definitely can follow their step-by-step process even if you don't consider yourself a tax master (although by now you should believe that you can do it!).

In case you have an extremely complex financial situation (lots of gains/losses, real estate investments, own a business, etc.), it may be beneficial for you to consider hiring a professional such as H&R Block to file your return. Although TurboTax is amazing, you may miss something by preparing your taxes on your own when there is so much data to wade through. Obviously there are pros and cons to each, so pick one that matches your level of complexity with one that is well-reputed.

Financial Security: Be Smart and Safe: 3 Simple Tips

I've spent countless hours in coffee shops, and, no joke, this scenario has happened twice just while writing this book: I'm pounding away on the keyboard and all of a sudden someone's phone rings near me and they start chatting. Normally I just ignore it, but twice it was clear that the person sitting near me was about to buy something with their credit card. Hand fishes around in bag or wallet and out comes the credit card and I'm sitting there thinking, "Please don't read your information out loud." Both times, the person proceeded to read out their credit card number, expiration date, 3-digit security code and all kinds of information including home (shipping) address, phone number, and even once, their birthdate! What did I do? Naturally, as you can imagine me doing something atypical by now, I grabbed a pen and a piece of paper and wrote it all down. Once they finished the call, I got up and walked over to slip them the piece of paper. Just imagine the look on their faces: they were shocked, confused, and a little more than disturbed. I'd add in a kind, yet stern, warning that next time they might not get someone listening who actually wanted to inform them of their reckless and irresponsible behavior. Both times, believe it or not, they said thank you and I went back to writing…

So, lesson learned? I hope so. Don't be a fool and don't assume that just because you're sipping your favorite latte that everyone around you is as happy and innocent. In the digital age, we indisputably have more access and opportunities to use technology for good, but like tax fraud and opportunities for identity theft highlighted above, we also have more exposure and risk as people engage in all kinds of technological malfeasance and trickery.

As such, be smart and safe and use these three tips to minimize the likelihood of a personal financial security breach:

- Don't verbally read out your personal or financial information in public and always use passwords on your personal devices such as your phone, tablet, and laptops. Lock your screens if you have to step away from them for any amount of time. If you do have to read your personal information out loud, read half in one room and half in another so no one person can hear the whole thing.
- Check your account statements each month. Fraudsters used to rack up huge charges as quickly as possible before

the card was shut off. Now they are getting smarter and will often charge in smaller, infrequent patterns so they are less noticeable. They know most people don't look over their debit and credit card information regularly so they keep a low profile in hopes that you don't notice. Report any suspicious activity to your bank or credit card company immediately.

- Don't transmit sensitive information on public Wi-Fi networks or computers and make sure that if you are, that you are on a website that's encrypted (it will have HTTPS instead of HTTP-the S stands for Secure which uses the ultra-safe Secure Socket Layer (SSL), meaning it's encrypted).

While this is the tip of the financial security iceberg, the lesson here is to be on guard and be smart. The cyber arena is a new field that will take decades to adapt to and understand. When there is uncertainty or lack of transparency, there is ample opportunity for individuals and criminal organizations/networks to abuse and capitalize on it via fraudulent and illegal means. There's almost nothing worse than getting your credit card or other financial information stolen. While it is a low probability event, it has huge negative ramifications that can take months or years to rectify.

Advanced Closing

Like the Rebels in Star Wars that are hanging out on the edge of the galaxy, you too are hanging out on the edge of the financial world if you are considering the concepts in the Advanced section. This is good news for you because it means that you are absorbing, learning, and considering areas that can significantly round out your financial lifestyle and enhance it beyond just the foundations that came before. While focusing on the foundations and becoming financially fit are crucial, the advanced section provides you with the full spectrum exposure to financial arenas and has hopefully allowed you to start to think about what's next and what's possible once you start to move outward from the core and enter secondary fitness layer. Start dreaming and asking yourself the bigger types of questions like "What would I do if I didn't have debt?" or "What can I do once I hit my savings goals and have a system set up for building retirement?" These are the questions that turn up the intensity and brightness of the light at the end of the tunnel. By working to implement the ideas in this book, you are no doubt accelerating to the day in which you can comfortably say, "Yes, I made it. Now that I'm outside of the tunnel, I get to choose what's next."

19. Welcome to the Club. P.S. What's Next!

There is no doubt a lot of information contained within this book. You shouldn't feel that just by reading it, you are all of a sudden going to become a perfect financial human. We're all flawed and we all struggle to reach our goals and visions, especially financial ones where the day-to-day demands, temptations, and opportunities are ever so real. Some guide us towards our goals and some steer us wildly off course. But if you can grapple with and come to accept the fact that financial security, health, and awesomeness will take years to achieve and that you'll have setbacks along the way, you will start to embrace a pliable and adaptable mindset that will set you apart and ultimately set you up for success in the long run – and that's where I hope you end up.

If you've made it this far, your journey has just begun, but henceforth you can officially consider yourself financially rogue and un-average – you are different and that's a good thing. You now know what rules to break so that you can take advantage of awesome opportunities while watching out for and avoiding deathly financial traps. I'll be the first to say:

Welcome to the club.

My goal is to help every single person in the U.S. work towards becoming financially rogue so that they too can join the club. There's no reason why people should have to wonder how to improve their financial situation – the key information is included in this very book. So do your friends and family (and maybe strangers on the street) a favor and tell them about this book so that they can become financially savvy too. Remember, it's not like you were born preloaded with this information in your head; you have to learn it. By telling someone about it, they too can undo the financial nonsense that they've been taught (or not taught at all). Just ask yourself, "What will happen to my best friend or family if I *don't* tell them about this?"

That's probably not a question you want to know the answer to, but I'm pretty confident that you do want to know what would happen to them if you *do* tell them about this book. It'll be no fun sipping margaritas on the beach by yourself if you end up being the only one that dared to become financially rogue! Get some friends together, read the book together, and start talking about ways to build your financial foundation and fitness together. It might feel awkward and hokey at first, but it'll feel pretty sweet when you and your friends are making awesome progress and crushing goals along the way.

In the famous words of Buzz Lightyear, "To infinity and beyond!"

What's Next?!

There is no try, only do.

Yes, that's right, the next thing to do is to lift your eyes from the pages of this book and go out into the real world. It's show time. In order to keep you fueled up and on top of your game, I want to leave you with some financial meditations and inspirational snippets that you can quickly re-read if you're feeling downtrodden, beaten up, or discouraged as you work your way through life. Enjoy them and feel free to create your own. (If you think they're good, send them to joe@holbergfinancial.com.)

Learn to fail. Fail to Learn

Failing isn't bad, but not learning from failure is. People fail all the time and you only have two choices: learn or don't learn. You will make small failures financially along the way (and maybe a big one or two), but you need to learn from them, adjust, and win next time.

Divide and Conquer

If you feel like you're not meeting your goals, pick and focus on just one. Knock it out of the park asap. Then, move on to the next *one*. Repeat this singular approach and build momentum until you can handle several simultaneously. The worst thing you can do is try to tackle several at the same time and not achieve any of them.

Honor Inertia

Inertia either works for you or against you. If you are "stuck" and feeling like you aren't making progress, just be honest with yourself and admit it. Sometimes inertia works against you. When you are making progress, take note and think of the surrounding factors that are helping you build so much positive progress. Noting them can help you through the tougher times later.

Be the Tortoise

Slow and steady wins the race both financially and for the tortoise. It's not about giant leaps, it's about one small step at a time. Be like Neil Armstrong, NASA legend, and take "one small step" for yourself and the giant leaps will come soon enough.

Avoid the Superstar Fallacy

I hate to break it to you, but if you think you're going to hit the Mega Millions jackpot, you need to accept the fact that the odds aren't in your favor. The probability of getting rich by *extremely low probability events* like becoming a YouTube star, starting the next sick band, or dunking the basketball for a living are too hyped up. This is absolutely *not* an endorsement to forsake your dreams. Pursue them with passion and with enthusiasm, absolutely. But from a financial standpoint, don't fall victim to thinking that you are going to get rich soon and that you can therefore not work to build a strong financial foundation and life. Waiting hurts and it hurts big. So take those small financial tortoise steps while you take massive life and dream steps. The two can coexist peacefully together.

Life Design Should Match Your Financial Goals

The day-to-day lifestyle that you live should be in line with helping you meet your financial goals. If you've got a couple hundred dollars left each month and you're using it to travel or have fun with friends, that's totally fine! But if your goal is to pay down debt and save more, then your life design is out of sync with your financial goals. Remember, you *can* have your cake and eat it too, but as we all know from childhood birthdays, eating too much cake can make you sick. Therefore, be smart about your decisions and work towards aligning your financial goals and life design.

Weeble Wobble

Do you remember the toys called Weeble Wobbles? No matter how many times you pushed them or knocked them around, they always bounced back up. If I achieve no other goal in life, I'll die happy knowing that I tried to be like the Weeble Wobbles (plus it sounds like the next big dance move...just saying). If you get knocked down, you have to get back up again. You're going to get knocked down in relationships, with money, at your job, and emotionally – but don't give up. As Harvey Dent says in *The Dark Knight*, "The night is darkest just before the dawn." So when you're feeling down, be the Weeble Wobble and bounce back up so you can continue to work towards your goals once dawn comes.

20. Financial Challenges (Not for the Faint Hearted)

Below are six financial challenges that I personally challenge you to do. I have designed these as ways for you to more actively and consciously engage with your finances and yourself. Be warned: they can be accomplished BUT they are not easy. Trust me, I made them up to challenge myself and while several of them took me multiple attempts, I ended up accomplishing each one. I know you can, too.

Each subsequent challenge takes the same number of months to enact as its number. So the first one takes one month to complete, the second one takes two, so on and so forth. I'd encourage you to try *at most* one or two of these at any given time as each one is difficult in its own right.

Have fun!

Spend Nothing Challenge (Duration: 1 Month)

The challenge is to spend absolutely $0 (that is spelled zero dollars, just to be clear) for an entire month –insane right? In this challenge, you are only allowed to spend money on *absolute* necessities like rent, utility bills, gas for your car, and food. There are some grey area items here like food, clothes, and other things. For example, you are not allowed to go out to eat, but you obviously can buy groceries and cook food at home. When cooking at home though, try to be as austere as possible. Don't starve yourself, eat healthy food and a healthy quantity, but ditch all the extras like beer, wine, extra fancy special cheese, and snacks, soda, etc. that are justifiably luxuries. The way I see it is that if you live to the average age of around 79 years old, you would have 948 full months on Earth and therefore you should be willing to try the Spend Nothing Challenge at least once in your life. This would account for just over 1/10 of 1%. Equivalently, if I asked you to give me 10% of a penny, would you really be giving up that much? You probably would.

I did this in October of 2010, which was also my birthday month, so bonus points if you do it over a holiday or birthday! I lived in Providence, RI and pretty much ate pasta for a month and read a lot of books. It's well worth the challenge and even if you fail, you'll learn something about yourself and you can always try it again.

Use the table below to track your expenses. Use the left column to plan out your month by writing down only the things you must spend money on during the month you tackle the Spend Nothing Challenge. Track every single expense for the month in the right column. The goal is to have nothing else written down that wasn't already planned for in the left column.

What are the absolute necessities?	What did I actually spend money on?

The Deep Freeze Challenge (Duration: 2 Months)

The challenge is to literally freeze your credit cards by putting them into a cup full of water and place it in the freezer.* Leave frozen for 2 months (or longer if you dare!). Freezing your credit cards is a great middle ground tactic between cutting them up and keeping them in your pocket. They are there and accessible if you truly truly need them, but they are out of reach for those impulsive and easy purchases that quickly add up.

Bonus: freeze all of your credit and retail cards, not just some.

I love this challenge and play it with myself at least once a year. When I first did it back in 2013, my roommates thought it would be funny to unfreeze my cards and hide them from me while refreezing just the water. After I completed the Deep Freeze Challenge I unfroze the water and found nothing but liquid H20 remaining. I stood there dumbfounded until they revealed their trick. We all got a kick out of it and now I'm going to be in two of their weddings-joke's on them! ;)

Let's keep this tracker simple. Use a pencil to tally how many days in a row you keep your credit cards frozen. If you unfreeze them, erase the tally marks and start over. Put a tally mark in the unfrozen section each time you unfreeze them.

Days Running Spent In Deep Freeze:
Number of Times Unfrozen During the Deep Freeze:

Tip: if you're thinking a full two months might be too tough of a challenge, make sure you try this with February being one of the months!

---

* I've never had my cards malfunction or not work after unfreezing them, in case you were wondering. There's a first time for everything though, so freeze at your own risk!

Master Tracker Challenge (Duration: 3 Months)

The challenge is to manually write down every single purchase that you make for three months. Write down a short description or the name of the place you bought something and the amount. Write all of it down whether it is repeated like rent, discretionary like a cup of coffee, or online like Netflix or clothes. Write all of it down. Before you think this impossible, I'll point out that it takes you less time to write it down than it does to actually buy something so you have no excuse.

The goal of the Master Tracker Challenge is to honestly record what's actually happening in your spending life. Doing this can help you gain massive insight into areas that you might not even realize you are spending a ton of money. Further, there are automated systems galore out there to track stuff. That's not the point. The point is to force yourself to do it manually for three months so you are more in tune and aware of what's happening! I guarantee you'll be surprised at what you find.

You'll probably need several of these tracker tables printed off, so open up Word or Google Docs and recreate a template and print them along the way (you can easily have hundreds of transactions over a three-month period, so be ready!)

Item Name, Description, or Place Purchased	Amount

4 Months Under $4.00 Analysis Challenge (Duration: 4 Months)

The challenge is to identify every single expenditure that is at or under $4.00 in value. It's the little stuff that adds up and this challenge is designed to help you analyze just how much of an impact items and transactions that cost less than $4.00 have on your financial life. Further, you are going to use your findings to extrapolate and estimate the lifetime impact of this on your financial life.

You can collect the data needed in one of two ways. One way is to use something like mint.com or another budget tracking tool to comb through and find all items at or below $4.00. This might take 30 minutes or so. Another way is to manually collect the data, which means, if you've already done the Master Tracker Challenge for 3 months, all you have to do is record your $4.00 and under transactions for one additional month.

After you collect your data, use it along with the following equations to estimate the yearly and the lifetime impact of those small $4.00 and under purchases. I've provided an example from my own life to support your calculations.

Step 1:

Write down the sum total of your $4.00 and under purchases for the last 4 months: _____

Step 2:

Multiply the value in Step 1 by 3 to get the annual cost: _____ x 3 = _____

Step 3:

Multiply the value in Step 2 by your estimated years remaining until age 79: _____ x (79-current age)

Step 4:

Ask yourself what you would do with the value in Step 3 if it were in your pocket or bank account.

My 4 Months Under $4.00 Challenge Example

Step 1: $426 (about $90/month on coffee, too many pit stops for French fries, and lots of other miscellaneous stuff)

Step 2: $426 x 3 = $1,278

Step 3: $1,278 x (79-29) = $1,278 x 50 = $63,900

Step 4: First, fix my broken jaw since it broke hitting the floor once I saw that number....then I'd use $2,000 to go to India and Southeast Asia, use about $5,000 to pay off my student loans, then I'd invest the remaining $56,000 or so!

Debt Destroyer Challenge (Duration: 5 Months)

The challenge is to take every single extra dollar, penny, and Benjamin, Lincoln, and Hamilton you can find and put it towards paying down debt. Use the Debt Snowball concept, write down your debt in the template below, and track how much progress you can make in 5 months. With a concerted effort and a little extra cash, set a target debt reduction amount either in dollars or a percent and go for it.

While you might want to destroy lots of debt items at the same time, focus on your top one or two highest interest rate debt items. Write down the name of your debt account and the balance. Then track the account balance at the end of each month (or after you make your monthly payment).

Debt Name	Debt Starting Balance	Month 1	Month 2	Month 3	Month 4	Month 5
(ex.) Visa Credit Card	*$1,254*	*$800*	*$643*	*$600*	*$415*	*$223*

Tip: This is a great challenge to conduct back-to-back or multiple times. This one also pairs well with the Deep Freeze Challenge or the Spend Nothing Challenge.

Tip: This is a great challenge to do around the tax season as you can strategically plan to use some or all of your refund to knock out portions of your debt.

Take notes on why some months you were able to make bigger or smaller payments on your debt. See if you can find any trends, opportunities, or weaknesses in your ability to pay down your debt.

Notes and Observations:

Emergency Savings Booster Challenge (Duration: 6 Months)

The challenge is to save as much as possible in your emergency savings account in six months. The goal is to be able to boost your emergency savings up towards and as close to 6 months' worth of your income as possible. While this amount may seem large, there are several key milestones that you can work towards to note progress along the way.

This challenge is similar to the Debt Destroyer Challenge. By rapidly increasing your savings, you will build up a stronger foundational pillar in your financial life.

Table 1: Emergency Savings Account Balance

Enter your starting balance in the first box below and then fill in the remaining boxes at the end of each month

Starting Balance	Month 1	Month 2	Month 3	Month 4	Month 5	Month 6

Table 2: Key Benchmark Achievements

Write down what 1 Month's Worth of Income is for you:_____

When you hit the key benchmark achievements below, write the date you accomplished it in the box.

$1,000 Savings Mark	1 Month's Worth of Income	3 Months' Worth of Income	6 Months' Worth of Income

Tip: To find 1 month's worth of income, take your annual salary and divide by 12. Alternatively, you can take your biweekly paycheck amount and multiply by 2. The latter will give you a slightly lower number, but that's ok. You can use whichever number feels good to you.

Tip 2: These amounts may seem really large, but remember, 62% of Americans have less than $1,000 saved. So hit that first savings mark and you'll have surpassed most Americans. Keep building to become un-average asap!

Notes

1 http://theskydeck.com/the-tower/facts-about-the-ledge/

2 http://www.bls.gov/news.release/hsgec.nr0.htm

3 For the general concept: https://en.wikipedia.org/wiki/Six_degrees_of_separation, for you movie buffs: check out the Six Degrees of Kevin Bacon Game at https://en.wikipedia.org/wiki/Six_Degrees_of_Kevin_Bacon, and for those mathematically inclined: https://en.wikipedia.org/wiki/Erdos_number

4 https://pbpcounselorconnection.wordpress.com/2014/05/27/25-shocking-statistics-about-personal-finance-in-the-us/

5 Q1 of 2016 BLS Report on weekly wages. http://www.bls.gov/news.release/pdf/wkyeng.pdf

6 http://www.economywatch.com/personal-finance/a-dozen-shocking-personal-finance-statistics.23-04.html

7 http://www.cfsinnovation.com/Find-your-topic/More-Topics/Underbanked-101

8 Stanford Social Innovation Review Webinar: The Hidden Financial Lives of America's Poor and Middle Class, Part 1. Thursday, January 21st, 2016. (https://ssir.org/webinar/hidden_financial_lives_part_one)

9 http://www.marketwatch.com/story/most-americans-have-less-than-1000-in-savings-2015-10-06

10 https://thebillfold.com/a-story-of-a-fuck-off-fund-648401263659#.wi0l27hgi

11 https://event.webcasts.com/viewer/event.jsp?ei=1086381

12 As of 2014: https://en.wikipedia.org/wiki/Demography_of_the_United_States#Ages

13 http://www.usbr.gov/lc/region/pao/brochures/faq.html#concrete

14 http://thirdmonthmania.com/

15 http://www.usatoday.com/story/money/personalfinance/2013/03/21/census-household-debt-report/2007195/

16 http://money.cnn.com/2013/05/17/pf/college/student-debt/

17 https://googleblog.blogspot.com/2014/05/getting-to-work-on-diversity-at-google.html

18 http://www.bankrate.com/calculators/credit-cards/balance-debt-payoff-calculator.aspx

19 https://www.youtube.com/watch?v=eGDBR2L5kzI

20 http://www.economywatch.com/personal-finance/a-dozen-shocking-personal-finance-statistics.23-04.html

21 https://www.newyorkfed.org/medialibrary/interactives/householdcredit/data/pdf/HHDC_2016Q3.pdf

22 https://www.nerdwallet.com/blog/credit-card-data/average-credit-card-debt-household/

23 http://www.wsj.com/articles/first-national-bank-of-omaha-to-pay-35-million-over-credit-card-practices-1472152186

24 http://money.usnews.com/money/blogs/my-money/2014/02/06/4-smart-ways-to-use-retail-store-credit-cards

25 According to the NY Federal Reserve as of Q2 2016 https://www.newyorkfed.org/microeconomics/hhdc.html

26 NCES Total undergrad stats ($17,490,000 – 16,365,738) / 16,365,738 http://nces.ed.gov/programs/digest/d15/tables/dt15_303.70.asp

27 According to data from the College Board, prices are in constant 2015 dollars, https://trends.collegeboard.org/college-pricing/figures-tables/tuition-and-fees-and-room-and-board-over-time-1975-76-2015-16-selected-years

28 According to a recent US News article, http://www.usnews.com/education/best-colleges/paying-for-college/slideshows/10-student-loan-facts-college-grads-need-to-know

29 http://investor.citizensbank.com/about-us/newsroom/latest-news/2016/2016-04-07-140336028.aspx

30 Blueprint for America, edited by George Schultz, p.28, published 2016.

31 Times Higher Ed Rankings, https://www.timeshighereducation.com/world-university-rankings/2016/world-ranking#!/page/0/length/25/sort_by/rank_label/sort_order/asc/cols/rank_only

32 http://www.dailymail.co.uk/news/article-2134783/President-Obama-Michelle-paid-student-loans-EIGHT-YEARS-ago.html

33 http://time.com/money/4173592/federal-student-loan-repayment-options-chart/

34 http://www.usnews.com/education/best-colleges/paying-for-college/slideshows/10-student-loan-facts-college-grads-need-to-know

35 http://investor.citizensbank.com/about-us/newsroom/latest-news/2016/2016-04-07-140336028.aspx

36 https://www.nslds.ed.gov/nslds/nslds_SA/

37 https://studentloans.gov/myDirectLoan/mobile/repayment/repaymentEstimator.action

38 https://en.wikipedia.org/wiki/Great_Society#Education

39 http://nces.ed.gov/pubs93/93442.pdf

40 In 2016 inflation adjusted dollars. http://cepr.net/documents/publications/student_debt_2005_09.pdf

41 https://studentloans.gov/myDirectLoan/mobile/repayment/repaymentEstimator.action

42 https://studentaid.ed.gov/sa/types/loans/perkins

43 https://studentaid.ed.gov/sa/repay-loans/forgiveness-cancellation/charts

44 https://studentaid.ed.gov/sa/repay-loans/forgiveness-cancellation/public-service

45 This is the case for about 96% of Americans. When I read this stat, I raised my eyebrows in disbelief, but upon reflection, I'm not terribly surprised. https://myhrprofessionals.com/2013/09/25/96-percent-of-americans-paid-electronically-via-direct-deposit/

46 American women as part of the labor force have dropped from 74% in 2001 to 69% in 2013. This is attributable to a variety of factors including gender inequality, substandard parental leave policies, and various economic trends and conditions. http://www.nytimes.com/2014/12/14/upshot/us-employment-women-not-working.html?_r=0

47 Ibid

48 According to the BLS, women comprise 74.6% of education and health service positions. http://www.bls.gov/cps/cpsaat18.htm

49 Previously cited, http://www.nytimes.com/2014/12/14/upshot/us-employment-women-not-working.html?_r=0

50 Women are earning 80 cents on the dollar compared to men and the gap is projected to exist until 2152, www.aauw.org/aauw_check/pdf_download/show_pdf.php?file=The-Simple-Truth

51 Women are earning 80 cents on the dollar compared to men and the gap is projected to exist until 2152, http://www.aauw.org/aauw_check/pdf_download/show_pdf.php?file=The-Simple-Truth

52 http://www.usnews.com/news/articles/2014/09/24/student-loan-default-rate-decreases-but-some-question-federal-free-passes

53 http://www.nytimes.com/2010/11/24/education/24colleges.html?_r=0

54 http://edtrust.org/wp-content/uploads/2013/10/For-Profit-Data-Summary.pdf

55 http://edtrust.org/wp-content/uploads/2013/10/For-Profit-Data-Summary.pdf

56 This was eventually reduced to ~$426 billion in size http://www.wsj.com/articles/ally-financial-exits-tarp-as-treasury-sells-remaining-stake-1419000430

57 http://www.economist.com/news/leaders/21705317-americas-housing-system-was-centre-last-crisis-it-has-still-not-been-properly

58 http://www.economist.com/news/leaders/21705317-americas-housing-system-was-centre-last-crisis-it-has-still-not-been-properly

59 From late 2007 to the end of 2008, Household wealth declined from a peak of $65.8T to $49.4T, representing a 24.9% decrease. http://money.cnn.com/2011/06/09/news/economy/household_wealth/

60 http://www.wsj.com/articles/many-who-lost-homes-to-foreclosure-in-last-decade-wont-return-nar-1429548640

61 http://files.consumerfinance.gov/f/201312_cfpb_mortgagerules.pdf

62 https://www.federalregister.gov/documents/2013/01/30/2013-00736/ability-to-repay-and-qualified-mortgage-standards-under-the-truth-in-lending-act-regulation-z

63 http://www.economist.com/news/leaders/21705317-americas-housing-system-was-centre-last-crisis-it-has-still-not-been-properly

64 http://www.economist.com/news/leaders/21705317-americas-housing-system-was-centre-last-crisis-it-has-still-not-been-properly

65 Rate quoted on bankrate.com on 10/4/2016)

66 The price of gold is $1312.00 per ounce, as quoted in the Economist Espresso app on 10/4/2016.

67 https://www.chicagofed.org/~/media/publications/profitwise-news-and-views/2010/pnv-aug2010-reed-final-web-pdf.pdf

68 https://www.chicagofed.org/~/media/publications/profitwise-news-and-views/2010/pnv-aug2010-reed-final-web-pdf.pdf

69 https://portal.hud.gov/hudportal/HUD?src=/buying/loans

70 https://kfcontent.blob.core.windows.net/research/83/documents/en/wealth-report-2015-2716.pdf

71 https://www.census.gov/content/dam/Census/library/publications/2016/demo/p60-256.pdf

72 https://www.investor.gov/additional-resources/free-financial-planning-tools/compound-interest-calculator

73 http://www.bankrate.com/calculators/retirement/retirement-plan-income-calculator.aspx

74 http://www.cnbc.com/2015/04/13/retiring-well-not-most-baby-boomers.html

75 http://www.investopedia.com/articles/personal-finance/011216/average-retirement-savings-age-2016.asp

76 http://time.com/money/4258451/retirement-savings-survey/

77 http://www.pewsocialtrends.org/2011/07/26/chapter-3-net-worth-by-type-of-asset/

78 http://www.bls.gov/opub/ted/2013/ted_20130103.htm

79 http://www.forbes.com/sites/ashleaebeling/2014/08/19/employees-are-falling-for-roth-401ks/#2916c9657b4c

80 http://www.nytimes.com/2016/10/23/your-money/403-b-retirement-plans-fees-teachers.html

81 You can read more about tax brackets, if you so dare, here: https://www.irs.gov/retirement-plans/plan-participant-employee/amount-of-roth-ira-contributions-that-you-can-make-for-2016

82 Check out the Roth IRA contribution limits and phase outs here for more info: https://www.irs.gov/retirement-plans/plan-participant-employee/amount-of-roth-ira-contributions-that-you-can-make-for-2016

83 Read more about IRAs here: https://www.irs.gov/retirement-plans/traditional-and-roth-iras

84 http://www.marketwatch.com/story/the-typical-american-couple-has-only-5000-saved-for-retirement-2016-04-28

85 https://investor.vanguard.com/etf/list?assetclass=stk&assetclass=stk#/etf/asset-class/month-end-returns

86 http://cordcutting.com/subscribers-watch-12-days-more-netflix-a-year-than-they-did-5-years-ago/

87 https://www.dol.gov/agencies/ebsa/about-ebsa/our-activities/resource-center/fact-sheets/dol-final-rule-to-address-conflicts-of-interest

88 http://www.bloomberg.com/news/articles/2016-05-02/put-buffett-s-advice-into-action-with-these-two-etfs

89 https://en.wikipedia.org/wiki/Burton_Malkiel

90 http://www.npr.org/2016/07/03/484562969/if-some-homeowner-trends-continue-signs-of-another-housing-bubble-ahead

91 http://www.nytimes.com/interactive/2014/upshot/buy-rent-calculator.html?_r=0

92 https://www.redfin.com/buy-a-home/classes-and-events and https://www.redfin.com/home-buying-guide/welcome

93 https://www.law.cornell.edu/uscode/text/26/72

94 http://www.bankrate.com/finance/taxes/when-its-ok-to-tap-your-ira.aspx

95 http://www.investopedia.com/university/insurance/insurance8.asp

96 https://www.nerdwallet.com/life-insurance

97 https://www.healthcare.gov/choose-a-plan/plans-categories/

98 For more and to see if you qualify: https://www.healthcare.gov/sep-list/

99 https://www.healthcare.gov/unemployed/cobra-coverage/

100 https://www.youtube.com/watch?v=oVngo_slWJ4

101 https://www.creditkarma.com/article/dispute-credit-report-errors

102 https://www.youtube.com/watch?v=zmg9NfsJelU

103 FICO has lots of great educational articles that can give you a glimpse into your score and how it's computed, for more: http://www.myfico.com/credit-education/whats-in-your-credit-score/

104 https://www.creditkarma.com/article/dispute-credit-report-errors

105 https://www.consumer.ftc.gov/articles/0151-disputing-errors-credit-reports

106 http://www.prnewswire.com/news-releases/lendingtree-survey-finds-nearly-60-of-americans-dont-know-their-credit-scores-300095483.html

107 http://cohealthinitiative.org/sites/cohealthinitiative.org/files/attachments/warren.pdf

108 https://www.irs.gov/publications/p502/ar02.html#en_US_2016_publink1000179029

109 http://www.forbes.com/sites/christinalamontagne/2015/07/13/my-employer-offers-both-hsa-and-fsa-whats-the-difference-and-which-should-i-use/#77a067b11c79

110 https://www.shrm.org/hr-today/news/hr-magazine/Documents/13-0245%202013_empbenefits_fnl.pdf

111 Read more here: https://www.irs.gov/uac/tax-benefits-for-education-information-center

112 According to the NY Federal Reserve as of Q2 2016, https://www.newyorkfed.org/microeconomics/hhdc.html

113 https://benefittrends.metlife.com/us-perspectives/the-millennial-benefits-perspective/

114 http://www.investopedia.com/terms/i/indexfund.asp?lgl=no-infinite

115 http://www.investopedia.com/terms/e/etf.asp?lgl=no-infinite

116 http://www.investopedia.com/terms/t/target-date_fund.asp?lgl=no-infinite

117 http://www.investopedia.com/terms/t/ter.asp?lgl=no-infinite

118 https://www.irs.gov/retirement-plans/retirement-plans-faqs-regarding-iras-contributions

119 http://finance.yahoo.com/news/u-etf-assets-hit-2-170010898.html

120 https://investor.vanguard.com/mutual-funds/index-vs-active

121 https://personal.vanguard.com/us/funds/snapshot?FundIntExt=INT&FundId=0968#tab=0 Accessed at 12:42pm Central Time on 12/6/2016

122 https://personal.vanguard.com/us/funds/snapshot?FundIntExt=INT&FundId=0968#tab=0 Accessed at 12:42pm Central Time on 12/6/2016

123 https://personal.vanguard.com/us/funds/snapshot?FundIntExt=INT&FundId=0681#tab=2 Accessed at 12:50pm Central Time on 12/6/2016

124 https://personal.vanguard.com/us/funds/snapshot?FundIntExt=INT&FundId=1 487#tab=2

125 http://money.cnn.com/2013/01/24/pf/unclaimed-money/

126 http://www.bentley.edu/newsroom/latest-headlines/mind-of-millennial

127 https://www.sec.gov/investor/pubs/intro529.htm

128 That is, your Modified Adjusted Gross Income (MAGI), which is generally different than your actual income as it takes into account some deductions and excludes others. You can read more here: https://turbotax.intuit.com/tax-tools/ tax-tips/IRS-Tax-Return/What-Is-the-Difference-Between-AGI-and-MAGI-on-Your-Taxes-/INF22699.html

129 That is, your Modified Adjusted Gross Income (MAGI), which is generally different than your actual income as it takes into account some deductions and excludes others. You can read more here: https://turbotax.intuit.com/tax-tools/ tax-tips/IRS-Tax-Return/What-Is-the-Difference-Between-AGI-and-MAGI-on-Your-Taxes-/INF22699.html

130 https://www.irs.gov/publications/p970/ch07.html

131 https://www.brookings.edu/interactives/earned-income-tax-credit-eitc-interactive-and-resources/

132 https://www.cityofchicago.org/city/en/depts/bacp/supp_info/refund_ anticipationloansinstantrefundswhatconsumersneedtoknow.html

133 https://www.irs.gov/individuals/find-a-location-for-free-tax-prep

134 https://www.irs.gov/uac/free-file-do-your-federal-taxes-for-free

135 http://money.usnews.com/money/blogs/my-money/articles/2016-03-17/6-scams-and-frauds-to-avoid-this-tax-season

Made in the USA
Monee, IL
07 September 2023

42328823R00208